Approaches to Popular Culture

Zev Barbu
C. W. E. Bigsby
Peter Burke
David Craig
Benjamin DeMott
Thomas Elsaesser
Sinclair Goodlad
Robert Hodge
Stuart Hood
G. R. Kress
Philip Melling
Paul Oliver
Bill Owens
Raymond Williams

Approaches to Popular Culture

Edited by C.W. E. Bigsby

Bowling Green University Popular Press
Bowling Green, Ohio 43403

First Published 1976 by
Edward Arnold (Publishers) Ltd
25 Hill Street, London W1X 8LL

ISBN: 0-87972-083-2 cloth
ISBN: 0-87972-084-0 paper

Text set in 11/12 pt IBM Journal

Contents

3 Examinations

Preface

Popular culture is so much a part of our daily existence that it is all but invisible. But, like other invisible forces, it loses none of its potency thereby. And though it may with justice be seen as evidence of a growing externalization of experience it is not itself wholly external to our experience. In large part it defines the texture if not the fabric of our environment. The design of our domestic appliances, our ready-to-wear clothes, our motor cars, our furniture; the nature and content of our daily newspapers, television programmes, films, best-sellers; the comics which our children read, the music which they listen to – all these constitute a series of statements about the relationship between self and society. They not only serve to mediate and define reality; they implicitly assert a series of values. As a consequence discussions of popular culture tend to resonate with moral fervour, a passion which may take political or philosophical form.

For some, who believe that men in the mass display a female passivity, popular culture is a weapon to manipulate or a force to deplore. Adolph Hitler was not, after all, the only one to treasure the conviction that 'the people, in an overwhelming majority, are so feminine in their nature and attitude that their activities and thoughts are motivated less by sober consideration than by feeling and sentiment.'[1] Indeed, the success with which Hitler translated politics into popular culture (and, one might add, popular culture into politics) has been imitated increasingly

[1] Adolf Hitler, *Mein Kampf*, quoted in The Frankfurt Institute for Social Research, *Aspects of Sociology*, trans. John Viertel (London 1973) p. 83.

by political managers for whom politics is a simple matter of packaging, marketing and, ultimately, consumption. But with the decline of the more simplistic models of human response the need for a more subtle investigation of popular culture and of the psychology of those at whom it is directed has become more apparent.

However, the individual wishing to decipher the symbols of popular culture, to assess its method, meaning and significance, is faced with a genuine dilemma. The conventional tools of the literary critic, historian and sociologist are revealed as inappropriate or as singularly blunt instruments of analysis, because they are themselves heavily influenced by class assumptions. Indeed, the very impulse to analyse such material is likely to be accompanied by coy apology.

This volume has a two-fold purpose. In the first section a number of writers outline possible approaches to popular culture, suggesting ways in which individual disciplines might most usefully attempt to encompass products inspired by or attuned to the popular mind. The third section consists of popular culture criticism in action. Six writers, not necessarily following the theoretical outlines of the preceding section, confront material as diverse as *The Clockwork Orange* and the media response to Watergate — the latter arguing against the conventional wisdom which sees that scandal as a morally liberating force in American life and a validation of political commentary on all levels in America. The effect is clearly eclectic; I hope that it is also instructive.

This book emerged from a conference held at the University of East Anglia in the summer of 1973. Half the essays derive from papers delivered on that occasion, the other half (with the exception of Raymond Williams's essay) were specially commissioned for this volume. Thanks are therefore due to the University of East Anglia and to the United States Embassy for the assistance which they rendered at that time. Acknowledgement is also due to UNESCO who have allowed me to reprint 'The Politics of Popular Culture' from their journal *Cultures*, where it first appeared in a slightly different form.

University of East Anglia   C.W.E. Bigsby
June 1975

1 Perspectives

1

The Politics of Popular Culture*

C.W.E. Bigsby

Political mass meeting: the stadium filled to the last seat, a veritable carpet of people and faces in the ascending tiers; the orator going full steam. He says: 'The mass culture is to blame for everything.' Tumultuous applause.[1]

Alexander Mitscherlich

As an area of study, popular culture has a reasonably long, if fragmented history, but uncertainty over method, the absence of any generally agreed theory and the persistence of an academic tradition suspicious of material so generally available, has created an air of defensiveness which has still not entirely dissipated. Forced to rebut criticism of the subject which they study and to justify a concern with data which by definition seems too frivolous to warrant serious investigation, students of popular culture have too frequently fallen into strategies which appear to concede a certain validity to the attacks of their detractors. Some have resorted to a self-deprecating brashness which in some degree reflects the form of the material which they examine. Others have sought respectability in the moral neutrality of the social sciences. Yet others have resorted to a mechanical application of Marxist analysis, seeing the popular arts simply as evidence of economic and social structure. The difficulty of studying popular culture (as opposed to peasant or folk culture) is that it tends to be associated, by both supporters and detractors, with the social forces which were

*Reprinted from *Cultures: An International Review*, I:2, by permission of UNESCO, © UNESCO 1973 where it appears in revised form.

[1] Quoted in The Frankfurt Institute for Social Research, Aspects of Sociology, trans. John Viertel (London, 1973), p. 72.

essential to its creation — namely urbanization and industrialization. Since the technocratic society has created not only the market for popular culture but also its form, techniques and subject matter, a reaction against technology is frequently confused with a rejection of its manifestations. Since art and technology are assumed to be in opposite camps, popular culture, the child of technology, has frequently been seen as a symbol of a new brutalism. To those convinced of the vital centrality of traditional culture, popular culture is, by analogy, granted an equal though opposite potency. It becomes evidence of a collapse of values and, by casual extension, the cause of that collapse. Thus, in the nineteenth century, the novel, itself both a symbol of the emergence of a new middle class and a mirror of its activities, was despised as a frivolous and immoral distraction — indeed, in true puritan form, immoral because frivolous. (There was, of course, a certain justification for feeling that a connection existed between social changes and artifacts made possible by new and improved methods of printing, distribution and sales which were themselves bringing about profound change in the social system.)

This view of popular culture as a form of barbarism derives partially from the changing perception of human history. The Hegelian system could regard everything as forming an essential part of a larger plan, but commitment to the idea of progress began to crumble at precisely the moment that conditions seemed to favour an emerging popular culture. Urbanization and industrialization were both the proof and in part the cause of a shift of view which saw human autonomy reduced and the ladder of existence plunge downwards towards anarchy and dissolution rather than soar upwards towards an unshakeable and pattern-forming divinity. Matthew Arnold's was in many senses a transitional generation. He read the signs which seemed to indicate impending collapse but could still draw confidently on values which had not succumbed to the irony which became the dominant mood of the twentieth century. Arnold's work essentially set the terms for the debate over culture which has continued to this day and which has tended to place the student of popular culture in the position of appearing to oppose the force of both aesthetics and ethics — or what Arnold chose to call 'sweetness and light'.

Thus the debate is concerned with far more than a consideration of aesthetics or descriptive accounts of technological models. It involves a clash of ideologies, philosophies and social and psychological theories. Popular culture is accordingly seen by turns as epiphanic and apocalyptic, as evidence of social cohesion and social dislocation, as proof of subversive energy and evidence of decadence. On the one hand the direct emotional appeal, the heightening of expression, the extremes of experience which we associate with popular culture are seen as serving identifiable psychological and sociological purposes, permitting the cathartic release of destructive passions and subversive feelings in a manner conducive to individual and social stability and hence, by extension, leading to the possibility of personal and public stasis: popular culture as adjustment syndrome. On the other hand, it is regarded as an expression of genuine needs not usually validated by a society which chooses to stress a view of man (rational, puritanical, socially-determined, inately moral) incompatible with an energetic emotionalism and an antinomian stance. The politics of popular culture, in other words, conceal a more basic concern with the nature of the individual and his society.

To Arnold culture was simply the 'disinterested endeavour after man's perfection'[2] while its motto, derived from Bishop Wilson, was 'to make reason and the will of God prevail'.[3] The association of culture with authority, established institutions and order, was natural and deliberate for he saw it as 'a principle of authority, to counteract the tendency to anarchy'[4] which he regarded as threatening his generation. It followed that he viewed with alarm both the material changes which seemed to imply a collapse of integral structure ('faith in machinery is . . . our besetting danger'[5]), and the flaccid thinking which wished to popularize culture and see it as an expression of freely exercised choice. As he remarked, in *Culture and Anarchy*, 'plenty of people will try to give the masses, as they call them, an intellectual food prepared and adapted in the way they think proper for the actual condition of the masses. The ordinary

[2] Matthew Arnold, *Culture and Anarchy* (Cambridge 1960) p. 27.
[3] *Ibid.*, p. 45.
[4] *Ibid.*, p. 82.
[5] *Ibid.*, p. 49.

popular literature is an example of this . . . but culture works differently. It does not try to teach down to the level of inferior classes . . . it seeks to do away with classes; to make the best that has been thought and known in the world current everywhere.'[6] Culture, in other words, is invoked as protection against a heedless democratization. To the members of the Frankfurt Institute of Social Research, writing a hundred years later, such an act was to be seen as an avowedly class reaction, final evidence of the dissolution against which Arnold and his spiritual descendants were allegedly fighting. The 'gesture of invocation,' they assert, 'the exalting of culture at the expense of mass society, the devoted consumption of cultural values as a confirmation of one's elevated internal spiritual equipment, these are inseparable from the decadent character of the civilization.'[7] To Arnold, however, the defence of civilized values was inextricably entangled with the assertion of cultural values. And since culture is decidedly not a 'having and a resting, but a growing and a becoming'[8] it follows that it tries 'not to make what each raw person may like, the rule by which he fashions himself; but to draw ever nearer to a sense of what is indeed beautiful, graceful, and becoming, and to get the raw person to like that'.[9] The assurance which lies behind such remarks, the conviction that beauty, sweetness and light are terms which carry not only a clear and agreed meaning but a moral force which brooks no dissent, strikes the modern ear a little strangely but, nonetheless, one encounters it again clearly enough in the 1930s, with the defiant protestations of Leavis, the atavistic longings of Eliot and the curious agrarian overtones of the New Critics. Arnold had created a germ which subsequently infected not merely a whole generation but a century of literary critics who accepted his Manichean view of the world and hence brought popular culture into existence by the simple act of defining its opposite. And the result of this was, on the one hand, an academic tradition of criticism which sought to identify the characteristics of 'sweetness and light' as expressed in literature, and on the other a conspiracy (by bourgeois society

[6] *Ibid.*, pp. 69–70.
[7] *Aspects of Sociology*, p. 94.
[8] *Culture and Anarchy*, p. 48.
[9] *Ibid.*, p. 50.

and its categorizing servants) to isolate, sight unseen, all those works excluded from the literary canon by virtue of assuming a form not sanctioned by the Arnoldian and Leavisite commitment to a personal view of human values and exquisite form. Yet in order to assess such a judgement it is necessary to examine the other components of the tradition, for Arnold was not alone in his 'elitism'. Professor Fiedler, a contemporary critic of popular culture, is ready to add Karl Marx, in one direction, and James and Lawrence ('crypto-Puritans'), in another.[10] From this it should be clear that the response to mass society and to mass art was by no means homogeneous. Wordsworth, equally, was appalled by the increasing accumulation of men in cities, recognized the pressures brought to bear on the common man and saw in Romanticism a force which could adapt itself to those excluded from patrician culture. William Morris strove to stem the movement towards the alienation of industrial society by reconstructing the dying craft tradition — in doing so using a language more democratic and expansive than the world he sought so eagerly to recapture, an irony which applies equally well to the naive references to unalienated and supposedly organic communities invoked by Leavis, Dover Wilson and Allen Tate in the 1930s, and by a similarly atavistic youth in the 1970s, delightedly discovering the joys of the nineteenth century agrarian commune. Curiously it was only when this craft tradition was related to the new industrialism, as it was by the Dutch architects and designers who formed *De Stijl* in 1917 and even more by those who taught and worked at the Bauhaus, that it gained any real substance.

Even the American poet Walt Whitman, anxious to celebrate democratic man, hailing the arrival of a technological age as bringing all men together in a mystical and physical union, and speaking with enthusiasm of the great popular newspapers, saw the popular culture of his age as depressingly mundane and unworthy of its setting: 'the main objects', he observed, were to 'amuse, to titillate, to pass away time, to circulate the news, and rumours of news, to rhyme, and read rhyme. . . . Today, in books,' he objected, 'success (so call'd) is for him or her who

[10] Leslie Fiedler, 'Towards a Definition of Popular Literature', in *Superculture: American Popular Culture and Europe*, ed. C. W. E. Bigsby (London 1975).

strikes the mean flat average, the sensational appetite for stimulus, incident, persiflage, &c, and depicts, to the common caliber, sensual, exterior life. . . . Behold the prolific brood of the contemporary novel, magazine-tale, theatre play, &c. The same endless thread of tangled and superlative love-story. . . .'[11]

Whitman always sought the unifying factor in the diversity of life, finding it in part in his own sensibility and in part, like Arnold, in culture, though his own definition differed from Arnold's in that it excluded the Englishman's respect for authority and for the various establishments which Arnold had seen as playing a crucial role in maintaining order. Arnold used culture as a bulwark against anarchy; Whitman as a defence against banality. Arnold feared a modern age which threatened essential values; Whitman welcomed it and recognized precisely that potential for spiritual unity which Arnold had considered rare enough in the Old World but despaired of finding in the New. Whitman celebrated the new 'daily electric communication with every part of the globe. What an age! What a land!'[12] This would have appalled Arnold, except insofar as the American retained a clear sense of the human potential of the new era. Yet, for all his calls for a foundation of 'the average, the bodily, the concrete, the democratic, the popular, on which all the superstructures of the future are to permanently rest,'[13] he was himself as disturbed by the standardization of man in America as Tocqueville had been decades before, and continued to insist on the strenuous effort demanded by a genuine art which he clearly juxtaposed to the popular literature which surrounded him. Whitman, like Karl Jaspers after him, feared that imagination might collapse when confronted with the rationalism of the first machine age and the vacuous mind produced by deadening labour. This was a more subtle point than Arnold was making in bluntly dismissing any tradition other than that which he sponsored. It was a point, too, which is not countered by Leslie Fiedler's refusal to grant any distinction between different symbolic expressions of values and traditions (though he has made a case for the libidinous vitality of the popular arts

[11] Walt Whitman, *Leaves of Grass and Selected Prose*, ed. John Kouwenhoven (New York 1950) p. 499.

[12] *Ibid.*, p. 453.

[13] *Ibid.*, p. 469.

which would have won at least part of Whitman's support). Jaspers has a keen enough historical sense to reject the apocalyptic imagery so prevalent in the 1930s. Yet he shared some of the fears of Arnold, Whitman, and, most directly, Ortega y Gasset. Like the latter he reacted against an age apparently based on 'the supply of mass-needs by rationalized production with the aid of technical advances.'[14] He also produced the most eloquent statement of a view which is reflected in the work of nineteenth century socialists like Morris, Marxist critics like Benjamin and Adorno, and the new liberal English critics of the 1950s, Richard Hoggart and Raymond Williams. Considering the growth of the new industrial state, he admitted that 'the technical life-order which came into being for the supply of the needs of the masses did at the outset preserve these real worlds of human creatures, by furnishing them with commodities.' But, he insisted:

When at length the time arrived when nothing in the individual's immediate real environment world was any longer made, shaped, or fashioned by that individual for his own purposes; when everything that came, came merely as the gratification of momentary need, to be used up and cast aside; when the very dwelling-place was machine made, when the environment had become despiritualized, when the day's work grew sufficient to itself, and ceased to be built up into a constituent of the worker's life — then man was, as it were, bereft of his world. Cast adrift in this way, lacking all sense of historical continuity with past or future, man cannot remain man. The universalization of the life-order threatens to reduce the life of the real man in a real world to mere functioning.[15]

This is the condition which Marxists have taught us to call 'alienation'. It is the condition, however, of maximum receptivity to a mass art, ideal for the production and consumption of a popular culture which no longer links man to his own past but which provides a temporary connection across class in the present.

It is precisely the kind of positivism outlined above which so disturbed Jaspers in 1931, for it seemed to him that the surge of blind enthusiasm for technical process (as evidenced, for example, by the Futurists), while creating the possibility of survival under the conditions of mass urbanization, simul-

[14] Karl Jaspers, *Man in the Modern Age*, trans. Eden and Cedar Paul (London 1951) p. 37.
[15] *Ibid.*, p. 44.

taneously denied the essense of human life. His lament is worth
quoting in full because it sums up so neatly a development
identified and deplored by right and left wing critics alike:

Essential humanity is reduced to the general; to vitality as a functional corporeality,
to the triviality of enjoyment. The divorce of labour from pleasure deprives life of
its possible gravity: public affairs become mere entertainment; private affairs, the
alternation of stimulation and fatigue, and a craving for novelty whose inexhaustible
current flows swiftly into the waters of oblivion. There is no continuity, only
pastime. Positivism likewise encourages an increasing activity of the impulses common
to us all: an enthusiasm for the numberless and the vast, for the creations of modern
technique, for huge crowds; sensational admiration for the achievements, fortunes,
and abilities of outstanding individuals; the complication and brutalization of the
erotic; gambling, adventurousness, and even the hazarding of one's life. Lottery
tickets are sold by the million; crossword puzzles become the chief occupation of
people's leisure. This positive gratification of the mind without personal participation
or effort promotes efficiency for the daily round, fatigue and recreation being
regularized. In becoming a mere function, life forfeits its historical particularity, to
the extreme of a levelling of the various ages of life. Youth as the period of highest
vital efficiency and of erotic exaltation becomes the desired type of life in general.
When the human being is regarded only as a function, he must be young; and if
youth is over, he will still strive to show its semblance.[16]

This is the nub of a central argument, for what Jaspers sees
as an atomizing and automatizing force, reducing the individual
to basic instincts, Leslie Fiedler, speaking one suspects for
precisely that youthful generation which is now inheriting not
only the popular arts themselves but also the study of those
arts, sees as a vital, subversive, exultant, anti-authoritarian,
liberating and joyously anarchic force. It is, Fiedler suggests, a
vital rediscovery of a dimension of human existence formerly
denied not so much by technology, which is merely a convenient
scapegoat, but by a persistent puritanism and a bourgeois power
structure intent on maintaining its control by outlawing and
denigrating those elements of existence over which it has
voluntarily relinquished control. To this degree, therefore, study
of popular culture today, for many cultural critics, is
inevitably to be seen as the advocacy of such a culture in the
face of those whose apocalyptic visions are as much an expression
of their own impending loss of control as of the imminent
collapse of necessary structure itself. The introduction of
popular culture into teaching programmes, with all its accompanying risk of fossilization, thus becomes an aesthetic and a

[16] *Ibid.*, pp. 49–50.

moral gesture because it is only traditional culture which need feel technology to be the enemy; the popular arts have long since adjusted and discovered resources with which to humanize the machine (witness the eroticism of many science fiction cover designs).

The 1930s were remarkably conscious of the implications of mass society, for though the nineteenth century had felt the first impact of industrialization, it was the early decades of the present century, with the birth of the movies, radio and television, which really began to recognize the profound social changes (beyond the mere multiplication of squalor which the naturalists had identified), which were threatening to change the profile of existence.[17] Many saw things in apocalyptic form. Spengler had warned in *The Decline of the West*, that the era of culture would be followed by a period of mere technical efficiency; Ortega y Gasset saw the rise of the masses as 'the greatest crisis that can afflict peoples, nations and civilization'.[18] In the face of this 'threat' it was not only T. S. Eliot who was prepared to assert that culture and 'equalitarianism', as he called it, were irreconcilable, though Eliot's definition of culture, starting with an impressive precision, shows an expedient flexibility as the book, *Towards a Definition of Culture*, progresses.

In England, the staunchest defender of Arnold's position, and hence the chief antagonist of proponents of popular culture was Dr F. R. Leavis, for whom the car became a symbol of a new technocracy and the popular press an image of the philistine 'levelling-down' which seemed its cultural corollary. He saw a quite definite split between the twin concepts of authority and culture which had seemed, to Matthew Arnold, so indissolubly wedded. In *Mass Civilization and Minority Culture*, Leavis saw the prospects for culture as rapidly diminishing and while recognizing that 'it is vain to resist the triumph of the machine', regarded it as 'equally vain to console us with the promise of a 'mass culture' that shall be utterly new.''It would,' he added, 'no doubt, be possible to argue that such a "mass culture" might be better then the culture we are losing, but it would be futile:

[17] See Philip Melling's chapter, 'American Popular Culture in the Thirties: Ideology, Myth, Genre.'

[18] Ortega y Gasset, *The Revolt of the Masses* (London 1961) p. 9.

the "utterly new" surrenders everything that can interest us.'[19]
He saw William Morris's notion that man freed from labour by
the machine would inevitable develop a love of art, as dangerously naive, and no less so when repeated by D. H. Lawrence.
For Leavis the future of Europe in general and England in
particular was contained in the American present. Indeed
American experience provided the material for the Catonian
warning which he has repeated throughout his work from the
1930s to the present. For in the United States, the links with
the past, the sense of continuity which was the essence of
culture, had been irrevocably sundered and as a consequence
a whole nation had been condemned, in his view, to an 'anti-
human reductivism that favours the American neo-imperialism
of the computer,'[20] so that America 'knows in its deep psyche
that it won't be happy even when it has solved its racial problem,
achieved a New Deal, landed men on the moon, and made a good
start towards beating Russia to the next planet.'[21] The charge
is a familiar one and he clearly speaks for many in identifying
the United States as the extreme example both of the industrial
process and the mass art which is the progeny of that process.
It explains, also, something of the extracultural implications of
the popular culture debate manifested in such phenomena as
the overly casual methodology of some popular culture
enthusiasts, and the single-minded and at times simplistically-
minded approach of what George Steiner has called the 'para-
Marxist school of criticism'.

As indicated above, popular culture has not only been
attacked from the right. But curiously enough there are several
points of contact between critics like Arnold, Eliot and Leavis,
defending the idea of a cultural elite and intent on resisting the
barbarian inroads of an unleashed democracy respectful neither
of established authority nor of the artifacts which they have
been taught to regard as constituting the basis of culture, and
those left-wing critics viewing the new mass art as an expression
of an unjust and inorganic social system. The Marxist conviction
that consciousness is determined by life rather than life by
consciousness, provides the rationale for an approach which sees

[19] F. R. Leavis, *Mass Civilization and Minority Culture* (Cambridge 1930) p. 31.
[20] F. R. Leavis, *Nor Shall My Sword* (London 1972) p. 206.
[21] *Ibid.*, p. 131.

popular culture as part of an ideological superstructure built on the foundation of a particular political and economic life. Just as Adorno recognized that chamber music required a particular social arrangement in order to function and declined with the passing of that arrangement, so other critics have investigated popular culture in terms of the society which produced it and have reacted to it accordingly. They, like Leavis, recognize the end of a particular tradition and the culture derived from it; where they differ is in their response to that fact and in the respect they are prepared to offer to a tradition which they would not choose to embrace.

As Walter Benjamin has pointed out, the work of art has always been reproducible, whether it be in the form of replicas produced by apprentices or merely die-stamped copies. But with the invention of various means of mass production and copying, the wide distribution of material became possible. This served not merely to undermine the unique quality of a work of art but also to shatter any concept of tradition built on the idea of a chain of autonomous artifacts. Hence, the machine age not only made the popularization of culture possible, it simultaneously implied the destruction of tradition and thus the idea of culture itself. For the word 'culture' had traditionally implied that the past had a genuinely authoritative role to play; its essence was thought to consist in the promotion of those abstract virtues (such as truth, beauty, moral probity) which were enshrined in discrete works of individual conception. But this is of course a limited concept of culture and at least part of the apocalyptic mood of Leavis and other 1930s critics derived from their particular definition of cultural values.

Since, as Adorno has pointed out, culture derives from a radical separation of mental and physical work (despite the 'organic' communities invoked by the cultural critics) the machine age has merely made apparent a division which has always existed. The destruction of temporal continuity, bewailed by Arnold and Leavis, is thus beside the point. The real problem is that culture, based on a radical disjunction while allegedly seeking synthesis, simply had no resources with which to resist the manipulators of the new consumer society since, almost by definition, these now constituted the new authority, and culture had always been defined by these critics in terms of authority. Thus culture had succumbed of its own internal weakness and the cultural critic had missed his aim, which should in truth have been directed at the changing basis of his society and not at the products which it generated; in curing the disease and not merely in recognizing the symptoms and prescribing an emetic. It was no use, in other words, for Leavis to concede the ineluctable state of the new consumer society and yet persist in his attachment to notions of humane values which would continue to survive within the walls of the universities, as a biological culture might continue its vestigial existence inside a glass tray. To Adorno, 'the disgrace of the present is not the preponderance of so-called material culture over the spiritual. . . . What must be attacked is the socially-dictated separation of consciousness from the social realization its essence requires. 'The struggle against mass culture,' he adds, quoting from Max Horkheimer:

can consist only in pointing out its connection with the persistence of social injustice. It is ridiculous to reproach chewing gum for diminishing the propensity for metaphysics, but it could probably be shown that Wrigley's profits and his Chicago palace have their roots in the social function of reconciling people to bad conditions and thus diverting them from criticism. It is not that chewing gum undermines metaphysics but that it is metaphysics — this is what must be made clear. We criticize mass culture not because it gives men too much or makes their life too secure — that we leave to Lutheran theology — but rather because it contributes to a condition in which men get too little and what they get is bad, a condition in which whole strata inside and out live in frightful poverty, in which men come to terms with injustice, in which the world is kept in a condition where one must expect on the one hand gigantic catastrophes and on the other clever elites conspiring to bring about a dubious peace. One day it will be readily apparent that men do not need the trash provided them by the culture industry or the miserable high-quality goods preferred by the more substantial industries. The thought, for instance, that in addition to food and lodging the cinema is necessary for the reproduction of labour power is 'true' only in a world which prepares men for the reproduction of their labour power and constrains their needs in harmony with the interests of supply and social control.[22]

Mass culture, in other words, is seen as a drug, like the soma of Huxley's dystopia, *Brave New World* — a society in which everything may be possessed and hence nothing has value. It blunts awareness and provides a spurious satisfaction for needs which no longer express fundamental human desires but are

[22] Theodore Adorno, *Prisms*, trans. Samuel and Shierry Weber (London 1967) pp. 109—110.

simply commercially stimulated demands for instant gratification. It is notable that Bellamy's utopia, *Looking Backward*,
and Paul Goodman's dystopia, *Communitas*, are structured on
a department store. This is a central expression of the modern
ethos. The drab inefficiency and patent inadequacy of such
stores for many years in Eastern Europe was by no means
accidental. It was a direct rejection of what were seen as
frivolous demands for irrelevant satisfactions. When Marcuse
distinguishes between 'true' and 'false' needs and defines false
needs as 'those which are superimposed upon the individual
by particular social interests' and asserts that 'most of the
prevailing needs to relax, to have fun, to behave and consume
in accordance with the advertisements . . . belong to this
category of false needs'[23] he implies, of course, a generally
agreed but deliberately subverted set of real values of a kind no
less absolute than those offered by Matthew Arnold. While he
is intent on resisting precisely those levelling tendencies which
had bothered Arnold, he does so for precisely the opposite
reason. Marcuse believes that popular culture becomes an
instrument of repression because it simulates a shared
experience which has the power to de-emphasize real class
differences and to assimilate cells of resistance. It has no
transcendent dimension, if we mean by this the capacity to
imply the existence of other values than those which provide
its own motor force. At best it creates the appearance of
criticism, but this is either an imposture or is instantly negated
by being institutionalized and presented as evidence of
liberality and a self-justifying pluralism. And since the autonomous personality and the integrity of imagination have, in his
view, as in that of Adorno, already surrendered to the brutal
demands of capitalist society, the maimed and standardized
citizens of today's consumer society are less the victims of mass
culture than the casualties of a society which has abandoned
any sense of human values. 'What is happening now,' he has
said, 'is not the deterioration of higher culture into mass culture
but the refutation of this culture by the reality. The reality
surpasses its culture,' it has 'betrayed the hope and destroyed
the truth which were preserved in the sublimations of higher

---

[23] Herbert Marcuse, *One-Dimensional Man* (London 1964) p. 5.

culture.'[24] Adorno singles out Auschwitz as his proof. Marcuse identifies no such precise historical moment. He sees only a process which has slowly destroyed the transcendent dimension, translating 'truth value' into 'exchange value', and materializing ideals, in the same way as F. Scott Fitzgerald's Gatsby had projected his youthful dreams onto the perishable Daisy Buchanan in *The Great Gatsby*. Since culture was traditionally committed to intercourse with the ideal, this process has destroyed its essence as, Benjamin insisted, had the reproduction of works of art, or as did the screenplay or television script of a classic. As the higher culture of the West was largely a product of a pretechnological age, it is scarcely any wonder that those who wish to sustain the one should find themselves in the position of advocating the other. Hence, from Matthew Arnold to F. R. Leavis, from Raymond Williams to Richard Hoggart, from Theodore Roszak to Charles Reich we are confronted with men whose commitment to cultural values seems ineluctably welded to a nostalgic regard for an organic community, whose work and culture are two aspects of a unified life. And since both left and right wing critics have been so deceived in their belief that a shorter working week would be the key to a new and fuller existence, the right has turned to the past, ignoring all too often the social cost of pretechnological culture, and the left to some distant future in which temporary restrictions would give way to a fully realized classless culture, unguided by rationalistic strictures. But in the last resort the latter is of course shaped as firmly by political necessities as are the vapid products of a television service whose primary purpose is to sell overpowered and dangerous cars to men who wish to live out the fantasies spun from the corporate mind of motor manufacturers and advertizing copywriters.

Up to now I have been talking as though popular culture were entirely a product of literate industrialized societies; that is, I have begged the question of the relationship between popular culture and folk culture, and, more importantly, I have yet to deal with the whole problem of definition. There are, indeed, those who reject the very idea of such distinctions, seeing the desire to distinguish popular culture from 'high' culture as merely evidence of a tendency to establish a gulf between the

[24] *Ibid.*, p. 56.

socially acceptable and the socially unacceptable; and who view popular culture not as the result of a fragmenting world scene but as an expression of the conscious desire for fragmentation on the part of a ruling bourgeois orthodoxy. Since popular culture is, in any case, defined primarily in terms of what it is not, it clearly requires a differentiated society in order to function. Yet these differentiations do not always coincide with the divisions between culture, meaning the 'high' arts as defined by a ruling social or intellectual elite, and the popular arts. It is, after all, worth recalling that the desire to create such distinctions is itself a recent phenomenon. It has been argued, for example, that while writers like Richardson, Cooper, Twain and Dickens (whose work contains abundant evidence of that resort to stereotype, melodrama and violent action which is normally taken to be a natural accoutrement of popular culture) have been accorded classic status because of an achievement which is intimately connected with their popularity, this status has been defended primarily by reference to the familiar terms of literary criticism — irony, tragic consciousness, structure, etc. A similar paradox is apparent in film criticism which often praises avowedly popular films for reasons which are not merely totally unconnected with their popularity but which would seem to be inimical to it. Popular culture, then, can apparently be transformed into 'high' art by a simple critical act of appropriation. Indeed so insecure are these categories that the popular culture of one generation can become the high culture of the next and vice versa — a fact which applies not only to individual artists but to genres (theatre, novel, film), subgenres (farce, science fiction, detective fiction) and styles (romanticism, realism).

Nevertheless, for all the justifiable assaults which have been launched on an overanxiety for definition, it is necessary to identify the perimeters of the discussion, particularly when dealing with terms which have proved so elusive. As I have pointed out elsewhere:

Part of the difficulty over the meaning of the term 'popular culture' arises from the differing meanings attributable to the word 'popular' itself, for as the OED makes evident it can mean both 'intended for and suited to ordinary people,' or 'prevalent or current among, or accepted by, the people generally.' The latter includes everyone; the former excludes all but the 'ordinary'. Hence popular culture is sometimes presented as that which appeals only to the commonality ('mass culture') or to the average ('middlebrow'), thus confirming the social fragmentation of society, and sometimes as a phenomenon cutting across class lines. For some, therefore, it is a simple opiate, for others a subversive and liberating force, linking those of differing social and educational background.

There is a further difficulty still in that the word 'culture' is susceptible both of a general and a specialized meaning. In the former sense it implies the attitudes and values of a society as expressed through the symbolic form of language, myths, rituals, life-styles, establishments (political, religious, educational); in the latter it is closer to the meaning implied by Matthew Arnold and defined by the OED as 'the training, development, and refinement of mind, tastes, manners: the condition of being thus trained and refined, the intellectual side of civilization.' . . . Thus, by analogy, popular culture is sometimes defined as the attitudes and values of those excluded from the intellectual elite and expressed through myths, rituals and life-styles specific to this excluded group, and sometimes as the popular, as opposed to the intellectual arts.[25]

By either definition the distinction between folk culture and popular culture may not perhaps seem a profound one, except in so far as we chose to regard the former as a communal art rooted in daily experience, a product of *gemeinschaft* in which the distinction between audience and performer is imprecise, and the latter an entertainment, a product of *gesellschaft,* in which that distinction becomes vital. Thus folk culture is in effect seen simply as pre-industrial, preliterate popular culture. Even then, it is worth reminding ourselves that the post-literate, post-industrial phase is not simply a product of the nineteenth century. The democratization of art, if we mean by that the mechanical reproduction of forms and images and their immediate availability, has a considerable history. The invention of movable type printing in the fifteenth century was merely the most important of many changes.

It was, however, the economic changes which brought about an increase in the middle class and the eventual spread of literacy which created the genuinely mass public which is a necessary precondition for post-industrial popular culture. Though there is considerable disagreement as to the date to which one can ascribe this development, Raymond Williams showing a preference for 1740 and others for the mid-nineteenth century, all are agreed in identifying the audience as the crucial factor, both because of its size and composition. For the mere existence of such a public makes the professional writer viable. In this respect

[25] C. W. E. Bigsby, *Superculture: American Popular Culture and Europe* (London 1975) pp. 23–4.

the popular literature of the eighteenth and nineteenth centuries
was merely harbinger to the mass media of the twentieth, whose
profitability turned on their ability to reflect and mould the
whims and desires of an apparently unvariegated audience. The
media thus become an essential element of popular culture.
Morris Janowitz has offered the following descriptive definition
of mass communications: 'Mass communications comprise the
institutions and techniques by which specialized social groups
employ technological devices (press, radio, films, etc.) to dis-
seminate symbolic content to large heterogeneous and widely
dispersed audiences. In other words, mass communications
perform essential functions for a society that uses complex
technology to control the environment. These functions include
the transmission of a society's heritage from one generation to
another, the collection of information for the surveillance of
the environment, and the correlation of the various parts of the
society in response to changes in the environment.'[26] Indeed,
by a predictable process and under the influence of structuralism and semiology, popular culture has increasingly come to
be regarded as simply a subdivision of communications, in the
sense defined by CECMAS, the centre d'études de communication de masse, on every copy of their journal,
Communications: 'Large circulation Press, Radio, Television,
Cinema, Advertising, Songs and Popular Novels, through all
these massive channels, the astounding development of which
characterizes the modern world, the man of the technological
civilization is building up a new culture' and the central questions
are those which the journal goes on to pose, namely 'What
are its contents? Its languages? Its functions? Its values? Its
effects? How does it define itself in relation to traditional
bodies of knowledge. In relation to other cultures?'

The study of popular culture drew at first on two main
traditions: that deriving from the methodology of literary
criticism and social history on the one hand, and that drawing

[26] Morris Janowitz, 'The Study of Mass Communication', in David L. Sills, ed.,
International Encyclopedia of the Social Sciences, III (1968) p. 41, and quoted in a
forthcoming UNESCO study by Dr Katzen, of Leicester University, on which I have
drawn widely in this section.

on the techniques of the social sciences on the other. Though the evidence is that these two traditions have in recent years drawn more closely together, historically they have been widely separated and even antagonistic.

Formal study of popular culture in most countries tended to start with a concern for the development of the press. This was particularly true of Germany and the United States. With the advent of movies and radio some of these centres broadened their activities and established centres for communication science. In Germany considerable stress has always been laid on the political implications of the media and hence ownership patterns and the issue of the public responsibility of a public medium. The same emphasis was less in evidence in the United States where the stress on moral concern tended to defer to the empirical value-free ethos of the social scientist, intent on pursuing the details of isolated aspects of this society.

The sociology of mass communications in the United States derives essentially from Harold Lasswell's dictum: 'Who says what in which channel, to whom, with what effects?' (The limitations of this approach are suggested by Raymond Williams in his essay in this volume, 'Communications as cultural science'.) This has tended to result, for the most part, in a strongly empirical tradition; in a concentration on audience study and content analysis, both at first somewhat mechanical exercises which lacked any genuine theoretical context. Certainly, Edgar Morin has objected that such studies lack any real insight into the transmission of cultural values or concern with the growth and nature of a culture industry, seen as part of a consumer society. And writing in 1964, Otto Larsen complained that such research 'tended to view persons as "targets" of communications impact rather than as part of a total communication process'.[27] This period from the 1930s to the late 1950s, therefore, was important primarily for its emphasis on the need to assemble quantities of data, a tendency which was encouraged by commercial firms who were themselves anxious to secure some rational means of assessing their market and planning their production, as well as by central government which began to require ever more information in order to

[27] Otto Larsen, 'Social Effects of Mass Communication', in R. E. L. Faris, ed., *Handbook of Modern Sociology* (Chicago 1964) pp. 368–9.

conduct its business. As had been widely objected, however, the mere assembling of information may add up to very little unless there is some kind of coordination of this material within the terms of a central thesis.

Such theories as did exist, in particular the simple cause and effect theory, denounced by Larsen, which presumed a direct and unmediated relationship between medium and recipient, have not survived the 1960s. In recent years a crucial emphasis has been laid on the mediators, or 'gate-keepers', an emphasis which has done something to dissipate the overly simplistic view of media effects which were a commonplace only a few years ago. Popular works, such as Vance Packard's *The Hidden Persuaders*, based on such research, were in some senses as misleading as the forces which they indicted in that they tended to create the image of psychosocial manipulators, armed with all the precise weaponry of social science, launching irresistible assaults on the subconscious of the suburban housewife. It is scarcely surprising that the same housewife treasured an inner conviction that many of the ills of her society could be traced to the media, thus creating public pressure for the kind of research which led, among other things, to the million dollar report on televised violence prepared for the Surgeon General's Office by researchers in fourteen universities.

The study of the mediating groups, (described by Professor Hood, in his essay in this volume, 'The Dilemma of the Communicators') who interpose themselves between the transmitters of material and its individual recipients, has had a profoundly important consequential result. It has brought the social scientist closer to a consideration of the general patterns of culture than had previously been the case. Analysis has become more subtle and even central cultural problems such as the way in which an individual performs the necessary task of distinguishing between reality and illusion in an electronic age have come under close scrutiny. Just as straightforward content analysis has given way to gratification studies, so these in turn have raised questions about the nature of gratification itself.

We have seen, then, a move towards the point at which the social scientist will tackle the kind of issues which Matthew Arnold had raised a century before; we have witnessed a shift from a concern with identifying the sociological structure and operational patterns of a society, to a consideration of its metaphysics. Accordingly, narrowly-based studies of indivdual media are giving way to rather more general studies which consider broader issues. Insofar as individual studies are concerned, the press, perhaps for historical reasons, remains the most popular area for research but there is evidence that over the next five years television will provide the main focus. Concern with the printed word seems to have been left to the Europeans, who, perhaps significantly, have always shown a greater interest in this field (viz. Raymond Williams and Robert Escarpit).

It is worth reminding ourselves at this point that, despite an early interest in the press, serious concern with the mass media in Europe, by social scientists, hardly began until the late 1950s. Some countries, like the United Kingdom, have been remarkably slow in this respect and this may in part account for the resistance which is still apparent in some quarters. Since about 1960, however, the Europeans in general, and especially the French, have pushed their research in a rather different direction. Reacting against the empirical method of the Americans, which for a decade or more has dominated French thinking, writers like Edgar Morin, Claude Lévi-Strauss and Roland Barthes have sought to push their investigations in a new direction: Morin stressing every aspect of the market situation, Lévi-Strauss applying the insights of structural linguistics and Barthes those of semiology. The precise importance, particularly of the approaches outlined by Lévi-Strauss and Barthes, are still being assessed but those who have followed in their footsteps have shown no hesitation in tackling such questions as the latent content of film and novel — subjects which, except in a mundane form, had evaded the American empirical tradition. In other words, American research has tended to concentrate most of its efforts on Lasswell's 'who', 'to whom' and 'with what effect', while European research has stressed the 'what' and 'in what channel' thereby, perhaps, discovering a middle-ground between the work of the sociologist and the cultural critic.

Also mediating between the work of the sociologists and that of cultural critics such as Hoggart and McLuhan (very different in approach as they obviously are), has been the phenomenon

of film study which has developed, in a more sophisticated
form, over the last two decades. In 1946, in his *Essai sur les
principes d'une philosophie du cinema*, Gilbert Cohen-Seat
established a distinction between what he called filmology,
a concern with the complex of imagery employed by the film,
and cinema, by which he meant the psychological, economic
and social implications of the medium. An institute was
established at the Sorbonne, though it subsequently closed
down in 1961. In a sense his movement was ahead of its time
and required the development of linguistics to provide a
language which carried real conviction. But Cohen-Seat was a
pioneer whose insights, absorbed into the structuralist
methodology, paved the way for the kind of work now conducted at the Centre d'études de communications de masse
at the École pratique des hautes études, in Paris. Now, of course,
film studies have established themselves widely, more especially
in France and the United States, while in the United Kingdom,
the Chair of Film Studies, established at London University in
1967, was the first chair concerned with teaching all aspects of
the medium ever established in the country. Such studies came
late to Britain, whose first university department for the training
of journalists, a commonplace in many European countries and
in the United States, was not established until 1970. Even the
more famous research centres were products of the 1960s. The
Centre for Contemporary Cultural Studies at Birmingham
emerged in 1964, while the Centre for Mass Communication
Research at Leicester University and the Centre for Television
Research at the University of Leeds were both founded in
1966.

The other main approach to a study of popular culture,
especially influential in Britain and the United States, has been
that rooted in a literary-historical tradition and drawing to some
extent on the humane assumptions of its nineteenth century
antecedents whose values in part it shares even while rejecting
many of its judgements. The essential difference between the
two approaches is that where the sociologist deals in value
analysis, the cultural critic tends to deal in value judgements.
The one observes phenomena with a view to constructing a
model of social interaction, the other evaluates and tests the
worth of transmitted cultural values. Until comparatively recent

times there has been a marked tendency to see the two approaches as to some degree antithetical but this breach is showing real signs of being closed. The tendency to see the sociologist's approach as descriptive and the literary historian's as prescriptive has in the past, however, been the cause of considerable animus. Cold objectivity has been contrasted with irresponsible intuition; mechanical content studies with cavalier generalization. In 1966 Richard Hoggart actually began an article entitled, 'Literature and Society', with two assertions: 'first, without appreciating good literature no one will really understand the nature of society; second, literary critical analysis can be applied to certain social phenomena other than "academically respectable" literature (for example, the popular arts, mass communications) so as to illuminate their meanings for individuals and for their societies.'[28] In other words he was identifying his two main antagonists as the social sciences and the traditional literary critics. And his attack on the social sciences became more overt as the article continued. For he contrasted the sensitive literary and cultural critic with those whose conception of the pursuit of knowledge turned on 'the effort after and the considered interpretation of objectively verifiable material, independent of the personality of the enquirer'. While conceeding that 'as a deliberately adopted professional position (a technical stance) this can, in certain circumstances be admirable,' he found that, 'as a general statement about human life it is one eyed.' For 'in some disciplines one must act as though all knowledge were scientifically verifiable (and in some subjects it can be so defined). In the study of society it cannot. Sociological and social-psychological techniques are already immensely sophisticated and rightly grow more sophisticated every day; they are still crude in comparison with the complexity of what an unskilled laborer feels on his pulses every day of the week.'[29] This last remark betrays a certain studied romanticism which has tended to characterize the literary approach, for Hoggart especially has tended to confront the conservative nostalgia of Arnold and his descendants with a liberal nostalgia, substituting the integrity of urban working-

[28] Richard Hoggart, 'Literature and Society', *The American Scholar*, XXXV, ii (Spring 1966) pp. 277–8.
[29] *Ibid.*

class life or regional distinction for the agrarian simplicities invoked by those for whom industrialization implied the necessary corruption of an organic community whose unity was an assumed if untested truth.

Three years after the remarks quoted above, however, the tune had changed and in a paper, 'Contemporary Cultural Studies', written for the Centre for Contemporary Cultural Studies at Birmingham which he now headed, Professor Hoggart advocated a close partnership between cultural critics and social scientists, reflecting thereby not only his own institution's growing commitment to sociology but also that move towards the consolidation of approaches which has been a mark of the social sciences themselves in recent years. Old assumptions that popular culture can be explained solely in terms of commercial or economic structures, or explicated only by application of content analysis or the rules of literary analysis, have given way to a pluralistic approach such as that to be found particularly at a number of French research centres as well as at the Birmingham Centre itself. Indeed part of the fascination of this subject lies not in the exclusive claims advanced by bellettrists, historians, sociologists, anthropologists, linguisticians or semi-ologists, but precisely in the necessary interdisciplinarity which alone holds the key to a real and full understanding of the popular arts and mass communications. The spread of multi-discipline approaches to central problems of the age has been a mark of educational innovation in Europe over the past decade and nowhere has this been more successful in exposing the springs of human action, needs and perceptions, than in this field which touches so directly on the everyday lives of the international community. While yesterday's battles have, seemingly, to be ritually refought whenever students of popular culture meet together, and though a certain air of defensiveness still seems to characterize the language of those who have long since validated both their subject and methodology, there is at last a clear sense both of the importance of the field and the need for an integrated assault on material which necessarily transcends both national boundaries and the divisions between disciplines.

2

Communications as Cultural Science

Raymond Williams

Human communication has been seriously and intensively studied as far back as we have records of organized thought. In western civilization the sciences of grammar and rhetoric were for two millennia at the center of education, and though the names have changed, studies of language and its practical skills have remained central. The study of communications — that significant plural — is by contrast, at least at first sight, a modern phenomenon.

There are two obvious reasons for this altered definition. First, the institutions of communications in modern societies are of a size and importance which give them, inevitably, social and political significance and, increasingly, economic significance as well. Second, there has been the well-known series of technical developments in communication, involving radical changes in the possibilities of transmission and reception and, as significantly, in reproducibility and reproduction. Because of these changes our kinds of attention and study have altered.

Necessarily, then, the communication scientist materializes in many specialized forms. He is a sociologist, concerned with these institutions and their effects. He is an engineer, concerned with these technologies and with the systems which are essential to design, understand and control. He is a cultural analyst, concerned with the meanings and values of particular artifacts and classes of artifact, from poems and paintings to films and newspapers, from buildings to fashions in dress. He is a psychologist, concerned with the basic units and patterns of communicative interaction, face to face (though if we always spoke face to face, in each other's presence, the problem would be very much simpler) or in the differential use of machines. Or he is a linguist or linguistic philosopher, concerned with the basic forms and structures of the acts of expression and communication.

The problems are so great — and not only great but extra-ordinarily subtle and intricate — that we ought first, in a general way, to welcome this diversity of emphasis and discipline. But this is rarely how it goes. That communication scientists cannot communicate with each other is by now one of those old jokes which with repetition becomes melancholy.

The situation reminds me of that perhaps apocryphal story of a conference on Latin studies, to be attended by Latin scholars from all over the world. Someone had the plausible notion that they should conduct their proceedings in Latin, but it didn't work. What they had in common as their subject was in practice less than the linguistic history that divided them. Some, I am sure, felt a kind of despair that there should have been this drifting apart. Others, I am also sure, went home and mocked those extraordinary others who said 'veer' or 'wire' or similar incomprehensible jargon for *vir*. But some at least, I would hope, came to reflect on their situation with some sense of the history which simultaneously united and divided them: the common interest and the divergent habits; and the need, as in all communication, to listen as well as to state and assert.

That is as much as can be done, in the short term. In Britain especially the waters of higher education are just now unusually brackish. You can go on doing, in effect without challenge, virtually anything that has ever been done, but if you propose anything new you are lucky if your integrity escapes whipping; your intelligence and sensibility will have been long given up as dead. For suppose you said, 'There are these different kinds of communication studies; shall we try, in some form — in a department, in a colloquium, in an interdisciplinary programme, to put them physically if in no other way in contact for say the next five years, and see if we learn anything?' — not only would you have committed an error of taste and judgement but you would find, rising from the ground like armed men or armed ghosts, tame literary scholars insisting on the paramount importance of keeping out sociology, tame sociologists saying the same thing the other way round — and to hear the curled sneer that can be got into 'sociology' or 'literary' is one of the communication experiences of our times. Fortunately, however, not all men, not even all scholars, are tame. Under whatever difficulties, the work will have to be done and is in some places being attempted.

The approach I want to describe is that of cultural studies, which is English for 'cultural science.' Here, centrally, communication is a practice. Communication study is open to whatever can be learned of the basis of this practice: the detailed processes of language and of gesture, in expression and interaction, and of course any general features of underlying human structures and conventions. It is open, also, to the effects on these processes and features of particular technologies which, since it is a modern study, it necessarily considers over a range from the printed book and the photograph to broadcasting and motion pictures and beyond these to the specialized electronic media.

Within a living culture, so many of these processes will have been naturalized, and those which have not will have been identified as conscious and isolable modernisms, that without this dimension of openness to the fundamental processes much of the working analysis will be naive, or will at best be limited to the unexamined conventions of its culture. Nevertheless, cultural study is concerned with practice. It draws to it a proportion — now markedly increasing — of those students whose received discipline is the understanding of cultural artifacts.

Over many centuries, ways have been found of talking to the point, though in varying and usually controversial ways, about poems, paintings, buildings, songs, novels, films, symphonies, newspapers, advertisements, political speeches, styles of dress; a whole range of cultural practice which may be separated as artifacts for more specific study, but which have also to be seen as the practical communication — or, more strictly, that special part of it which has survived because it is in some way recorded — of a particular people or class of a people at a particular place and time.

Many of the disciplines which deal with these artifacts are remarkably developed in their own terms, and in an academic context can separate out from each other and from that more central perception that they were made by real men in real places in real and significant social relationships. More crucially, in their concentration on artifacts, the disciplines, especially as they develop in scholarly and historical ways, can convert all practices to artifacts, and in the shadow of this delusion suppose themselves absolved, in the name of the excellence and achievement of the past, from the comparable practices of their own time.

It is then not only, to take an example, that in the study of literature at Oxford there was for many years a classical time-stop at 1830, since the practice of our great-great-grandfathers and their embarrassingly pressing descendants was altogether too turbulent and uncertain; or that in the study of the history of the English language at Cambridge there is in effect a time-stop at the point in the late middle ages when the language became that which we now write and speak and keep changing. It is also that a practice has to become an artifact, and moreover an artifact of the kind that is conventionally found in libraries and museums, to deserve much attention. A seventeenth-century political pamphlet deserves disciplined attention; a current party political broadcast does not.

There is, then, a resistance, in the name of standards, to a very wide area of contemporary cultural practice; but moreover, from the habits of mind thus induced (the conversion of practices into artifacts, of real expressive and communicative process into isolable objects) several modes of analysis which depend on the recognition of practice — the reconstruction of composition, the study of social relations within which the practice occurred, the study of related practices which lead to distinguishable artifacts but which are still related — all these and other modes become attenuated or unattempted and the discipline narrows, losing its touch with life.

We say cultural studies because we are concerned with practice and with the relations between practices. Culture itself was originally a practice: the growth and tending of wheat or the growth and tending of minds. The significance of the emergence of the modern meaning of culture — that meaning which took it beyond specific cultural practices to a general process or state — is that the individual practices were seen as related parts of a general development or achievement. Culture became, in the eighteenth century, an idea which expressed a secular sense of general human development, and its advance, in this respect, over metaphysical notions of a providential or aberrant civilization is remarkable.

But almost at once it encountered the central problem of all subsequent cultural theory: that of the relations between different practices, within what was nevertheless seen as a general development. The first form of this difficulty was the use of culture to indicate all general human development — in the popular form of the universal histories, which recounted the growth of civilization — and the alternative and almost contemporary use of the same term, 'culture,' to indicate the specific development of a particular people, a national culture.

This difficulty has persisted, and is still of radical theoretical importance in anthropology and in history. But the next phase of difficulty was even harder. In idealist thought it had been assumed that the guiding element in this general cultural process was spirit or consciousness (although in its later forms this was a human and not a divine spirit). Marx challenged that by naming the guiding element — even, in language he inherited, the determining element — as material production and the social relations it embodies. That theoretical conflict is also, still, of profound importance. In our own immediate terms, it underlies all questions about the relations between practices, and unless these questions are faced, no studies of communications can get very far.

Out of this argument, about the relation between practices, came the new concept of cultural science and with it a significant part of modern sociology. Dilthey, for example, was concerned to distinguish between the natural and cultural sciences, in respect of their fields of research, their forms of experience, and the role of the attitudes of the investigator. His distinctions, I believe, are still fundamental, though they leave many problems unsolved.

Weber, even more extensively, was persistently concerned with the relations between fundamental social and cultural practices, and his hypothesis of elective affinities — at times in the more modern guise of 'correspondences' and 'homologous structures' — has proved an attractive halfway house in cultural analysis; halfway, or so it seems, between simple idealist theories and the simpler kinds of materialist determinism.

Now the spirit of this whole inquiry — to which literally thousands of people have contributed — is profoundly open, alert, and general. It has had its bitter and even its squalid controversies, and this is understandable; but in temper and approach it is in a wholly different dimension from what seems our own world of small cultivators, heads down to their own fields; or if they have their heads down, good luck to them, for some at least are much busier at the walls and fences, erecting improbable signs that trespassers will be prosecuted, or exploiting the natural desire of young men and women to be qualified and certificated by a self-interested definition of the discipline and its boundaries.

I recall the spirit of cultural science because I am interested in its heirs — who will change its methods but will still inherit its vigorous and general humanity. If I speak with some feeling it is because until quite recently opportunities were missed here in Britain — in a country which has a very rich tradition of just this kind — for the effective reconstitution of cultural studies, within which, as I am arguing, a central kind of communications study should be pursued.

The opportunities were missed, largely, because of a demarcation dispute. People coming to communications analysis from the tradition of cultural studies were looked up and down and eventually identified as literary types. Some part of this error was explicable. Literary study itself, for the reasons I gave earlier, had been in some places reduced to the specialized analysis of isolated artifacts. Indeed there has been a critical culmination of a long process of narrowing-down. Literature itself, as a concept, was a Renaissance specialization from the more general area of discourse in writing and speech: a specialization directly related to the printed book. In the late eighteenth and early nineteenth centuries there was a further specialization: literature, which had till then included all forms of writing, came to be specialized, though with some exceptions and overlaps, to imaginative literature. (The theoretical complications of that limitation are only just beginning to be grasped.) As modern literary study entered the universities there was a further specialization; literature was the 'good' or 'serious' part of such work.

So the natural area of interest of this kind of person — an interest in all discourse in writing or speech — had been specialized and even restricted to printed imaginative compositions of a certain quality. Of course, when people looked around, most of these had been written in the past. Today — it was said — there was only television and all that rubbish, so that literature, in some places, came to resemble that proverbial bird which flew in ever-decreasing circles until it finally and fundamentally disappeared.

Now this definition of a discipline had undoubtedly made some of its disciples strange. It was no wonder they got looked at. But who was doing the looking? I remember a friend of mine being rebuked for having attempted some cultural analysis on the grounds that this was wanton and ignorant trespass into sociology, by the practitioners of a discipline which in this country at that time had produced not a single piece of cultural analysis of its own and indeed showed no signs of wanting to try.

There was a central area of overlap — more or less adequately recognized and negotiated — between these varying cultural studies and the specifically aesthetic or specifically social studies which lay in either direction. What the practice of aesthetic analysis contributed was a capacity for sustained and detailed analysis of actual cultural works. What was much more open to question was the extension of this kind of analysis and insight to matters of cultural and social generalization where, quite properly, there were other real disciplines to act as a check, or, better, as an incentive. The study of cultural institutions or of cultural effects could not properly be pursued by projected aesthetic analysis.

Yet for a generation this problem was masked by a notion which, as it happened, was widely shared by those who had approached modern communications from what was called 'high culture' and by orthodox social and political scientists. This notion — an ideology if ever there was one — was that of a 'mass society,' based on deep social, cultural and political assumptions and experiences.

And so it came about that the study of communications was deeply and almost disastrously deformed by being confidently named as the study of 'mass-communications'. 'Mass-communications' is a term which seems to have got into every language and into the most diverse schools, which describes and too often predicts departments and research programs and conferences, and which it is time to bury. Not only is it disastrous in its limitation of communication studies to a few specialized areas like broadcasting and the cinema and what it miscalls popular literature, when there is the whole common area of discourse in speech and writing that always needs to be considered. It is also disastrous in its consequent definition of the 'mass media'. The 'mass' metaphor overtook us in its weakest meaning, of the large ultimate audience, and then positively prevented the analysis of most specific modern communication situations and of most specific modern communication conventions and forms.

But it had one lingering effect. If most people are masses, they are inherently stupid, unstable, easily influenced. Sex and violence not only rear but propagate their ugly heads. The only question worth asking, it seemed, about jazz or television or cinema or even football (for a while they left out politics) was first how, then whether, it corrupted people. The residual result is that it is still easier to get resources for impact-studies — perhaps we should call them corruption-studies — in television and the like than for any other single kind of work. Much of what is then called the sociology of communications is this kind of impact-study, and indeed some of it is valuable, though it is always necessary to add, as everyone trained in really precise observation of behaviour will confirm, that the scientific discovery and demonstration of effects is one of the toughest areas you can enter.

For, again, there is corruption and corruption. I would like to see a system of parallel grants: for every inquiry into the consumption of television or the like, equal resources for an inquiry into production. The great or at least large institutions of modern communications need intensive and continuous study. This has so far been done only in part-time and occasional ways. And I should add while I am saying this that it seems to me very significant that the most detailed information that exists in Britain about reading habits, and some associated behavior, is in the regular and highly specific surveys and reports of the Institute of Practitioners in Advertising: a highly intentional form of research, to say the least, but one which puts any comparable scholarly work in this country to shame.

Studies of institutions, in the full sense — of the productive institutions, of their audiences, and of the forms of relationship between them — will have to be carried out by procedures of social science from which, in result and by example, all cultural analysts will learn a great deal. Indeed in this respect the orthodox suspicion of cultural studies can be seen as justified, and it can only be overcome, from both sides, by practical work. But, of course, this kind of study does not exhaust cultural analysis, or leave it merely to describe, to analyze, and to generalize particular works. Detailed aesthetic analysis tends to be continued and extended. But the real questions arise when we come to forms. Questions about forms in communications are also questions about institutions and about the organization of social relationships. Let me give an example.

When I first started reading social and political science, at about the time when I was getting interested in communications, I came across a formula which I was told was standard for communication sciences: 'Who says what how to whom with what effect?' I was reasonably impressed, after some of my literary studies. That there was a 'who' and a 'whom' as well as a 'what' seemed encouraging, and 'effect,' of course, we were all talking about anyway. But as I went on, I noticed what might be called a diminution of the 'what': a problem that arises, incidentally, in many communication studies, where the relationship — the 'who' and the 'whom' that communication postulates — can come to override the full substance of the communication, though the relationship and the substance must be seen as in fact inseparable.

To anyone with literary experience, the 'what' is irreducible, as well as active, and needs precise attention as a way of understanding the 'who' and the 'whom' in their most significant senses, and certainly as a way of understanding 'effect'. And I suppose it was this that led me to noticing the formula's most extraordinary omission: 'Who says what how to whom with what effect' — but 'with what purpose?' Nobody seemed to be mentioning or inquiring into that. I know now that this exclusion of *intention* was characteristic of a whole phase of functionalist social theory, in communications as in much else. But I noticed the exclusion first because I knew nobody could answer questions about the 'what' or give reality and specificity to the variables abstracted as 'who' and 'whom', or speak in other than unconsciously manipulative ways about 'effect', unless intention — not necessarily conscious intention, but the intention informed in the 'what', the shaping intention, the active composition of what is always more than an object — the practice of communication — was seriously and continuously investigated. So I amended the formula, in a paper in a social-scientific journal; but the amendment would have happened anyway, for new people were coming and new frontiers were being crossed.

There is a sense that we are only beginning. It is in this spirit that I offer my example of what communication study involves. It occurred to me recently that the television discussion — the sort of thing we see in Britain on *Panorama* or *Midweek* or *Nationwide* — is now the principal medium of formal social and political argument for the majority of our people. Now I know, as I say that, that the old high-cultural reflex is waiting — I wonder how many of you experienced it: something along the lines of — 'Then God help us!'

But I don't feel it like that, if only because I'm glad that so many people now have at least that minimal access to general discussion. I don't, that is to say, write it off as beneath investigation; on the contrary, even when I agree about its limits and its faults, I see the case for investigation. And how this investigation would be done seems to be to set the task, by example, for communication studies.

First, there is a necessary approach through social and political science. Even highly educated people know comparatively little about the precise social structures within which such discussions are arranged — I mean the formal research, editing, and production relationships; the departmental relationships within the broadcasting institutions; the structures of those institutions and their relations with others. There is this factual description and analysis and social questions arising from it: the critical comparison of models of institutions, models of audiences, and models of representative viewpoints, to take only these obvious examples.

And with these we begin to enter an area where conscious and unconscious models would have to be analyzed and distinguished. Take the model of an active chairman, for example, and the wealth of questions around his role in this precise situation: questions that could be approached, among other ways, by analyzing the notions of presentation and introduction, of chairing and interviewing, or the older notions of mediator and moderator.

Some of these could be tackled with known tools of social analysis; others would require a different dimension of analysis. Someone trained in the analysis of language would in any case have much to contribute: descriptively, as with someone noting and analyzing the conscious politics; critically, to attend to the forms of the discourse — the diction and imagery but also the basic strategies of address, the encounters and evasions, the mode of question and answer and rhetorical question and non-answer: for all of which, if we would use them, we have very serviceable tools.

We would need someone sensitized to dramatic analysis: to the significance of physical groupings, to take only one example, and to the modulation of these by the specific television environment both internally, within the studio, and in quite different ways in the transmitted version (whether edited or live); a recognition of the significance of viewpoint, close-up, variation of angle, cutting — a technical yet central kind of analysis of the precise communication situation.

We would need an understanding of the positive require-ments of the technology and the overlapping but not identical version of those requirements adopted by the professionals now using it. For very close work we would need the techniques developed by experimental psychologists for precise analysis of verbal and nonverbal interaction; indeed, their com-bination with dramatic and cinematic analysis would be extraordinarily instructive. And we would have to go on to include the other part of the communication situation — the viewers: not only studying persistent effects and influences but recording and discussing them in more precise ways while the process is still alive.

We can describe all these methods serially, but most of the really interesting questions would only arise when we came to put the findings together or, more likely, to push each other's findings around: around the proposition, for example, that the television discussion is not only a political event but also a cultural form, and that the form indicates many overt and covert relationships.

The work will be done because I think there are now enough of us who want to work in these ways to survive the defenses of vested interests, the general drizzle of discouragement, and even the more deeply-rooted inertia of contemporary orthodox culture; to announce in effect an open conspiracy: that in new ways, by trial and error but always openly and publicly, we shall do this work because it needs to be done.

3

Popular Culture: A Sociological Approach

Zev Barbu

Considering the present state of sociological theory in general
it would be somewhat disingenuous to begin by apologizing for
the highly circumspect and tentative manner in which I intend
to approach the subject matter of this paper. It is nonetheless
necessary to emphasize from the very outset that lack of a
coherent theoretical framework constitutes only part of my
difficulty. To follow a Durkheimian manner of approach, one
can say that the sociology of popular culture has not yet fulfilled
the first two basic requirements of any systematic enquiry, a
clear definition and a comprehensive classification. Not only is
there an alarmingly wide range of 'operational' definitions, but
the very meaning of the term 'popular' differs so greatly from
author to author, from context to context, indeed from
language to language, that no amount of sociological imagination
is great enough to construct a complete picture. Particularly
alarming is the tendency noticed in many recent works in the
field, to confine the phenomenon of popular culture to its
most recent version, namely popular culture in advanced
industrial societies, and consequently, to apply to it interpretative models and analytical tools relevant for this and for
no other type of society. Whatever its initial justification might
have been, it has by now become sufficiently clear that this
type of approach is inadequate in a two-fold way: first, it tends
to overemphasize those aspects of popular culture which are
amenable to an empirical type of enquiry; second, it has, in
the long run, prepared the ground for a purely negative, moreover 'subversive', conception of the phenomenon, a

conception rooted in and leading to an emphatic preception
and appraisal of the antinormative tendencies and values in
contemporary societies, as well as of those (cultural) activities
and products which are not, or actively resist being, included in
the dominant culture of these societies. Although this is a
point which will be discussed in some detail at a later stage, it
is important to mention it at the very outset so as to bring into
immediate focus the rationale, and indeed the prime mover of
the present enterprise, namely, the necessity of making a new
start in the study of popular culture. Lest the task may appear
overambitious, I hasten to specify that the main intention is to
pose or re-open, rather than to solve a problem, and for this
purpose I intend to follow established sociological procedures.
More precisely, I propose to survey and examine this area of
study from a historical comparative point of view paying
particular attention to the following main themes: the major
varieties or types of popular culture in relation to their specific
social framework; the specific nature of contemporary popular
culture and the methodological problems raised by it. But
before anything else I should like to comment briefly on the
meaning of popular culture.

Let me start with a point just mentioned regarding the
definition of the concept of popular culture. Even from a quick
glance at some representative works in the field one can form a
pretty clear idea that the concept is often no more than a broad
umbrella covering a wide range, almost an open series, of
phenomena, such as, for example, ancient romances (second
century AD), religious, hagiographic literature in seventeenth
century France, didactic literature in seventeenth century
England, peasant art in contemporary Romania, Scottish
country dance, horror, pornographic, or scientific fiction in
contemporary industrial societies, cinema as well as most forms
of entertainment, and on the whole any form of cultural activity
and product which is by one criterion or another reckoned to
arouse a relatively widespread interest, or achieve a high degree
of consumption in a given society. To put it differently, the
epithet 'popular' is equally applied to the *Bibliothèque Bleue* in
seventeenth century France, working-class culture in Elizabethan

England, English eighteenth century drama, and, according
to de Tocqueville, the American culture as a whole; even the
Weimar culture was an essentially popular culture, as one of
its latest historians believes.

Needless to say my main concern here is not with the
underlying logic but with the sociological relevance of such a
mental operation. Does this type of conceptualization, this
broad categorization provide me with a basic insight, an initial
theoretical hypothesis or useful interpretative tool in this field
of enquiry? The answer is a categorical no, for the obvious
reason that these phenomena belong to so many and varied
social contexts and types of society that they cannot, and do
not, constitute one single analytical unit. In other words, the
groundwork of any systematic sociological enquiry and above
all a systematic classification of phenomena is, in this case,
either incomplete or entirely lacking. Admittedly, this is a
complex and difficult operation which requires a great deal
of detailed investigation in order to be properly carried out. A
brief discussion of some guiding principles and general framework will, however, be in order.

At the risk of appearing pedantic it is necessary to begin by
drawing a distinction between 'popular' and 'popularized', that
is between the notion of a popular culture and that of a
popularized culture. Whether this is real or a purely analytical
distinction should for the moment remain a moot point. The
fact is that the terms popular and popularized are often used
in the same or similar contexts, and that this creates the
impression that they belong to the same category. Now,
whatever the methodological merit, such a position is based on
a naïve, often unexamined, type of generalization and as such
constitutes a main source of ambiguity and confusion in many
contemporary studies of popular culture. Briefly, to the
sociologist the differences between a popular and a popularized
culture are at least as important as are the similarities. Granted,
as commonly used, the terms signify popularity, or simply, the
quality of being widespread. But even from a most cursory
semantic analysis one can deduce important differences. While
the former (popular) indicates an implicit state or condition,
more precisely, a phenomenon which is widespread owing to
some intrinsic or at least nonspecified condition, the latter

(popularized) presupposes a specific process inside which one could discern a certain degree of autonomy, moreover a certain degree of internal differentiation between a set of initiating circumstances, on the one hand, and a final product, on the other. Putting it differently, and, at the same time, moving away from pure semantics, the term popular signifies a widespread condition or state of affairs which, even when exhibiting a certain degree of change or growth, has as its main characteristic the fact that it is given, and consequently, offers little, if any, ground for a clear conceptual distinction between 'now' and 'then' between 'actuality' and 'potentiality'. Thus, if pushed to an extreme, the difference of meaning between the two notions could be as great and radical as to constitute a basis for a diochotomic classification of cultures on the dimension of historicity. More precisely, while the term popular normally connotes a type of culture of a more or less static character, hence, with a weak, hardly noticeable historical dimension, the term popularized connotes the very opposite, namely, a type of culture which is both widespread and widespreading as a result of organized social action. So much for semantic considerations which owing to their abstract nature are bound to overstate if not exaggerate the difference between a popular and a popularized type of culture. But the exaggeration may serve the positive purpose of highlighting an important point of sociological procedure. To start with, and this bears directly on the foregoing comment, even from a rapid survey of the field one can notice a sharp division, and consequently, the necessity of a broad binary classification, of the phenomena belonging to it. There is, on the one hand, an area, indeed a category of phenomena, which belongs to what is commonly called a traditional, mainly rural, type of society. There is, on the other hand, a not less distinct area belonging to a modern industrial type of society. To explain the difference between the two areas is a complex enterprise involving nothing less than a detailed account of modernization itself. For a quick understanding, however, it should be enough to mention those aspects of modernization which are particularly relevant. There is first of all the spread of literacy, or in terms more pertinent to our present concern, the transition from a preliterate to a literate stage in the development of a given society. Parallel to this, although not necessarily synchronized, is the transition from a dominantly oral to a dominantly written culture, a process, which needless to say is intimately related to, if not entirely dependant on, a series of other more central aspects of modernization, such as, for instance, urbanization, industrialization, as well as various forms and degrees of democratization, which, together or separately, produce a qualitative change in the structure and functioning of a given society. Briefly, any study of popular culture has to begin from a phenomenological duality, more simply, the objective existence of two kinds of popular culture separated, better said, differentiated, from each other by the process of modernization. This, I hasten to add, should not be taken to imply that they do not share a series of important characteristics, still less that they exclude each other. However, even when they coexist — which is often the case — they derive their specific character from the fact that they are genetically related to two types of society or to two different stages in the development of one and the same society, traditional and modern.

Traditional popular culture

That peasant and primitive cultures are two more or less distinct varieties of traditional culture can hardly be disputed. Can they also be described as popular cultures or varieties thereof? Although on the whole positive, the answer is neither a single nor simple one. In a strict sociological sense a peasant or primitive culture is not only popular but universal or communal, that is, shared by all members of the community. However, taken in isolation, the criterion of popularity raises some important questions. One is aware for instance, that the term normally implies a degree of relativity in a demographic statistical sense, that, within a given framework, normally a societal unit, something which is popular requires for its definition something which is not popular, i.e. restricted, marginal, minority. Thus, this would seem to imply that the existence of a so-called popular culture requires an intracultural and naturally intrasocietal differentiation between a 'high' and 'low', a majority (mass), and a minority (elitic) culture, a phenomenon which is hardly visible in a peasant, or primitive culture. Similarly, one can legitimately ask whether a common or commonly shared culture can in principle also be a popular culture. The difficulty in this case seems to lie in the fact that while the former normally presupposes a highly integrated social structure, the latter does not. Would it not therefore be useful from a sociological standpoint to make a distinction between common and popular culture?

It is hoped that the answers or some of these questions will emerge gradually. It would, nonetheless, be useful to state in advance that significant as they may be, the difficulties raised by this and other similar questions cannot and do not alter the substance of the argument put forward in this section, that primitive and peasant cultures are not only particularly instances of popular culture, but that because of their analytical relevance, they should be included in any social study of the subject. The argument can be carried out at two closely interlinked levels, cultural and social. Bearing in mind the point just made in connection with the notion of popularity, it would be useful and at the same time more accurate to refer to primitive and peasant cultures as protopopular cultures in a mainly descriptive rather than genetic historical sense, more specifically, in the sense that they contain strong if not dominant features of popular culture. Now, I fully realize, as the reader must, that clear as it may be this is something of a *non sequitur*; that in trying to advance an idea I have unwittingly jolted the whole argument into new and unprepared positions. In other words, to state that primitive and peasant cultures contain elements of popular culture is not very helpful if the very notion of popular culture has so far only tentatively been defined. It is therefore necessary to transpose the argument into a more interrogative key and ask what are the criteria according to which peasant or primitive culture can be considered as popular culture? More precisely, what are the intrinsic characteristics of this culture and to what extent are they relevant for the understanding of popular culture?

Most studies pay particular attention to the question of the strong, relatively direct and spontaneous appeal of popular culture. Lest this may look too obvious a point, it is necessary to specify that there is a considerable variety of opinion about the nature and explanation of the phenomena. Some convergency of views can nonetheless be found which is all the more significant since it is rare. Namely, a strong direct or spontaneous appeal seems to be meaningfully (i.e. more logically than psychologically) related to two thematic trends in most varieties of popular culture. This is often seen as an inner contradiction, a polarity between a strong orientation towards the concrete and particular, on one side, and a not less strong orientation towards the general and universal, on the other.[1] The former theme has a dominantly social character, and if popular literature is taken as an example, consists of a strong concern with everyday life in a didactic and descriptive manner, a perception — and feeling-bound reflection of a given social situation involving common, normally lower-class people, as in eighteenth century popular drama, or nineteenth century melodrama, to mention two well-known instances. It was with the idea of popular (read democratic) culture in mind that Diderot worked out his programme for a new drama and theatre in general as an unadulterated transposition to the stage of perceptually defineable slices of everyday life. The latter theme, on the other hand, consists of highly sublimated, normally symbolic-mythic, representations of a universal human condition, a biopsychological drive, a deep seated emotional or intellectual state aroused and permanently fomented by man's relation to the world and himself. And since his name has just been mentioned, one may as well add that Diderot's life-long pre-occupation with 'la littèrature licencieuse' was on the whole animated by the same idea of popular culture. That his own writing in the genre was only marginally popular only serves to prove that popularity is seldom, if ever, an entirely statistical concept. As will be shown later, in this, as in many other areas of cultural production, individual or collective, the concept of potentiality is an indispensable interpretative tool.

To return to the main point, do primitive and peasant cultures have the kind of appeal just outlined? Do they justify from this particular point of view the epithet of popular? The answer is a mildly qualified yes. To start with, and this sheds direct light on the nature of the qualification, both primitive and peasant cultures are complex systems expressing, thereby

[1] A detailed discussion of this can be found in W. Worringer, *Abstraction and Empathy* (London 1956).

satisfying in a coherent manner, the totality of life's conditions of a well-established community of people, a fact which makes it difficult to isolate and to discriminate clearly — be it for the purpose of analysis only — between various constituents, functional and structural. This applies with particular intensity to those aspects of primitive and peasant cultures which refer, or are supposed to refer, to everyday life for the obvious reason that they are intrinsically bound, often dissolved, in the highly metaphoric style of these cultures.

And yet this is only one side of the truth. Obviously, terms such as, 'descriptive', 'realist' and even 'didactic' have a very relative meaning. Following a code of their own, both primitive and peasant cultures reveal a deep concern with everyday life and social life in particular. The point can be illustrated in more than one way. Thus, in his unfortunately too brief comparative study of cognitive and social systems, G. Gurvitch makes the important point that 'the cognitive system of the peasant class' is rooted and organized around the perceptual knowledge of the external world, and a common sense knowledge of the world as a totality, two cognitive processes which determine the concrete and particularistic character of peasant culture.[2] Similarly, the *savage mind*, a rough equivalent for primitive culture, is characterized, to use C. Lévi-Strauss' words, by 'a mode of knowledge which is roughly adapted to that of perception and imagination'.[3] Finally, and admittedly in a considerably broader context, a sociologist such as Talcott Parsons refers to traditional cultures in general as cognitive and emotional systems dominated by particularistic values.

The fact that Gurvitch, like many others before him, pays particular attention to the cognitive-practical character of peasant culture should not detain us here. Taking into account the highly metaphoric-transfigurative character of peasant culture — and here one may add, primitive culture — it would be more appropriate to say that its undoubtedly great relevance for everyday life and its strong appeal for *all* members of the community, lies not as much in its cognitive, as in its ritualizing and liturgic functions, in its capacity to give a

[2] G. Gurvitch, *The Social Frameworks of Knowledge*, trans. M. and K. Thompson (Oxford 1971).

[3] C. Lévi-Strauss, *The Savage Mind* (London 1966), 15.

perfectly integrated expression — cognitive, emotional and practical — to all aspects of human life.

There are other perhaps more obvious grounds on which the epithet of proto-cultural can be used in the context of a peasant and primitive type of culture. To begin with, no less visible is the presence of the second thematic appeal just referred to, that is, the symbolic representation of the human condition *per se*. Although adducing relevant evidence would, in this case, be both easy and pleasant, the point is so self-evident that the temptation should be resisted. For the purpose at hand it should be enough to highlight the significance of the problem by mapping out the key positions reached in this field of studies as a result of intensive research carried out by people belonging to various disciplines but sharing in common, apart from a strong belief in the deep existential significance of various forms of traditional literature (peasant and primitive), a series of interpretative techniques and methods devised or adapted to this end. It is difficult to find a simple label, but what I have in mind is a whole range of structuralist interpretations (semantic, existentialist, experiential, sociocultural and psychological) of myths, folktales, legends, romances, ballads, to mention only some of the best known forms of creative imagination dominant in traditional literature, oral or written. Although the battle is still on and the front of the attack too broad to be properly coordinated, some directions are sufficiently clear and some achievements significant enough to deserve to be mentioned here.

To start with a general point of approach, it has become increasingly clear that these basic forms of popular imagination are something more and perhaps something else than accidental outcomes of recreational activities. accidental or intentional crystallizations of free-floating fantasies which, owing mainly to their inherent entertaining or pleasure rousing potential, have acquired an enduring, often super-historical, character as well as a degree of autonomy. Parallel to this, one notices a steadily growing body of evidence and theoretical awareness that they can and should be regarded as global pictures of the world characteristic of various, mainly early, stages in the development of mankind. Admittedly, one may easily object that, formulated in general terms such as these, this kind of approach is neither entirely new nor sufficiently relevant for the present argument. That is why it is important to state at once that my present concern lies with the various specific manners in which this initial position has been worked out. Despite its obvious interpretative value, the theoretical hypothesis that myths or folk-tales are imaginative constructions, or unifying images of man's experience of the world and himself, cannot and does not explain the dynamic potential and universal appeal of these products of imagination. How can one explain, for instance, the fact − and this is obviously a fact of observation − that myths, like rituals, have a built-in tendency for re-enactment? Although the answer to this and other similar questions are not easy to find one can detect a general trend which may briefly be formulated as follows: At a first level − the surface level − myths, and this stands for all other products of popular imagination, are composites of images and signs held together and organized in a meaningful form, that is, a narrative form. That this constitutes a visible totality hardly needs demonstrating. However, beneath this, hence, at an invisible level, myths are something more and something else. It would perhaps be useful to mention that this trend of thought is animated by the analytical principle of coexistent, superimposed, yet interpenetrating levels of meaning, which if properly applied reveals that myths are, structurally, systems of signs, and, functionally, basic codes of communication between man and the world. And, as the word code clearly suggests, myths are dynamic, moreover, open systems in that they contain a set of cognitive and emotional schemes which provide a permanent framework for man's experience of the world. In other words, myths constitute basic modes in which man structures (identifies, classifies and interconnects), as well as evaluates, his experience of the world. As has been often said, myths are not simply structures but generative structures of man's relationship to the world and himself.

From what has just been said one can draw the conclusion that myths derive their significance not as much from their formal qualities as from their intrinsic expressive capacity, from the fact that as systems of signs they refer to complex human situations, or, putting it differently, as codes, they contain in a simplified yet highly concentrated form not only modes of feeling about, but also modes of perceiving and representing, the world as a whole. Now, although this sheds considerable light on the relationship between myths and popular culture, one important point still remains to be clarified. Namely, it is well known that of all major cultural forms, myths are the least amenable to what may be called a classical type of sociological analysis, which assumes the possibility, first, of situating, hence of classifying myths according to their social contexts — be they ethnic groups, social classes, or global societies — and secondly, of interpreting them in terms of such contexts. Granted, there have been various attempts of a more or less systematic nature to identify the social origins of various myths, and classify them accordingly. But whatever their intrinsic merits may have been, such enterprises have contributed little to the sociological understanding of myths. It is important to point out that most sociogenetic studies in this field have sooner or later arrived at the same place: a highly fluid, grey, insufficiently differentiated, social reality which defies sociological analysis as much as a Rorschach test defies accurate perception. The same could be aid about those elaborate studies, so fashionable a few decades ago, concerned with the diffusion of myths. It would, therefore, hardly be an exaggeration to say that neither the milieu of birth nor that of adoption seem to affect myths deeply enough as to make a comparative study of them meaningful in sociological terms: like snails, myths slither through the history of mankind safely protected by their shells.

It was perhaps a simple image such as this that stimulated the beginnings of what is now commonly considered as one of the most exciting and fruitful intellectual enterprises of our time, Lévi-Strauss's comparative study of myths. For, needless to say, from the very outset his attention had been focused on what was common, permanent and general rather than individual, changeable, and particular in myths. Moreover he started from a vague intuition and arrived at a demonstrable conclusion that myths are essentially trans-societal and trans-historical products and that a proper understanding of their structure throws light on human nature as something specific and unique. Since this aspect of Lévi Strauss's work is well known, I confine myself to a formulation of its dominant theses. First, man is a culture-creating animal, and, hence, his specificity and uniqueness lie in his capacity to make a radical break with a natural order in the cosmos, and a simultaneous and irreversible integration with an artificial order, an order which, while fulfilling a signifying and codifying function relative to the order of nature, has a dynamic of its own. Closely related to this there is another not less well known thesis, namely, the priority of culture over society. This should be taken in a logical rather than ontological or chronological sense, meaning that according to Lévi-Strauss the order of culture, the order of signs and symbols, constitutes a more comprehensive and authentic manifestation of human nature than that of society, and consequently, the latter cannot explain the former.

As for the more specific relevance which the above ideas have in the present context the following points ought to be emphasized: to start with, myths, or rather myth-making, constitutes a first decisive step away from, indeed the very breaking-point with nature and, hence is a basic modality of becoming human. Putting it differently, myths are the original maps, the only reliable maps of a vast territory lying between the heart of the forest and the first 'clearing', between 'day' and 'night', 'raw' and 'cooked', 'hunted' and 'hunting', 'wild' and 'domesticated', 'sex' and 'love', 'instinct' and 'intelligence', to mention only the main signposts on the road leading from nature to culture. Secondly and more importantly, to the extent to which myth-making is rooted in man's capacity to express at an imaginative level, hence, transcend the trauma of separation from nature, myths are depositaries of primary modes of experiencing the world, primary modes of self-awareness and awareness of the world, briefly, primary forms of consciousness. It remains only to specify that primary means universal, or as Lévi-Strauss would have it, myths contain the *a priori* structure, the chromosomes regulating and controlling the process by which man moves from a natural to an artificial, symbolic, or conceived thought-of order in his existence.

Now we can return to the question of the relationship between traditions and popular culture. The main idea emerging from the foregoing argument is that myth-making constitutes a paradigm of culture formation, and, as such, a vantage point from which culture, like language in general, can be seen as an anthropological constant, a *sine qua non* in the definition of man. Two implications of this idea are particularly relevant in the present context. First, elements of myth, or a mythic substratum, could and should be found in all cultures, in all societies and all historical periods. Second, the mythic component, or substratum, of a given culture should be taken as a reliable index of its popularity.

But reasonable as these statements may appear, they have to be proven and this raises important problems of approach and method. It is perfectly reasonable to postulate, as Lévi-Strauss did, that, at a symbolic level, 'raw' and 'cooked' constitutes a polarity of such an intensity of meaning that the bridge, the mediation between them, represents the journey between nature and culture, which is the quintessence of the human project of life, provided that one has adequate means by which to identify such a project in various social contexts including our own. Similarly, to be aware, as many of us are, that Oedipus 's'est nous' is one thing, to demonstrate the particular manner or manners in which the ancient myth operates through the imagination of contemporary man, is another. That these are genuine warnings can hardly be denied. Their importance could, however, be easily exaggerated if one is not ready to admit that in an enterprise of this sort, rigorous methods are not always and not necessarily an advantage, that precise techniques have, at times, to give way to 'occultations', to 'wild practices', as a psychoanalyst facing an enigmatic case would say. Bearing this in mind one could confidently maintain that the results achieved so far are far from insignificant. Leaving aside the contribution made by psychoanalysis as a whole, and the Jungian approach in particular, as well as by Lévi-Strauss's followers, the following two trends deserve special mention. The first may briefly be described as a structural-existential interpretation of literature and art of the sort illustrated by F. Kermode, or M. Raimond to mention only two variations on the same theme.[4] The purpose of the exercise is twofold: first, to discover or reconstruct the structure of human experience embodied in a literary work, and secondly, to reveal its existential significance.

[4] F. Kermode, *The Sense of an Ending: Studies in the Theory of Fiction* (London 1967) and M. Raimond, *La Crise du roman des lendemains du naturalisme aux années vingt* (Paris 1965).

This is normally achieved by establishing a participatory relation between the human situation as revealed by a literary work, on one side, and a myth, or mythic world, on the other. Thus, in describing the sense, or rather the project of life characterizing a particular literary work, or author, the proponents of this type of approach normally use terms such as anxiety, dread, hope, despair, and a series of other existential categories which apply, needless to say, equally well to the structure of human experience revealed by most myths. In this sense, Kermode and Raimond define the significance of an individual work, or of a trend or period by identifying their mythical framework and orientation in terms such as 'apocalyptic', 'paradisiac', 'deluge'. That this says a great deal about their appeal hardly needs mentioning.

The other trend refers to what has lately come to be known as the world-view conception of literature. As this is often described as a sociological, sometime scientific type of approach, the term myth may appear out of place unless taken in its broadest possible connotation. I hasten to say, however, that this should on no account be considered as a purely arbitrary still less as a distorting view of the position held by the protagonists of this type of approach. On the contrary, I am inclined to believe that G. Lukacs or L. Goldmann, to mention only two such critics, stand only to gain if this aspect of their work is brought to light and acknowledged. For, leaving aside the more general theoretical and ideological orientation of their work, their key concept is, analytically speaking, similar to and often interchangeable with that of myth, that is literature seen as 'consciousness of the world as a totality', in the one case, and literature seen as a metaphor of the world, in the other. Consider, for instance, what Lukacs has to say about the value and significance of the novels of Balzac as compared with those of Kafka. The work of Balzac, Lukacs maintains, has a universal significance, social and aesthetic, because the vision of man derived from it transcends the present in a manner analoguous — homologuous is Lukacs' work — to that in which proletarian consciousness transcends the conditions of capitalist society. The novels of Kafka, on the other hand, have only a minor artistic value because the vision of man derived from them is glued to the present as lived by an isolated, hence, nontypical individual. But since Lukacs does not hesitate — and rightly so — to add to this a series of emotional categories such as, for instance, forwardlooking-optimistic, and inwardlooking-pessimistic, one wonders whether this type of approach reveals anything more and anything else than the mythic motive underlying the existential significance of Balzac's and Kafka's novels, that is, the paradisaic and apocalyptic motif respectively. Although the reasons that Lukacs cannot accept such an interpretation appears to be many and varied, they could be reduced to one, namely his interpretative model of literature makes little if any sense outside the framework of a modern industrial type of society, which by contrast with the traditional community is a highly differentiated and divided type of society striving toward, or in terms of literature, dreaming of, a future unity. Within such a social framework, a forwardlooking-paradisaic mythology is implicitly loaded with a positive value and universal significance, whether it is shared by a majority, a minority or by nobody. In the next section I shall explore the main implication of such a position for the concept and indeed the phenomenon of popular literature.

Popular culture and modern society

Traditional culture is popular to the extent to which it is the expression of an integrated community which constitutes the hallmark of a traditional society of a primitive or peasant type. Within the framework of a traditional society, the notions of popular, common and universal have convergent if not over-lapping connotations, as far as cultural products and values are concerned. This, needless to say, does not imply that traditional culture should be seen as a direct reflection of social reality, or of the world as a whole. Thus, the significance of this culture may be, and often is, a function of its capacity to express an alternative to reality, a compensatory myth, to use an expression which Freud applies to folk tales in general. But it is a consensual compensatory myth, and herein lies its universality and popularity. Equally inadequate would be to maintain that because of the nondifferentiated character of traditional society, traditional culture depicts an harmonious and peaceful universe. On the contrary, the popular hero, the hero of the fairy tales and legends, is more often than not born and grows

up in a world of struggle, a world in which he has to choose
between opposing goals and temptations. But, again, it is a
consensual opposition and struggle — normally between good
and evil, or between life and death — and consequently a consensual choice.

With this in mind one can look now more closely at the
phenomenon of popular culture in modern societies. I say with
this in mind because one way, perhaps the most usual way, of
tackling the question is by following the logical principle of
opposition and contrast. As just suggested, the fact that modern
industrial societies have a highly differentiated, moreover
internally divided, structure has led to a general assumption
which lies at the basis of most if not all studies in this field. It
is that there is an analoguous or homologuous differentiation
and inner division in the culture of these societies. Whether and
to what extent this is a justified assumption is a question which
lies beyond the scope of the present discussion. In what follows
I shall concentrate attention on the sociological aspects of the
question with special reference to the methodological principles
involved.

Starting with the point just made, most authors in this field
adhere to a binary classification of culture which they con-
ceptualize in a great variety of ways starting from a series of
more commonly used dichotomies, such as, learned versus
unlearned, highbrow versus lowbrow cultures, and continuing
with a series of more systematic binary classifications, such as
mass and elite culture (the phenomenon identified by de
Tocquville in the context of democratic and aristocratic
societies) popular culture and genuine art (L. Lowenthal) or to
end up with something fashionable, Gramsci's distinction
between popular and dominant or hegemonic culture. Now,
terminology apart, these classifications have two things in
common: they all involve in various degrees a dichotomic
criterion and a value judgement. A possible exception from
the first rule is Lowenthal who argues that the distinction
between genuine art and popular culture consists in the fact
that the former is concerned with 'the truth' while the latter
emphasizes 'the nature of the effect'.[5] Much more significant

[5] L. Lowenthal, *Literature, Popular Culture and Society* (Engelwood Cliffs, 1961).

is the deviation from the second rule, namely, the reversal of hierarchy between popular and dominant culture.

Brief as it is, it is hoped that the above list of binary terms is clear and representative enough to allow me to move to the central question of this final section: What are the main socio-logical criteria for distinguishing between two levels or types of culture, or, more to the point, what are the main sociological criteria used in the study of popular culture in modern societies? Although it is far too early to arrive at definite conclusions there is enough evidence to suggest that the criteria used so far can be grouped around three main points. These are variations on the relationship between class and culture, between the author and his work and between the market as an economically organized institution and cultural production.

In its broadest, and at the same time most abstract, formu-lation, the first criterion postulates that cultural division is rooted in and runs along the lines of class division, that learned, or high, culture corresponds to upper classes, while popular culture corresponds to lower classes. Within this broad formulation one can find a number of variations mainly concerning: the precise nature of the relationship between class and culture, i.e. direct or mediated; the relationship between the two types of culture, i.e. whether the former is historically speaking a refined form of the latter, or conversely, the latter is a degraded form of the former; the sociological index of classification, the author, the content or other characteristics of literary production. All this is obviously relevant, but the main point with which I am concerned here, and which has direct bearing on the argument as a whole, refers to the development in time of this type of approach. To repeat, by postulating a correspondence between high culture and upper classes, and popular culture and lower classes, the class criteria also imply a relationship of superiority-inferiority, and minority-majority between the two cultures. In other words, the former is the culture of a few, hence the expression elite culture, while the latter is the culture of the many, the people. This distinction has in time undergone such a change as to produce a radical shift in the meaning of the notion of popular culture. Two relatively recent studies, one by P. Bourdieu, the other by N. Birnbaum illustrate the point.[6]

In examining the relationship between social class and the perception of cultural artefacts, Bourdieu puts forward the argument that the perception of a work of art involves the ability to decipher a code, and this ability is limited by knowledge and education, hence by class. By this standard the 'holy places' of art (galleries) are accessible to a chosen few, while the great masses have the choice of either joining the few, a choice severely limited by education, or living in permanent cultural starvation. But this is not all. Bourdieu continues to argue, and in this he echoes a widespread opinion, that in contemporary industrial society there is one culture only, the culture of the dominant classes, and that consequently, the great masses have to define their cultural status by simply opposing and rejecting this, i.e. without possessing a positive alternative.

A similar idea is put forward by Birnbaum who after demonstrating that, in modern societies, education has produced a cultural stratification of the population, argues that in Britain, unlike the continent, a public conception of culture is lacking, that, since the end of the nineteenth century, there has been only 'a particular version of high culture developed by a national elite for whome culture meant what the lower and middle classes and even more the workers lacked. Not surprisingly these developed a counter culture of their own. [7] But since it is obvious that today the British working classes can no longer claim a culture of their own of the type described, or rather postulated, by R. Hoggart among others, an expression such as 'a counter culture of their own' can mean only one thing — the culture of a political minority created on behalf of, or simply, imputed to, the working classes.

The second criterion for distinguishing between a highbrow-elitic and lowbrow-popular culture refers to the relationship between the author and his work. It is a complex, and at times, ambiguous criterion on two grounds: first, it contains a strong psychological often irrational element, and secondly, logically speaking, it occupies an intermediary position between the class

[6] P. Bourdieu, 'Outline of a sociological theory of art perception', *International Social Science Journal*, XX, 1968.
[7] N. Birnbaum, *The Crisis of Industrial Society* (London 1969), 133.

and market criteria. It deserves nonetheless to be mentioned separately because it sheds additional light on the development of the concept of popular culture in modern industrial societies. The idea can briefly be formulated as follows: The popularity of an author is a function of certain intrinsic and, in principle, identifiable qualities of his work taken as whole, or individually. I am, needless to say, aware that a statement such as this begs a series of important questions of method and approach. For this reason the best I can do is to illustrate the idea by a few concrete instances. One example is offered by R. Escarpit who argues that the popularity of a literary work can and should be assessed in terms of readership, a notion which includes the number of reprints, number of individual readers and number of references in periodicals, newspapers or recorded conversations.[8] Although this is not the place to give a critical account of Escarpit's work, the following comments are necessary in order to bring into focus its relevance for the present argument.

While agreeing that social classes contribute to cultural bifurcation (highbrow-lowbrow) Escarpit does not establish a determining link between the lower classes and popular culture. On the contrary, under certain circumstances, highbrow literature can also be popular. Thus, Escarpit has the merit, which is by no means small, of eliminating from the definition of the concept of popular culture the ambiguity aroused by a mixed criterion, factual-quantitative and valuative-ideological. Unfortunately, his own position is not completely free from difficulties and even obscurities. Leaving aside the technical problem involved in any enterprise of this sort, Escarpit's manner of approach says relatively little about a series of questions starting with 'why'. Obviously, he is right to assume that popularity depends on a cluster of conditions which includes the relationship between the author and his work, as well as the relationship between readership and the work, in terms of interest and values. However, assuming is one thing and demonstrating is another, or, putting it differently, Escarpit cannot help creating the impression that popularity is an objective-quantitative phenomenon, and as such, can be

[8] R. Escarpit: *Sociology of Literature*, trans. E. Pick (Painesville, 1965).

explained in objective terms such as, the invention of print, the spread of literacy and the organization of libraries.

Another example of a similar type of approach can be found in Lowenthal's study of popular culture in eighteenth century England. As mentioned elsewhere, he distinguishes between true art and popular culture, the novel and drama of the period being examples of the latter. Further, he establishes a close relationship between popular culture and the lower classes of society not only in terms of readership — a criterion which he takes for granted — but in a series of other terms referring mainly to the status of the writer, and those attributes (form and content) of his work which mediate the relationship between him and his audience. Stating Lowenthal's argument simply, he suggests that the drama and novel of the period were popular because, and to the extent to which, the playwright and the novelist projected in their work patterns of behaviour and structures of experiences and fantasies shared by the members of the lower classes, which needless to say, constituted a majority of the population. He singles out for special consideration two sets of factors. The first, referring mainly to the content of the works analysed by him, consists of an open and persistent preoccupation with sex and violence. The second, of a more complex nature in that it involves both content and form, refers to the predominantly entertaining effects of these works. The latter aspect constitutes the basic criterion whereby Lowenthal distinguishes between true art (a term roughly corresponding to highbrow culture) and popular culture.

Two comments are particularly relevant in the present context. First, it will be noticed that as far as the content of popular literature in eighteenth century England is concerned, Lowenthal lays particular stress on concern with sex and violence, thus coming very near to what, in an earlier section, was described as a general characteristic of popular literature. This raises the question of the relationship between traditional and modern popular culture, and the possibility of working out a general concept based on their common traits. As this is a particularly important point I should like to comment briefly on it.

Tedious as it may be, it is necessary to repeat that a strong stimulation of senses, hence, the concept of man as a sensuous being, is a basic characteristic of popular culture in general. Concern with sex and violence is perhaps the most obvious aspect of this, and consequently its presence can be tested in the popular literature of all times, as for instance, ancient romances (which according to Perry were an offspring of both, the pornographic and adventure literature of the period), the picaresque and, above all, the early modern novel (centred on the love-and-death theme, as L. Fiedler tells us), contemporary pornographic and scientific fiction, and to come to the main point, the folk literature of all times.[9] In other words, popular literature can be seen as a coherent whole to the extent to which it expresses an anthropological constant. But this being said, it is necessary to look in the opposite direction and ask: What are the differences between the traditional and modern popular literature with regard to the sex-violence motif, or the image of man as a sensuous being? While not claiming to possess the full answer, one point emerging from Lowenthal's work seems to be relevent in this respect. It refers to the meaning or meanings which such a motif has in the context of human existence as a whole. Admittedly, at the level of desire, to use a fashionable terminology, the sex-violence theme expresses a strong claim put by man to extend his universe, to suspend any predefinition of his existence, to dislocate anything that has been located, to undo anything that has been done so as to make available everything, in every place at and any time. But the direction and the final goal of such an imaginative project differ considerably from traditional to modern popular literature. To start with, in traditional literature the project is essentially extrasocietal, more precisely, it involves the whole community in a utopian world, a world in which the 'fair maid' is the dream of everyone, as the husky witch is the nightmare of everyone: hence, the highly metaphoric mode of expression of traditional literature. I deliberately say 'mode of expression' in order to avoid a facile distinction between form and content, for in this more than in any other literary form, language is a mode of being which, like the dream, is infinitely polymorphic, and like the metaphor, infinitely

[9] E. B. Perry, *The Ancient Romances*. (Berkeley, 1967) and L. Fiedler, *Love and Death in the American Novel* (New York, 1960).

polysemic. If the expressive power of the myth of Genesis may be invoked, the world depicted by traditional literature is the world on Friday, just before its creator decided to rest, just before he arrested and imprisoned his dream in the black box of his skull.

By comparison, the project of life emerging from popular literature in modern societies, including eighteenth century England, is predominantly intrasocietal in two alternative or complimentary senses: as a genuine cultural expression of the lower classes of society, or as an artifact produced by a minority for the consumption of a majority. But before going any further with this aspect of the subject, one principle has to be made clear. It is that modernity does not start with industrialization, but with a much broader process which permeated human consciousness long before expressing itself in various social institutions. This is a growing awareness — a process set up by the Renaissance — that society can and should be understood in terms of, and to a certain extent, shaped according to, conscious rational goals. Briefly, the idea of popular culture in the modern era is almost inseparable from the idea and practice of instrumental rationality. To be sure, this manifests itself under a great variety of forms, but the basic principle is the same, namely, the production or adaptation of culture carried out by a minority on behalf of society as whole, and for the specific aspirations, taste and standards of a majority. To make this clear it is necessary to stress the intimate, indeed the codetermining relation between means and goals, that is, between cultural production and the aspirations and values as well as the cultural standards of those individuals, groups or classes, who constitute a majority in a given society. To understand this is to understand why the popular culture of the *Ancien Régime,* or to follow more closely Mandrou's study of the subject, why the *Bibliothèque Bleue de Troy* contained mainly religious hagiographic books, adventures stories (romances, legends, fairytales), and books of improvement, or, to give another example, why the popular culture of eighteenth century England put a special emphasis on the 'story' and 'drama' of the underprivileged and uprooted who in their struggle for survival or success are more often than not compelled to fall back on their natural resources — sex and aggression – as well as on the multiple emotional derivations of them.[10] In the early stages of urbanization and industrialization, when England was a nightmare for some and a dream for others, the sense of adventure was less hagiographic (extrasocietal) and more entrepreneurial in a picaresque or practical sense. This was a world in which the human imagination seemed to be either fascinated or horrified, but at any rate arrested, by a society in turmoil which, for this very reason, was more unstable and unpredictable than imagination itself. Within this general framework the following more specific points deserve special consideration.

As Lowenthal rightly maintains, 'concern with the nature of the effect' lies at the very core of popular literature whose central if not exclusive aim is to entertain. In the case of the eighteenth century novel and drama, this aim was achieved by two apparently contradictory means: flat representation of everyday life, hence, exclusive concern with the detail and the common, as against the problematic, in human existence; a heightened expression of basic, that is, common, emotions and fantasies, hence, concern with sex and violence. Now, apart from the fact that it constitutes a point of contact with traditional popular culture, the phenomenon has a significance and history of its own. Briefly, concern with entertainment tends to become a dominant, and at times unique, feature of popular culture in the modern era. One aspect of this is the rapid growth of pornographic literature and literature of violence, a process which has been taken over and further developed by contemporary cultural industry. But the main point which I wish to make refers to the heightening of expression as a principal means of communicating, and thus, of increasing the appeal and circulation of cultural products. A relatively recent, and admittedly exaggerated instance will illustrate this.

In his recent study of German culture during the Weimar regime, W. Laqueur argues that this was also a popular culture.[11] Laqueur's reasons can be summarized as follows. There was a sustained effort particularly by the Dadaists to break down the traditional art forms including the basic rules of prosody, to

---

[10] R. Mandrou, *De la culture populaire aux 17ᵉ et 18ᵉ siècles* (Paris 1965).
[11] W. Laqueur, *Weimar. A Cultural History, 1918–1933* (London 1974).

deformalize the entire process of artistic creation in favour of direct and spontaneous expression, of improvisation and amateurism, as against elaboration and professionalism. This brought about a series of innovations which have a great deal to do with the popular character of Weimar culture. One of the dominant features of this culture was the concern with topicality — topicality of subject matter, as in Brecht's plays, topicality of theme (the workers' revolution for instance) or topicality of situation, so typically illustrated by the prominent part played by the cabaret in the cultural scene of the period. That this was a kind of art which appealed to large audiences need hardly be demonstrated. But, the rejection, moreover the deliberate destruction, of traditional art forms was responsible for another dominant feature of Weimar culture which, following Lowenthal's manner of approach, could be described as 'concern with the effect' provided that one bears in mind that, in this case, there is a deliberate intention to *shock*, to create an ecstatic state, a 'new euphoria'. More precisely, heightened feelings and intensified expression were natural consequences of one of the guiding principles and practices of the art of the period and of expressionist art in particular: the priority of content over form.

Now, without denying Laqueur's contention that Weimar culture was also a popular culture, one cannot help questioning its meaning. That spontaneity of expression, simplicity of style and topicality facilitate communication can hardly be doubted. Similarly, heightened emotionality is a well-known device of popular art, of melodrama, for instance, and the box-office success of German expressionist films like *Doctor Caligari's Cabinet* can be taken as a proof of this. But one has to admit that the so-called Weimar culture was an urban, predominantly middle-class phenomenon; moreover, it had a distinct elitic character. Firstly, it was the product of a tiny minority, a cultural elite who employed a great deal of energy and skill to reach new and wider audiences. Secondly, and more importantly, the core of their audience, the disseminators, were also a minority consisting of culturally sophisticated and politically enlightened people.

The case of Weimar culture and above all its dual character, popular and, at the same time, elitic, has a particular significance in the present context. As just suggested, one aspect of the phenomenon was political in the specific sense that many writers and artists were politically minded, and a substantial proportion of their audience had well-defined political leanings whether of the left, or of the right. But most importantly, the general framework of Weimar society — an advanced industrial society ridden by internal conflicts — was such that politics became *ipso facto* a predominant preoccupation and consequently an important factor in the production, circulation and appreciation of art and literature. More precisely, politics became a vehicle, and on the whole the main index, of popularity. Although relatively well known, the phenomenon is more complex than it would appear at first sight. For one thing there was a deliberate and persistent use made by the artists — Brecht is an outstanding example — of political devices for the purpose of heightening the effect and increasing the circulation of their works. As well as a great simplification of style, this involved a considerable amount of straightforward political comment, if not agitation, in terms determined by the general social situation which meant concern for the oppressed be they the lower classes or the German community as a whole. This meeting point between art and politics constitutes a watershed in the development of modern popular culture, described at an earlier stage as the transition from an extrasocietal to an intrasocietal significance of the phenomenon. Here in the Weimar Republic we have an exaggerated version, or, more accurately, a caricature of this process because it is manufactured by a minority, not for a majority as a distinguishable social category (the lower classes of society), but for the people at large, an amorphous and passive entity. It is a caricature, because the popular culture of the time turned almost overnight into a *populist* culture of the right, or of the left. The significance of this will be shown presently, but not before dealing very briefly with another characteristic aspect of popular culture in advanced industrial societies: the role of the market in the process of cultural production and consumption.

To start with a point just made, it is obvious that the popularity of Weimar culture was not a purely political phenomenon, i.e. achieved by political means and for

political ends. Rather, the politicization of culture, to use
an expression coined by W. Benjamin, came later in the day
and with ambiguous results as far as the popularity of Weimar
culture was concerned.[12] As in many other advanced industrial
societies, in the Weimar Republic, the process of cultural
production, individual or collective, was to a great extent
sensitive to and often determined by the market. To illustrate
this, one should bear in mind the many and laborious transformations suffered by the famous story of Doctor Caligari
before it reached its final, box-office success in a film version.
Indeed there is much to be said about the thesis that some of
the essential features of expressionism can be best accounted
for in market terms, such as competition, advertising and
fashion. As is often maintained, in modern industrial societies
art has become a commodity. Even if this is an exaggeration,
and I am inclined to think that it is, it would still be true to say
that under the circumstances the concept and indeed the
phenomenon of popular culture makes little sense unless one is
prepared to believe in miracles, that is, that the phenomenon
has suddenly risen from its deathbed and begun a new and
vigorous life under the name of mass culture. That some authors
manage to refer without any hesitation or qualification to
contemporary pornographic literature and science fiction as a
modern version of popular culture is an example of this kind
of belief. But this is beside the point. Whether the causes of
the process lie in the market, or the political structure of
modern society the end product is the same, and may briefly
be described as follows.

   The first thing to be noticed is a gradual reversal of
positions with regard to the social framework, or simply the
social location of the phenomenon of popular culture. What
once was an expression of global society, what for de
Tocqueville was a dominant trait of a democratic society,
moreover what in the early stages of the modern era was a
majority phenomenon, has gradually turned into its opposite,
a conscious product of a ruling minority. Further, what once
was an integral and integrating vision, a code, a language
expressing the experience of the world and the seat in life
of a whole community has gradually shrunk, first, to a

[12] W. Benjamin, *Illuminations*, trans. H. Zohn (London 1970).

partial vision, normally a class vision, then to the vision of a minority different from if not opposed to the rest of society. What once was unifying has now become a divisive vision and project of life. As far as conceptualization is concerned this has resulted, first, in a minimal, then, in a negative definition of popular culture.

As this is admittedly, an abstract formulation it would be useful to illustrate its meaning with a few concrete examples. As suggested in an earlier paragraph referring to the relationship between a popular and a populist culture, in those modern societies in which the concept of popular culture still has a positive content this is more often than not political and ideological in character. In such a context, the concept of popular culture has no specific descriptive function. It is in fact a normative, moreover, prescriptive concept signifying what the people, the majority, the great masses, ought to feel, think and be. From this to a negative definition of the phenomenon is but a short step. In general terms this can be seen as a theoretical consequence of two observable processes taking place in modern industrial societies, the decline, one may say extinction, of what was earlier called traditional culture, on the one side, and working class culture, on the other. Whether the causes of this are mainly technological, the spread of literacy, for instance, or mainly social, is a moot question. The fact is that it has become increasingly difficult to speak in meaningful terms about the existence of an 'alternative' culture in contemporary industrial society. Exaggerated as it may appear, the idea of cultural unidimensionality is, under the circumstances, an adequate and useful theoretical hypothesis. But ideas die hard and the idea of popular culture is no exception.

The future historian of contemporary industrial civilization will undoubtedly be tempted to put forward the thesis that the concept of popular culture was on the whole a revolutionary concept. The body of evidence lying at his disposal is impressive. There is first of all, the ideological connotation of the concept, the roots of which could be traced back to an early state of modernization in the democratic cult and romantic myth of the 'people' and the 'popular' — to the folkloric age of the modern mind. But, like all cults, the cult of the people had gradually turned into an empty ritual, a mask hiding rather than revealing something. Thus, in fascist societies, the concept had no function other than that of conjuring up an exalted state of feeling about something that refuses to be known, save in a symbolic form — a leader or a charismatic elite. In socialist societies, the concept has admittedly a more specific and deliberate ideological connotation, but despite, or just because of this its referential function is even more ambiguous. In Soviet Russia, the notion of popular culture, a very popular notion indeed, has a mainly evocative connotation; it is a requiem for a dead cultural past performed by professional enthnographers.

The future historian will also be able to collect new and important evidence in support of the so-called convergency thesis, since the same kind of development has taken place in most modern liberal or democratic societies. In the early days of modernization, and owing mainly to the romantic reaction, the notion of popular culture acquired a distinct protest flavour which has subsequently been embedded in a variety of cultural trends and movements, such as antirationalism, anti-industrialization, antiurbanization, to mention only a few. Most of these have had their positive counterparts, thus creating a general climate of opinion favouring not only the preservation but also the revival of a popular culture which with few exceptions meant traditional, mainly peasant, culture. The exceptions are, however, highly significant because they indicate at a relatively early stage the future development of the phenomenon.

The first exception refers to American society where for obvious reasons the notion of popular culture has a history of its own as the culture of the common man, or common people, a broad and fluid social category. It has nonetheless had a distinct and at time strong protest, if not revolutionary flavour as the long and complex history of the blackface minstrelsy movement clearly shows. Much more significant, because more specific, is the second exception typically illustrated by England, the first industrial country, where owing to the disappearance of peasantry as a distinct category, the sociological connotation of the phenomenon of popular culture has undergone a radical change. Since the middle of the last century one can notice a growing tendency to identify both the vestiges and metamorphosis of an old traditional culture in an urban and industrial setting. The result was a relatively new concept of popular culture, the so-called traditional working-class culture, a complex if not explosive conceptual construct referring to a highly transitional cultural relativity, i.e., a fading collective memory of a traditional rural culture (old songs and ballads), on the one side, and an *ad hoc* interpretation, often an original expression of an impinging urban middle-class culture, on the other. And transitional it was, for, during the last decade or so, it has become increasingly clear that the notion of a traditional working-class culture connotes hardly anything save the memory of a memory: more precisely, present generations recollecting the recollections of their parents and grandparents. Thus, both a traditional working-class and a traditional peasant culture are things of the past.

But the idea has survived, and the tautology permitted, this means that, in the democratic societies of today, the phenomenon of popular culture has an even more conspicuous ideological character than it has in other types of industrial society. This leads to a new stage in the understanding and conceptualization of the phenomenon previously referred to as a negative definition of popular culture. The first and certainly the most significant step in this direction was made by A. Gramsci.[13] Briefly, in an attempt to assess the chances of a proletarian revolution in advanced industrial societies, Gramsci uses the concept of popular or people's culture in order to indicate not so much an active as a potential force, a position of resistance against the hegemonic rule of an established (middle-class) culture. But since Gramsci was not able, and perhaps not altogether willing, to define either the concrete contents, or the social framework of popular culture — on the contrary, he lay particular stress on its illusive nature — his concept suggests a potential rather than a manifest function and structure of creative imagination, a carefully disguised arsenal of mental states whose *raison d'etre* is to resist inclusion and actively subvert the dominant culture of contemporary capitalist societies, and, more importantly, any form of cultural domination. This is the sad-heroic ending of a great idea: popular culture *sive* the culture of absence.

[13] A. Gramsci, *Letteratura e vita nazionale* (Rome 1950).

References

Benjamin, W. *Illuminations*, trans. H. Zohn. London 1970.

Birnbaum, N. *The Crisis of Industrial Society*, London 1969.

Bourdieu, P. 'Outline of a sociological theory of art perception', *International Social Science Journal*, XX, 1968.

Escarpit, R. *Sociology of Literature*, trans. E. Pick, Painesville, Ohio 1965.

Fiedler, L. *Love and Death in the American Novel*, New York, N.Y. 1960.

Gramsci, A. *Letteratura e vita nazionale*, Rome 1950.

Gurvitch, G. *The Social Frameworks of Knowledge*, trans. M. and K. Thompson, Oxford 1971.

Laqueur, W. *Weimar. A Cultural History, 1918–1933*, London 1974.

Lévi-Strauss, C. *The Savage Mind*, London, 1966.

Lowenthal, L. *Literature, Popular Culture and Society*, Engelwood Cliffs, N.J. 1961.

Mandrou, R. *De la culture populaire aux 17ᵉ et 18ᵉ siècles*, Paris 1965.

4

Oblique Approaches to the History of Popular Culture

Peter Burke

Until a few years ago, the history of popular culture would have seemed a contradiction in terms to most professional historians. Do the people have a culture? Did that culture really have a history? 'History' meant essentially Ranke-type history, the political history of nation states. There was also cultural history, Burckhardt-type history, which was concerned with attitudes and values and their embodiment in symbolic forms such as paintings and plays. Both kinds of history were concerned with elites. The political historian studied the doings of kings and statesmen; the cultural historian studied artists and intellectuals. Neither of them was concerned with the attitudes and values of shopkeepers and factory workers, peasants and craftsmen, servants and fishermen, beggars and thieves.

The attitudes and values of men and women like these, and their embodiment in folksongs and folktales, devotional and satiric images and in such diverse, but at least partially symbolic, activities as witchcraft, pilgrimages and carnivals, were not neglected altogether. In the nineteenth century (to mention no more than three famous works), Wilhelm Soldan published a history of witchtrials in 1843, Charles Nisard published a history of French chap-books in 1854, and Giuseppe Pitrè published a large work on Sicilian folklore and festivals in 1889. However, Soldan the historian looked at witch trials from above, from the point of view of the judges. Nisard, an antiquarian, did little more than describe the contents of particular almanacs and romances. Pitrè, a folklorist, was not particularly interested in developments over time.[1]

These books and others like them tended to deal with the popular beliefs and festivals, songs and stories of a given period in relative isolation from the economic or social or political history of the period. It is as if there were two histories: mainstream history — the Renaissance, the Reformation, the French Revolution — and the historical backwaters of the prophecies of Merlin, or the old Danish house, or the Feast of Fools. On one side the professional historians neglected the attitudes of the majority of the population as beneath the dignity of history, and on the other the antiquarians and folklorists made few references to political events or even to social change. Giuseppe Pitrè studied nineteenth century Sicilian popular culture without discussing the impact of the unification of Italy, in which he had taken part, or of the rise of capitalism in the Sicilian countryside. As if acknowledging that their work was beneath the dignity of history, three distinguished students of French popular culture wrote under pseudonyms: 'Champfleury' (the novelist Jules Husson); 'Paul Saintyves' (the publisher Emile Nourry); and 'Henri Davenson' (the ancient historian H.-I. Marrou).

In the last few years, a good deal has been done to end the split between these two kinds of history. Political historians have begun to write their history 'from below', as well as from the point of view of the ruling classes. Brecht's worker is getting his questions about history answered at last. Thus Christopher Hill has approached the English revolution of the seventeenth century by looking at 'the attempts of the common people to impose their own solutions to the problems of their time'. Albert Soboul and George Rudé have looked at the role of the *sans-culottes* and of the crowd in the French Revolution. Jesse Lemisch has looked at the American Revolution from the point of view of the merchant seaman. Nathan Wachtel has studied the 'vision of the vanquished', the Spanish conquest of Peru as seen by the Indians.[2]

---

[1] W. Soldan, *Geschichte der Hexenprozesse* (Stuttgart 1843); C. Nisard, *Histoire des livres populaires* (Paris 1854); G. Pitrè, *Usi e costumi, credenze e preguidizi del popolo siciliano* (Palermo 1889)

[2] C. Hill, *The World Turned Upside Down* (London 1972); A. Soboul, *Les Sans-culottes parisiens en l'an II* (Paris 1958); G. Rudé, *The Crowd in the French*

Cultural history too can be seen from below. The Little Tradition (in Robert Redfield's useful phrase) has a history, no less than the Great Tradition. It is possible to study changes in popular culture and to relate them to the history of the time. Some studies of this kind have been written by folklorists. Will-Erich Peuckert is a folklorist who has made a deliberate attempt to combine the approaches of 'Volkskunde' and 'Geistesgeschichte' in a study of Germany in the age of Luther. David Buchan is a student of folklore (or as he would prefer to say, 'Folklife'), whose book on the ballad is centrally concerned with processes of economic, social and cultural change in northeast Scotland in the eighteenth and nineteenth centuries.[3]

Historians have also made their contribution, and particularly in the last few years. In France, Robert Mandrou's study of the *Bibliothèque Bleue* in the seventeenth and eighteenth centuries has attracted a good deal of attention. Where Nisard did little more than describe French chap-books, Mandrou is concerned to reveal the world view implicit in the texts (emphasizing how conformist it was), and to relate this world view to the rest of the culture and society of the old regime. In a similar way, Carlo Ginzburg's study of witchcraft and agrarian cults in Friuli and Keith Thomas's study of English popular beliefs are both concerned with the world views of peasants and craftsmen and with the changes which took place in the sixteenth and seventeenth centuries.[4]

The rise of a 'history of the inarticulate', which includes their cultural history, is a new, exciting and fashionable development. Is it also valid? The crucial problem is the problem of the sources. How on earth can we find out what the popular culture of past generations was really like? This is the question which the present essay will attempt to answer.

The problem of the sources is naturally more or less awkward according to the region and the period in which a given historian

---

[3] W.-E. Peuckert, *Die grosse Wende* (Hamburg 1948); D. Buchan, *The Ballad and the Folk* (London 1972).

[4] R. Mandrou, *De la culture populaire aux 17e et 18e siècles* (Paris 1964); C. Ginzburg, *I benandanti* (Turin 1966); K. V. Thomas, *Religion and the Decline of Magic* (London 1971).

Revolution (Oxford 1959); J. Lemisch, 'Jack Tar in the Streets', in *William and Mary Quarterly*, 25, 1968, and 'Listening to the Inarticulate' in *Journal of Social History* 3, 1969–70; N. Wachtel, *La Vision des vaincus* (Paris 1971).

is interested. Sometimes the problem is not acute enough to be methodologically interesting, and sometimes it is too acute. For western Europe about 1850 there is not much of a problem. By then there was 90 per cent adult literacy in Sweden, 70 per cent in England, 65 per cent in France. Museums of popular art are full of objects dating from this period. It is no more difficult to study English popular culture in the nineteenth century than to study the culture of the English gentry in the seventeenth century. On the other hand, the historian of the popular culture of the middle ages has too much of a problem for discussion of his methods to be fruitful. In his mosaic too many stones are lacking.[5]

In between comes the historian of early modern Europe, from the Gutenberg Revolution to the Industrial Revolution. For him, the difficulties are great enough to make him think about method but not great enough to frustrate him altogether. There are obstacles and even traps, but they can be surmounted and avoided. For this reason (apart from the more personal one that I specialize in the history of the sixteenth and seventeenth centuries), I shall take most of my examples from the early modern period. Concentration on this middle period enables one to avoid the opposite sins of presumption and despair, of overestimating the difficulties of the enterprise and of underestimating them.

Essentially this enterprise is one of reconstructing and interpreting the attitudes and values, the myths, images and rituals of the peasants and craftsmen of early modern Europe. The majority of them were illiterate. Much of their culture was oral culture, so we cannot know it directly. Much of their culture took the form of festivals which were equally impermanent. What is left? There are the usual written and printed sources which historians use — the documents. But what does it mean to have the 'documents' when one is studying people who were mostly illiterate? It means, for one thing, that we see popular culture through alien eyes, through the eyes of mediators. We

[5] Some brave attempts have been made, like J. Le Goff, 'Culture cléricale et traditions folkloriques dans la civilisation mérouingienne' in *Annales economies, sociétés, civilisations* 22, 1967 and C. Morris, *Medieval Media* (Southampton 1972).

are in much the same position as historians of black Africa, since the written sources for African history until quite recent times were also the work of outsiders. They were written by travellers or missionaries or officials, who often did not know the local culture very well and were sometimes trying to suppress it.

The historian of early modern Europe is in a similar position when he approaches popular culture through the sermons of friars such as St Bernardino in fifteenth-century Italy, Olivier Maillard in fifteenth-century France, Abraham a Sancta Clara in seventeenth-century Austria.[6] The friars were often the sons of craftsmen or peasants; Abraham was the son of a serf innkeeper. They preached in a colloquial style, drawing on folk tales for their *exempla*, and sometimes behaving quite literally like buffoons in the pulpit. St Bernardino imitated the buzzing of flies. However, friars are not peasants. They were often university men, trained in scholastic theology and interested in passing on the Great Tradition to the people. Their colloquial style was not spontaneous talking, but a conscious literary choice from the three possible styles, the others being the ornate and the plain. They might transmute a tale to point a moral. They were mediators between two traditions, learned and popular, rather than representatives of either.

If the sermons of friars do not give us direct access to popular culture, what about chap-books? What about the famous *Bibliothèque Bleue*? We have been told that it expresses the mentality of the French peasants of the old regime. It certainly reached some of the peasants. The better-off bought chap-books, the literate read them and others may have listened when the books were read aloud. The chap-books were also bought and read by craftsmen. However, these booklets were not composed by craftsmen or peasants, nor are they in most cases the printed versions of an oral tradition. In many cases we know that the books were composed by priests, nobles, doctors or lawyers, sometimes centuries earlier. Someone revised, abridged or translated the book, and someone else chose to print it. A pedlar selected it for his pack, and thus it arrived in a given village. There is thus a whole chain of mediators between a

[6] For example, M. Michel, *Die Volkssage bei Abraham a Sancta Clara* (Leipzig 1933).

particular text, let us say a romance of chivalry like *Pierre de Provence*, and the peasants whose mentality it is supposed to express. We cannot be sure that the 'conformist' attitudes to the king or the nobles or the clergy which are expressed in the texts were the attitudes of most of the audience.[7] A German example may make the point more obvious. The surviving broadside ballads about the German peasants' war of 1525 are hostile to the peasants. Perhaps they are an attempt at propaganda, perhaps they simply express the hostility of the town to the country. In any case they do not express the values of the rebels.[8]

If chap-books do not give us direct access to popular culture, perhaps witch trials do. Since most people accused of witchcraft in the sixteenth and seventeenth centuries seem to have been peasants (women in particular), their trials and confessions are obviously an important source for popular attitudes and values. In the trial records one can hear them talking, protesting, even laughing, and when the records were kept in Latin, some of their untranslatable comments had to be left in the vernacular. Yet here again there were mediators. The confessions were not often spontaneous but made after interrogation. The interrogators were men from the upper classes, usually clergy. They had their stereotypes of witches, their expectations of what the accused must have seen and done, stereotypes which often derived from Latin manuals on the subject, like the notorious *Malleus Maleficarum*. The interrogators had the initiative and asked the questions, which might be leading questions like, 'By what means came you to have acquaintance with the Devil?' They were in a position to impose their definition of the situation, often by torture or the threat of torture, and thus to discover what they had set out to discover. It is hard for the modern historian to get behind the stereotype and to find out what the accused herself thought she had been doing.[9]

[7] R. Mandrou, *op. cit.*, argues for a predominantly peasant audience. Some doubts are raised by G. Bollême, 'Littérature populaire et littérature de colportage au 18e siècle' in *Livre et société*, I (Paris 1965) and by H.-J. Martin, *Livre pouvoirs et société*, Paris 1969, 955ff.

[8] R. von Liliencron, *Die historischer Volkslieder der Deutschen*, 3 (Leipzig 1867), ns 374–93.

[9] Ginzburg and Thomas, *op. cit.*, xi and 516f, discuss the evidence of confessions.

If witch trials are tainted evidence, perhaps riots and rebellions give us a more direct access to popular culture. Actions speak louder than words. Rebellions have long been studied by historians — Wilhelm Zimmermann's classic work on the German peasants' war goes back to the early 1840s — but they have only recently been studied as part of popular culture. Riots and rebellions can be seen not only as explosions of blind fury but as dramatic expressions of attitudes and values. Their symbolic elements are well worth the historian's attention; the banners, the effigies, the mock executions and the real executions in mock-legal forms. Riots often developed out of festivals, such as Carnival, and prolonged their ritual with more serious intent. Emmanuel Le Roy Ladurie and Natalie Z. Davis have both studied the French religious wars of the sixteenth century from this perspective. Le Roy Ladurie has described a riot which developed out of the carnival at Romans in 1580, where craftsmen and peasants 'danced their revolt in the streets of the town', declaring that the rich had been profiting at the expense of the poor. Natalie Davis has emphasized the concern with pollution shown by both Catholic and Protestant crowds. For Protestants, images polluted and iconoclasm was a way of ridding the community of this pollution. For Catholics, heretics polluted, and to burn them or drown them was a rite of purification.[10]

There is no doubt that this approach to the wars of religion is a fruitful one, but here too the historian has to remember the mediators. Catholic and Protestant witnesses and chroniclers sometimes gave extremely divergent accounts of the same episode. Often we know about peasant revolts only through the reports of the officials who were trying to suppress them and whose values, so different from the values of the peasants, may have affected not only the judgements they passed but the whole description they gave. They might have seen as a blind fury what was in fact a planned defence of specific rights. Modern historians who have more sympathy with rebellious peasants may attribute anachronistic aims to the rebels if they cannot discover what they really wanted. In some cases, notably the German peasants' war, the demands of the rebels have

[10] E. Le Roy Ladurie, *Les Paysans de Languedoc* (Paris 1966) 393f; N. Z. Davis, 'The Rites of Violence' in *Past and Present* 59, 1973.

survived, but we do not know how they were drawn up. The famous Twelve Articles begin with the demand for the parish to choose its priest. Was this what mattered most to the peasants, or only to the clergyman who drew the demands up? The leaders of peasant risings were often not peasants but nobles or priests, and sometimes they were not even voluntary leaders, but forced into it. Thus even the leaders of the movement were mediators.[11]

If we cannot have direct access to the attitudes and feelings of craftsmen and peasants through their riots and rebellions, perhaps we can do so through oral tradition. Since the historian of early modern Europe is on the wrong side of the industrial revolution and the rise of literacy which followed it, it is too late for him to take up field work with any hope of success. In compensation, he can profit from the late eighteenth-century discovery of popular culture and use the notes of the folksong and folktale collectors of the years around 1800, such as the brothers Grimm and Sir Walter Scott. Once again, he has to remember the mediator. The collectors did not always print what they found just as they found it. They censored, they polished, they 'improved'. They are mediators, and not the only ones. The Grimms, for example, did not do all their collecting themselves, but relied on their friends – more mediators. Then there are the informants. Mrs Brown of Falkland (1747–1810) provided versions of no less than thirty-three ballads, of which five are not found elsewhere. It comes as something of a shock to discover that she was no peasant woman but a professor's daughter and a minister's wife, interested in the poems of 'Ossian' and acquainted with Percy's *Reliques.* She too is a mediator.[12]

Thus there is some force in the traditional historian's objection that it is impossible to write the history of popular culture because the documents are lacking or untrustworthy. We have to study the oral through the written and the illiterate through the learned. However, this does not mean that we should despair – historians can never trust their documents

---

[11] E. B. Bax, *The Peasants' War in Germany* (London 1899), 75.

[12] W. Schoof, *Zur Entstehungsgeschichte der Grimmschen Märchen* (Hamburg 1959); D. Buchan, *op. cit.*, chapter 7, and D. C. Fowler, *A Literary History of the Popular Ballad* (Durham, N.C. 1968), chapter 10.

completely anyway. What it does mean is that we can never afford to forget that we are employing indirect or oblique approaches to popular culture.

The point is not that the documentary sources are worthless, but that they are distorted, and this distortion can be allowed for. Thus in his study of Italian witch trials, Carlo Ginzburg pays particular attention to occasions when the interrogator was disconcerted by the answers of the accused, precisely because they did not conform to the stereotype. Inspired by British social anthropology, Keith Thomas and Alan Macfarlane use English witch trials to study the villagers who brought accusations of witch craft, their relation to the accused and the situations out of which accusations developed. David Buchan continues to rely on the ballad texts provided by Mrs Brown, but is aware of the dangers of doing this. He meets objections with the argument that in eighteenth-century Scotland it was possible to keep two languages in one's head, English for writing and Scots for speaking, without one contaminating the other. The moral seems to be that popular culture is an elusive quarry for the historian to hunt, but that a consciously oblique approach is the least likely to put him on the wrong track.

In fact there are several oblique approaches. So far I have been discussing the socially oblique, the study of the attitudes of craftsmen and peasants through the testimony of nobles or priests or lawyers. A second approach is to use popular art as a source. There are woodcuts and painted icons, spoons and jugs, chairs and tables, caskets and cradles, samplers and bed-spreads, ploughs and saddles. Many of them are decorated, and some of them are dated. There are even whole houses, preserved in open-air museums at Aarhus, Arnhem, Bucharest and else-where. These artifacts are our most immediate contact with the dead whose world we want to reconstruct and interpret, so it is odd to call this approach oblique at all. I do so mainly because few members of the historical profession take visual evidence as seriously as 'documents' or know how to handle it, apart from art historians and archaeologists. The historian of popular culture has something to learn from both these groups.

From the art historian he can learn the techniques of
iconography, defined by one of its greatest practitioners, Erwin
Panofsky, as 'that branch of the history of art which concerns
itself with the subject matter or meaning of works of art as
opposed to their form'. It includes relatively pedestrian tasks
like the identification of saints by their attributes, but at a
deeper level of analysis, which Panofsky came to call 'iconology',
it also involves the diagnosis of the attitudes and values which
works of art embody.[13] If the proportion of paintings with
secular subjects increases in Renaissance Italy, this suggests
that values too were becoming more secular. Popular imagery
can be studied in the same way; for example the hand coloured
woodcuts produced at Épinal and elsewhere in France in the
eighteenth century, or the painted carts which became common
in Sicily in the nineteenth century. The interesting questions
are again questions of iconology. What does St Martin or
St Yves mean to a French peasant? What do Orlando, Rinaldo
and other paladins mean to the Sicilians who had them painted
on their carts? Does the secularization of French popular
imagery at the end of the eighteenth century reflect a secularization of values? Iconology even offers an approach to rebellion;
we understand the Pilgrimage of Grace better when we notice
the crusading imagery on the banners of the rebels.[14]

It may not be fruitful to look at chairs or houses in this way,
for their meaning is their use. Yet they too may have something
to tell us. The history of the Tuscan peasants, as an Italian urban
historian has recently suggested, is 'written on the fields where
they worked and the houses where they lived; that is where we
can read it'. How can we learn to read houses and fields? This is
where the archaeologist comes in, for he studies the culture of
peoples without writing almost entirely from this sort of
evidence. He studies types of axe-head or beaker and plots
their distribution on maps. Historians of early modern Europe
can make use of similar methods if they wish. Indeed, the
English farmhouses and cottages of the sixteenth and
seventeenth centuries have been studied in precisely this way.
It turns out that there were marked differences in rural housing

[13] E. Panofsky, *Meaning in the Visual Arts* (New York 1955) chapter 1.
[14] J. Adhémar *et al.*, *Imagerie populaire française* (Milan 1968); S. Lo Presti,
Il carretto (Palermo 1955).

between the highland zone of the north and west and the low-land zone of the south and east; these went with differences in family life, working habits and standards of comfort and convenience, all part of popular culture.[15]

It may yet be possible for the historian to be more ambitious still. Social and cultural anthropologists have made studies of the spatial symbolism of houses as a reflection of the values of the people who live in them. Thus the Berber house, we are told, is organized according to a set of oppositions. The dark lower part of the house is associated with sleep, death and animals, and opposed to the light upper part of the house, associated with men and with life.[16] Could such an analysis be made of a farmhouse in Wales or Provence or Tuscany?

It is easy to be carried away be these new possibilities and to forget the pitfalls. We cannot enter an eighteenth-century house. What we see in an open-air museum is a reconstruction by a museum curator who arranges the objects according to his idea of the eighteenth-century peasant. Before we jump from painted jug to popular culture there is a whole series of questions which need to be answered. Did the peasant make the jug himself or buy it from a professional craftsman? Did most villagers own such jugs or only the richest? Was the jug for everyday use or was it brought out on special occasions?

A third approach to popular culture is chronologically oblique; it is the 'regressive method'. The term was coined by the great French historian Marc Bloch when he was studying French rural history. He tried to read the history of the French peasants from the fields they tilled, and found that the evidence was good for the eighteenth century, when field maps, for example, were common, but fragmentary before this. So Bloch proposed to read history backwards. 'Is it not inevitable that in general, the facts of the most distant past are also the most obscure? How can one escape from the necessity of working from the better to the less well known?'[17]

[15] P. Pierotti, *Urbanistica: storia e prassi* (Florence 1972), 88; M. W. Barley, *The English Farmhouse and Cottage* (London 1961) xviii, 269.

[16] P. Bourdieu, 'The Berber House or the World Reversed' in M. Douglas, ed., *Rules and Meanings* (Harmondsworth 1973).

[17] M. Bloch, *Les Caractères originaux de l'histoire rurale française* (Paris 1964 edn) xii.

The historian of popular culture is in a position much like Marc Bloch's. In a number of European countries from France to Denmark, popular prints, broadsides and chap-books of the eighteenth century are very much more common than earlier ones, whether because more were printed or because a greater proportion have survived. A high percentage of the objects preserved in museums of popular art which date from before the year 1800 are in fact of eighteenth-century origin. Again, it was only in the late eighteenth century that ballads and stories were systematically collected from oral tradition and that peasant customs and festivals were systematically described. Thus there is a strong case for writing the history of European popular culture backwards and for using the late eighteenth century as a base, reconstructing the whole popular belief system and then moving back to consider the more fragmentary evidence from the sixteenth and seventeenth centuries.

Please do not misunderstand me. I am not suggesting that we return to the methods of Sir James Frazer and other nineteenth century scholars who took the customs of the peasants of their day as a basis for the reconstruction of what they liked to think of as the primitive religion of the Aryans. That really is presumptuous, because it demands from the evidence more than the evidence is able to give. The historian knows that he cannot jump thousands of years in this way, because so many changes have taken place in that long period. It is possible that in the plays still performed by English mummers there are 'traces of ancient mystery', but we cannot be sure how ancient those traces are. In any case the historian's main preoccupation is not with the study of origins, but rather with the attitudes and values of each generation. He is not so much concerned with the question whether the hero-combat enacted by the English mummers was originally a fertility rite, as with the question of what it meant to the people who performed it in specific places and centuries. Of course 'meaning' need not be confined to 'manifest meaning'; the latent meanings of symbolic action have also to be considered. But 'latent meaning' must not be confused with 'original meaning'.[18]

[18] Contrast A. Brody, *The English Mummers and their Plays: Traces of Ancient Mystery* (London 1970), especially chapter 6.

The more modest aim of Marc Bloch and of other historians who would like to follow in his steps is not to jump millennia but to walk back a century or two by means of the regressive method. There are still dangers, of course. The method assumes the basic stability of popular culture. Now the idea that the attitudes and values of the French peasants remained totally unchanged from 1500 to 1800 is demonstrably false. We know that some of them became Calvinists, notably in the Cévennes. We know that a higher proportion of them were literate in the late eighteenth century than had been in the late seventeenth century. We know that the subject matter of the *Bibliothèque Bleue* changed, and that in the eighteenth century chap-books reveal more interest in history and love, more concern with the useful and the natural, less emphasis on the marvellous and on death.[19] In other words, the idea of an unchanging popular culture is a myth, a myth created by the educated townsman who sees the peasants as part of nature rather than as part of culture, as animals rather than men.

Marc Bloch did not make this mistake. His point was rather that change in the French countryside was slow. Similarly, it is reasonable to argue that popular culture in early modern Europe changed slowly relative to the minority culture of the day, from Renaissance to Rococo, let alone relative to us. In village communities where a majority of families remained from generation to generation in the same place, tilling the same soil their fathers and grandfathers had done, one can presume a good deal of cultural continuity. This geographical stability was not always the case in the villages of early modern Europe, but it was probably the case quite often.

In this kind of situation, it is likely that oral traditions are less unreliable than Ranke-type historians believe. They are interested in the precise dating of political events, but the chronology of oral tradition is inexact. They live in societies where there is no mechanism to ensure the correct transmission of oral tradition, and do not think that in this respect other societies may be better organized. However, the ethno-historians of black Africa and elsewhere suggest that in some societies oral traditions are transmitted with care, and that the

[19] Bollême, *op. cit.*, 70f; G. Bollême, *Les Almanacs populaires aux 17e et 18e siècles* (Paris and The Hague 1969) 110f.

historian can learn a good deal from them, in particular about cultural history. Oral traditions give the insider's view.[20]

Of course oral traditions gradually change as they are handed down, but the historian who is conscious that he is imploying the oblique, regressive method will remember to make some allowance for this. It is easier to do so now that a group of French historians have developed the method of what they call 'serial history', studying slow changes over the long term through a series of relatively homogeneous data. Thus a two-hundred-year series of wills from a given region might reveal a good deal about continuity and change in attitudes to God or to the family. A long series of chap-books might offer similar revelations, and in fact the *Bibliothèque Bleue* has been studied in precisely this way.[21] The method is much like that of the archaeologist studying the distribution of axe-heads over space and time.

The conclusion seems to be that there are enough cultural continuities to make the regressive method a useful one for the historian, but enough changes to require him to use it with great care. It is more reliable for the interpretation of attitudes than for the reconstruction of attitudes; more reliable for the reconstruction of whole structures than for the reconstruction of specific details. The basic problem is that of making ends meet, of knowing exactly how much to allow for change. Take the English mummer's plays, for example. Over six hundred texts survive, almost all of them from the nineteenth and twentieth centuries. A number of them have St George as the hero, and in Norfolk in 1473, Sir John Paston referred to a man he had kept 'this three year to play St George'. It is likely, though not certain, that he was referring to a similar kind of play. Can we make ends meet and reconstruct the mummer's play as it existed in the fifteenth or sixteenth century? There are so many nineteenth-century versions that for once it seems safe to start from this side of the industrial revolution. We can begin by subtraction. In different nineteenth-century versions of the play, the characters included Oliver Cromwell, King William (probably William III) and Admiral Vernon. These people can be

[20] J. Vansina, *De la tradition orale* (1961): English trans. (London 1965).
[21] P. Chaunu, 'Une histoire religieuse sérielle' in *Revue d'histoire moderne* 12, 1965; Bollême (as note 19).

eliminated. Textual criticism can enable us to recover some of the older names or turns of phrase which have become corrupted in the process of oral transmission, to read 'Turkish Knight' for 'Turkey Snipe'. We may allow something for the fact that some nineteenth-century versions were recorded in bowdlerized form (the problem of the mediator). Like a picture restorer stripping off layers of over-painting, the historian employing the regressive method finds himself penetrating to the fundamental structure of the action; the sequence of combats, the slaying of the hero and his revival.[22]

In this last example and elsewhere, the regressive method may be eked out by a fourth oblique approach — comparison. Thus the earlier forms and the possible meaning of the English mummer's plays, in particular the Wooing Ceremony plays, have been illuminated by a study of the *Haghios Gheorghios* play in Thrace, as it was performed in the first years of the twentieth century. The Greek play makes it considerably easier to imagine what the English play was like before bowdlerization. Again, Child ballad 4, *Lady Isabel and the Elf-Knight*, is brief and somewhat cryptic. There are fuller versions, older versions, and more numerous versions elsewhere; in the Netherlands, for example (*Heer Halewijn*) and in Hungary (*Molnár Anna*). From these comparisons we can derive a better idea of what used to be sung in Britain and what it meant than we can from an eighteenth-century Scottish text alone.[23]

Like the regressive method, the comparative method seems a sin against some of the most essential canons of the historian — his interest in the specific, in all its individuality, and his emphasis on regional variation. The historian of popular culture certainly cannot afford to neglect regional variation. Students of popular art can often place a painted jug to within a few villages on stylistic grounds alone. However, all these variations of detail often coexist with very important similarities.

[22] E. K. Chambers, *The English Folkplay* (Oxford 1933); Brody (as note 17).

[23] R. M. Dawkins, 'The Modern Carnival in Thrace' in *Journal of Hellenic Studies*, 26, 1906; H. O. Nygard, *The Ballad of Heer Halewijn*, Helsinki and Knoxville, Tenn. 1958; L. Vargyas, *Researches into the Medieval History of Folk Ballad* (Budapest 1967) 129f.

Folklorists have shown that the same ballads, the same folk-tales can be found all over Europe. They are often given local colouring, yet the common plot or structure remains. Think of the famous stories about the foolish men from one particular village. In England the anecdotes cluster round the 'mad men of Gotham' (in Nottinghamshire) who were already immortalized in a collection of tales printed in the sixteenth century. In Germany it was the men of Fünsing or Lappenhausen who were considered the greatest fools, as we know from the stories and plays of Hans Sachs. In Denmark it was the men of Mols, and in Italy it was the men of Cava, near Salerno. Underneath the local colouring the stereotype of the fool is the same right across Europe. We cannot assume the homogeneity of European culture any more than its stability over time, but there are enough similarities for the comparative method, like the regressive method, to be fruitful. If the comparative method seems too speculative, it should be remembered that it is not to be used by itself but in conjunction with the other methods, and in particular to make sense of surviving fragments of evidence, not as a substitute for them.

The popular culture of early modern Europe is elusive. It can only be approached in a roundabout manner, recovered by indirect means, and often needs to be interpreted by analogy. To write its history it is necessary to draw for concepts and methods on disciplines such as archaeology, folklore, iconography and social anthropology. It is necessary to mix up different places (the comparative method), or different periods (the regressive method) or different social groups and media, looking at peasants and craftsmen through the eyes of mediators from other classes and studying the written to find out about the oral. All this is breaking the traditional rules of historical method, but then these rules were codified when history meant essentially what Ranke wrote, the political history of the nation states of the West. If the history of popular culture (like social history or the history of black Africa) cannot be written in terms of these rules, this need not mean that there is something wrong with these subjects, that the history of popular culture is a contradiction in terms. Perhaps there is something wrong with the rules.

5

Structuralism and Popular Culture

G. R. Kress

Structuralism exists in two distinct though related forms. It exists as a form of analysis, and here it is prominently and correctly associated with linguistics and anthropology, it also exists as an 'ism', an 'ism' like Marxism, existentialism, etc. In the latter form considerations which are intrinsic to this philosophy are often more prominent than the desire to display the structure of the object under investigation. So, for instance, questions about the reality of objects and their structures, of the ideological motivation of analysis, of problems of reading, and the like, tend to be focal in discussions of 'ism' structuralists. The former tends to push such considerations very much into the background; the emphasis is empirical rather than theoretical. Over the course of some forty or fifty years this difference in emphasis has developed into significantly different kinds of endeavour.

In this essay it is my intention to show the range of analytical tools which, I take it, both kinds of structuralist use. I will also attempt a tentative definition of the term popular culture arising both out of a structuralist analysis, as well as out of specific criticisms of the limitations of structuralist analyses. Assigning a 'structural value' to popular culture (in the context of the larger structure *culture*) and discussing the structural items and relations within popular culture inevitably demands discussion of ideological motivations underlying such an activity, and some space is given over to this.

It has become convention to trace both forms of structuralism to Saussure, and in particular to his posthumously published

Cours de Linguistique Generale. It is true that Saussure provided crucial concepts for the analysis of structure: it is equally true that problems of structure had been dealt with before Saussure. Any analysis assumes that there is structure in the object analysed. And while Saussure became central in the development of linguistics, his place in the development of structuralism outside linguistics is nowhere near as focal. In fact the contribution of linguistics generally to structuralism has probably been overrated (as may have happened in the case of Lévi-Strauss; here the mythical event is the encounter between Lévi-Strauss and Jakobson in New York after the Second World War which led to Lévi-Strauss's adoption of Jakobsonian binary feature analysis). Saussure made a seminal remark in the *Cours* about the (not then existent) science of semiology, whose place, he stated, was already assured in advance. Roland Barthes's *Elements of Semiology* (Barthes, 1967) specifically takes up this idea, and develops it, following Saussure's advice that 'language, better than anything else, offers a basis for understanding the semiological problem' (Saussure, 1966 p. 16). But Lévi-Strauss is at the very least as crucial in the development of structuralism as Saussure, and his indebtedness to linguistics is overstated. His work in the analysis of myth was started ten years before the meeting with Jakobson. The reasons for the continuing persistence of the myth of the close relation between structuralism and linguistics are themselves an interesting area for investigation by mythologists.

Reacting against the historical preoccupations of linguistics during the nineteenth century, and responding to Durkheim's notion of social reality beyond the individual, Saussure focused the attention of linguistics away from process (that is, change through time) and toward the concept of an *état de langue.* The task of linguistics was seen in the twofold task of describing this *état,* and of simultaneously developing the methodology for doing this in a manner akin to that of the natural sciences. Saussure saw this *état* as a selfcontained, discrete, and static entity as far as any individual speaker of the *langue* is concerned: that individual receives his *langue* from the community, whose property it is. Thus it exists outside the individual 'who can never create nor modify it by himself' (Saussure, 1966, p. 14). It is social, not individual. Language is not an abstraction, nor, indeed, are linguistic signs: 'though basically psychological (they) are not abstractions; associations which bear the stamp of collective approval . . . are realities that have their seat in the brain' (p. 15). Saussure predicted that linguistics would be subsumed under the general science of signs, semiology, though language was the paradigm case of a semiological system, in which problems as well as methodologies could be worked out. But it would be subject to the general laws applying to semiology. Conversely, statements about the structure of language — both substantial and formal — would have general validity in the study of other sign systems.

To restate, linguistics, following Saussure, saw as its object a discrete entity, set off clearly from other phenomena; static, not in process; real, not abstract and certainly not the fiction of an analyst; social, not individual; *langue* as against *parole*, which was subject to the speaker's wilful, and contextually determined uses. Thus the conception of the entity, and the methods developed for describing it, were intimately linked. The two crucial notions pointed to by Saussure were *syntagm* and *paradigm*. Relations between one item and other items present in the same entity are *syntagmatic*. Relations between an item and other items not present in the entity (but which might replace it) are *paradigmatic*. In the development of structuralism, in both senses outlined at the beginning, the focus has tended to fall on the syntagmatic aspect of structure, by and large. That is, the structure of an object is seen as essentially a statement about the items of which the entity is composed, and of the relations obtaining between them. This is not a question of absolutes, but of the main thrust of the movement. In Lévi-Strauss's practice different structures are contrasted, but treated as transforms of each other, so that the focus is not on paradigmatic contrast, but on structural (logical) similarity. 'On the Motlav-Mota—Aurora system, the relevant term in the first opposition is birth. In the Lifu-Ulawa-Malaita system it is death. All the terms in the other opposition are similarly reversed. . . . The two systems are therefore in the position of exact opposites within the same group' (1972, p. 80). Paradigmatic relations have been used most frequently to define the value of items in a structure, or the values of the structure itself in the context of larger structures. As an example of the latter use, one might consider the meaning of 'popular culture', by showing the terms which might contrast with popular culture in the structure 'culture': 'high culture', 'folkculture', 'subculture', 'mass-culture', 'counter culture'. The value of the term popular culture is thus a function of its contrast with terms in the same paradigm. As far as the value of an item within a structure is concerned, again a paradigmatic contrast is established. To consider another simple example[1]: in the structure *evening meal,* the structural elements might be *first course, main course,* and *desert.* The structural relations would be those of simple sequence in the structure *evening meal;* the structural value of the items however is established by the potential contrasts (for any given family, considered as representative of a larger social group). If *first course* is always realized by the substantial item 'tomato soup', then its significance differs from the case where *first course* can be realized by various kinds of soup, which in turn differs from the case where *first course* can be realized by any kind of soup, or fruit, or some savoury dish.

Although the significance of the item *first course* differs according to the paradigmatic structure in which it operates, its value in the syntagmatic structure *evening meal* remains constant. It remains first course in a structure comprising three terms. However, the syntagmatic value of *first course* would be altered in a syntagmatic structure into which a new term was introduced. Thus if the syntagmatic structure *evening meal* were to consist of *first course, main course, sweet,* and *cheese and biscuits* the value of all the items would be altered. The value of popular culture could, similarly, be established syntagmatically. First one would specify the structure in which popular culture is a structural term, let us say culture generally. We would then get an inventory of the other structural items in that structure, and the relations between them. To take an analogy: The sentence *Rod Stewart has released a new single* consists of three main structural items: two nominal ones *Rod Stewart* and *a new single,* one verbal/process item *has released.* Structurally they are arranged as shown in Figure 1. *Rod Stewart* is directly dominated by Sentence; *a new single* is directly dominated by *Predicate.* Thus the relations of the

---

[1] This is an echo of an example discussed in detail in Halliday 1961. The methodology there exemplified could itself be used to establish typologies of cultural forms.

two nominal items within the sentence are fundamentally different. (In addition there are the subsidiary relations *has — released* and *new — single*, instances of *modification*.) Similar relations would have to be established in the case of *culture — popular culture*. A hypothetical 'configurational' description of popular culture is shown in Figure 2.

Both terms, syntagmatic and paradigmatic, are thus crucial to the definition of a structure; and each in a distinct manner. The paradigmatic dimension links the structure outwards, so to speak, and is one indicator of meaning; the syntagmatic dimension establishes the internal order of the entity, as well as the syntagmatic value (function) of items. It has been claimed (P. E. Lewis, in Ehrman, 1970) that structuralist analyses cannot deal with meaning. This is obviously not true, unless we restrict the term meaning in an idiosyncratic manner. One kind of meaning that structuralism cannot deal with successfully is the 'functional meaning' of a structure operating in a larger structure, for the moment we look at this we are looking at a new structure. But this is simply saying that functionalist analysis is fundamentally different from structuralist analysis.

As I have said, most structural descriptions concentrate on the syntagmatic dimension of structure. The reason for this is not far to seek: a structuralist analysis can only apply to an entity defined as an entity. That is, one assumption that all structuralists have to make is that there are discrete entities (and that the problem of establishing these entities is a minor problem). Once an entity is clearly partitioned off from other phenomena, the task seems to be to describe the internal relations of this entity only. This is in fact a major shortcoming of structuralist analyses: in order to be able to enumerate items, state relations between them, establish their syntagmatic and paradigmatic values, in short, to display the structure, one has to proceed as though the object contracted no external relations. This gives to many structural analyses their peculiarly formal and sterile feel: it is difficult to link statements about a structure outwards. Saussure's dictum against the study of context has remained willy-nilly with structuralist analysis: 'Language must, to put it correctly, be studied in itself.' He had wanted to focus on those aspects of language which were *not* voluntary, which 'in some way always elude the individual

Structure	:	Sentence
Example	:	*Rod Stewart has released a new single*
Structural Items	:	(Nominal) (Verbal) (Nominal)
Structural relations	:	Subject/Actor process Object/Goal

No further structural items are involved or implied.

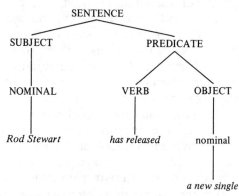

Figure 1. Configurational description of sentence

will' (p. 17), in an attempt to discover general laws, beyond the influence of the individual.

However, the problems associated with the definition of the entity have not gone unnoticed by structuralists. Their answers have differed. Levi-Strauss, in *Le Cru et le cuit*, meets the problem of the artificial 'closing off' of an object with an offer of a minimal set of analytical tools, and the destruction of the boundaries around the object whenever they threaten to firm up; or even perhaps, not to recognize the object. 'In order to obtain equally dense scanning, the procedure would have to be renewed several times, *by drawing new circles* at points situated on the periphery . . . In the process the mythical territory would of course be enlarged . . . the books are never closed'. Thus his methodology denies, or comes very close to denying, the existence of the discrete object. Levi-Strauss like Saussure, is interested in the set of rules which generates instances of the object; but while the set of rules may have stability, the generated entities do not: 'We are dealing with a reality in

Structure	:	Culture		
Example	:	'Pop World'	Means of production	Pop record
Structural Items	:	Social group	Process	Product
Structural relations	:	Producers	Process of Production	Commodity

Structural item 'consumer' is implied in structural item 'commodity'.

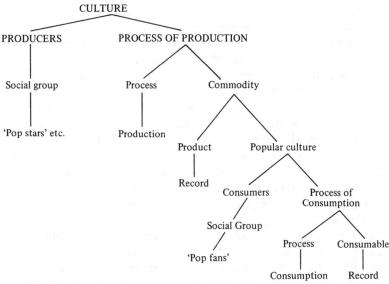

Figure 2. Hypothetical configurational description of culture (popular culture)

process, a reality which is perpetually under the attack from the past which ruins it, and a future which changes it' (1970, p 14). He touches on the question of process here: entities undergo change of form, are in constant process. What motivates this change? The individual cannot affect the underlying rule system, according to him. Also, of course, in as far as it is true of entities that they are constantly changing, then every item in the structure inherent in the entity is in process of change. And a structuralist description will be both out of date and false the moment it is attempted. And this applies to the underlying set of rules as much as to the surface structure. But just as no linguist would insist on having a set of all texts before beginning the analysis of a language, simply because this would be both an impossible and a pointless demand, so Lévi-Strauss infers general laws from the shifting and infinite number of surface entities.

Other practitioners have been concerned with this problem, but have expressed it in terms of the *focus* of the entity (Lévi-Strauss's 'equal density of scanning'): this is perhaps true especially of some adherents of the *Tel Quel* movement. If the focus of the entity is shifted, we get a totally new structure, and thus, in theory, the potential number of structures of any one entity is infinite. One might for instances look at a game, let us say darts. If we take the *board* as the focus of the structure, the other items associated with it are the *darts*, the *blackboard* on which the score is kept, *pieces of chalk*, possibly also a *light* above the board. However, this last item functions in a structure with a different focus, namely the *game and the players*. Here the focus might be a *team captain*; it might be a *social occasion* (i.e. 'Wednesday night is darts night'); it might be a *team*. If the latter item is present it is likely that the focus has already shifted: onto the *league* in which teams compete. If I were the manager of the local brewery, however, the focus of the structure might be *sale of beer*, in which *dartsclubs based on pubs* is one of a number of structural items. A sociologist on the other hand might be interested in *social cohesion* in a specific area, and he would see the *darts team* as a structural item in yet another structure. All of these structures would deal with the same substantial items: but the items would occupy totally different places in the various structures.

The ideological aspect of this selection is obvious. Objects do not meet the analyst, he needs to define them. Here we come to one of the crucial aspects of a structural approach to popular culture: the definition of *popular culture* is an ideological act. And in at least two ways: first, the analyst proceeds from within an ideology; second, the analyst may have a specific purpose (e.g. control, mystification). Thus some practitioners of structuralism question the reality of the entity and of the structure they describe, regarding them as the construct of the analyst, or of the method of analysis. In some modern treatments this has been regarded, by Barthes and others, as a problem of 'reading'. That is, the question how any reader extracts significance from a text (or how he imposes structure on the text) has been made the focus of attention, and the problem of 'signification' raised to primary position. Just as in an ambiguous utterance I will normally 'read' one meaning, the one which the context has most facilitated perhaps, so in a larger and more complex structure I will normally read one meaning. But the moment someone points out the ambiguity of an utterance to me I will see it immediately: *visiting aunts* will become either *I visit aunts* or *Aunts visit me*. In any one sentence the number of readings is of course finite. But in a larger text, a novel say, the number of readings is huge, and perhaps infinite. This is undoubtedly a complex question. But one sometimes gets the impression that the response on the part of many structuralists has been to mirror the complexities of the problem in their descriptions. That is, the explanatory model is at least as bafflingly complex as the problem, and the relation of the model to the problem as mysterious as the reading process. This representational mode of procedure shows a great love of mystery and builds mystification into the approach as a theoretical term. It conveys very effectively the sense of the mystery surrounding the reading process, but is not strong on clarification.

Because they focus on a closed-off entity, structuralist analyses cannot answer this question; and the view one adopts amounts to a simple affirmation of faith (though never simply affirmed). A solution is possible only if one looks at systems of structures (i.e. a new structure); then it will become apparent that networks of relations exist between the structures of certain entities, and not between others. Or at least that the density of the relations is greater between certain structures than between certain others.

So for instance, if one looked at the structure of soap opera television serials, it would be apparent that there existed systematic links with the structure of other forms of popular culture: fashion, systems of food, pop music, at every level; but that the density of the links between the structure of the same television serials and the structures of e.g. church fetes, garden parties and jumble sales in England would be far less dense. There is thus a necessary first assumption that the entity has reality, and that this is going to be borne out empirically in the density of the relations in systems of structures. This provides no answer to the ideological definition of popular culture; it does provide a working methodology. Structural analysis would have to incorporate this methodology: not to confine itself to the analysis of discrete entities, but to take as its proper object of attention systems of structures (which is in fact the practice of anthropologists). A second assumption would be that the entities, and the systems in which they participate, are ideological constructs, and that readers and analysts are 'locked into' ideological constructs, and that that fact too is to be accounted for.

If then we assume as a working hypothesis in a particular investigation that there is reality in the entities we look at, and that consequently the structures inherent in the entities have reality, a further question arises: do the structures, and the systematic arrangements of structures, signify anything beyond themselves? Are they exponents of signs of a different order? In linguistics, there is little debate nowadays over the distinction between deep and surface structure (though there is much debate over the precise nature of the two levels): broadly speaking, deep structure is closer to a semantic structure, of which the surface structure is an expression. For example, on the level of surface structure we might have the sentences (1) *Jane likes her new job*, (2) *the new job pleases Jane*, (3) *Jane is pleased by her new job*, (4) *It's the new job that Jane (really) likes*, (5) *What Jane is (really) pleased by is her new job*, etc. On the level of deep structure on the other hand, these surface forms are represented in a non-linear, non-temporal, non-syntagmatic structure consisting of three items: an abstract *PROCESS* (more specifically mental process PLEASE) (where caps are meant to indicate that these are abstract linguistic items), a nominal *PROCESSOR*, and a nominal *STIMULUS* (of the mental process), with the structural relations as indicated in the labels themselves. Thus the variety of surface structural forms are all realizations of *one* conceptual/cognitive/semantic structure. This is, I believe, not unlike Lévi-Strauss' conception of the relation of differing forms of one myth. (In talking about the Ge of Central America in *Le Cru et le Cuit*.) He postulates a relation between an abstract form of a myth, and its various manifestations across a vast range of communities and geographical locations. Furthermore, he also cites evidence of transformations of myths performed by individuals, so that tellers of the myth appear to have considerable freedom to alter the surface form of the myth. However, most importantly, the myth itself is a transform of one system of logical order into another, so that the myth represents one mode of conceptual manipulation of (aspect of) reality. Thus underlying the myth is a deeper and significantly different conceptual, psychological, universal order.

Figure 3 gives a schematic representation. The underlying myth is thus the first transform (transform stage 1); the tribal variations of that form of the myth represent a further transformational stage (transform stage 2). Both of these trans-

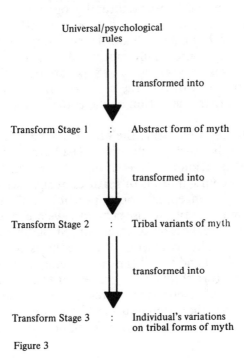

Figure 3

formational operations are significant. It is only the transforms performed by individuals in the telling of the myth (transform stage 3) which Lévi-Strauss does not regard as significant.

Going back to the linguistic example for a moment, we can ask whether the surface forms are in fact wilful and non-significant, unmotivated variations on the deep form. A little reflection will show that this is not so. For one thing, each surface form is, as it were, a response to differing questions, and thus each would be appropriate for a different discourse. Sentence (1) presupposes that the hearer knows that Jane has a job, but not whether she likes it or not. (5) assumes that Jane is really quite extraordinarily chuffed generally, but that the new job has capped it all. The point is that the various forms are (a) motivated by different contextual demands, and (b) thus carry significance over and above that carried by the underlying structure. Transferring this to Lévi-Strauss's discussion of myths it seems apparent that precisely the same process is at work; the transforms of the myth (transform stage 2) are due to different (cultural/geographical) contextual demands. What one would like to know is whether the transforms which the individual performs (transform stage 3) are not similarly contextually motivated: and if not, why not. Here what seems to be crucially at stake are two things: the relation of the individual to the cultural form in question and, dependent on that, the notion of the entity as static or in process.

To sum up for a moment: the object to be explained turns out not to be the (surface) structure. The latter stands in a relation of realization to a level of underlying structure, and there we find configurations of features of significance of different kinds: conceptual, social, psychological, cultural, depending on the entity whose structure we are investigating. This then is the real object of attention. Structural analysis which does not take cognizance of this point is doomed to remain superficial and trivial. The underlying form is realized in surface structure through the process of transformation. This process itself responds to contextual constraints and demands, so that the ensuing surface forms are not simply wilful variations of the underlying form, but are appropriate to specific contexts.

This account can be readily transferred to the study of popular culture. Bearing in mind the methodological requirements made above, the analysts task is as follows. In the first instance he meets an entity, intuitively defined. He has to place this entity in a system of structures. Thus even in considering one manifestation of popular culture, he must place it, in the process of analysis, in the system of structures in which it functions, i.e. culture. Furthermore, if he regards the entity he studies as analogous to transform stage 2 of myth, he knows that he is attempting to uncover the more abstract form corresponding to transform stage 1 of myth. Analytically this process depends on the fact that transformations operate on specific configurations of structure: thus the structure of the previous transformational stage is recoverable. In the case of popular culture this demand is fulfilled specifically only at transform stage 1. The entities at transform stage 2 are in many cases objects, material products. These products do not bear indications of their internal structure; the structural specification is lost, and consequently the transformational relation to stage 1 is opaque. It is clear why the analyst needs to place the particular entity he is looking at in the largest context. Figure 4 represents a hypothesis about the relation of popular culture to its underlying form; it also represents a hypothesis about the relation between forms of popular culture and myth. (The consumer of popular culture is in a different position. He confronts the individual and varying forms of popular culture as discrete objects, often as physical objects, but objects, as we have seen, without structure. As he is not an analyst of culture, the path to recovering transform stage 1 is cut off to him, and with it the possibility of recovering the 'content' of transform stage 1.)

Thus the multiplicity of forms of popular culture should lead the analyst to a single underlying configuration of meanings. The surface variations are not without significance: they lead to the further question as to what kind of context any specific surface form is appropriate for. Or, to turn it the other way around, what specifically it is in the context that demands this particular surface realization of the underlying form. The process of analysis is thus two-directional: from the multiplicity of surface forms one wishes to get to a unified underlying structure. This underlying structure will show what the *content* of the surface forms is, that is, show what the surface structures are expressing. From there one can then work towards an

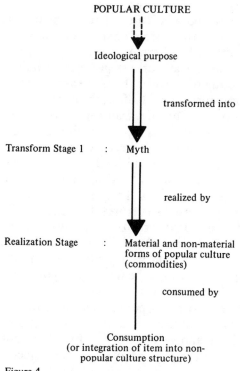

Figure 4

understanding of the various contexts in which forms of popular culture appear, by asking what specifically it is in any given context that demands that the content be expressed in one form rather than another. Thus two kinds of information will be revealed by the analysis: the content of the underlying structure, and the range of significant contexts (and the significances of that range). An examination of a range of entities such as *dress fashions, pop music, (design of) consumer goods, popular writing* (womens magazines, westerns, comics) should reveal the common content, as well as the motivations for the varying surface realizations of the common content.

So far this is similar to Lévi-Strauss' methodology in analysing myths; analogous to the spread and variety of surface forms of the 'same' myth (transform stage 2), we have the variety or surface expressions of popular culture: underlying both, one common content (transform stage 1). In the case of myth, the common content is the abstract form of the myth (transform stage 1) which is itself an expression of the content underlying it: universal psychological rules. In the case of popular culture, the common content of the various realizations of popular culture is the content of the myth (transform stage 1) underlying the multiplicity of forms. Content is here meant in an abstract sense: characterizations of the status of the individual, characterizations of activities which confer status on individuals (e.g. attitudes to marriage, motherhood, notions about the structure of the society of which the individual is a member) which may be expressed in material or non-material forms, e.g. advertising, supermarkets. Underlying this stage in popular culture are however not universal/psychological rules, but a specific ideological purpose which is in itself a transform; that is, the transformation of a content from a deeper level. Figure 4 is a schematic and hypothetical representation.

This account makes strong analogies between the structural place of myth in the Lévi-Strauss sense, and popular culture. An abstract myth gives rise to specific forms of myth in one case, and a myth (probably equally powerful and abstract), underlies the surface forms of popular culture. There are however crucial differences: at transform stage 1 the underlying contents are structurally completely different — in one case universal psychological rules, in the other, an ideological purpose. Transform stage 2 of myth is paralleled in the case of popular culture by a realization stage. The importance of this is that the structural description of the entity is completely lost at this stage in popular culture. The Amazonian Indian has the structural specification of the myth available to him: he can see that one form of the myth (i.e. the way he tells it) is in some non-trivial sense the same as another form of the myth (i.e. the way his neighbour tells it). The consumer of popular culture cannot perceive this, because the entity he consumes is without structure. Thus pop records do not seem like dress fashions; and the local supermarket does not to him have similarity to Tarzan films. Thus while the Indian can be creative, in the sense of being able to perform the transformation from stage 2 to stage 3 (and different versions of these), the consumer of popular culture can only consume – or abstain (when he is of course not consumer, and thus structurally already occupying a different place).

As a hypothesis, I would draw a closer analogy between the structural place of folk culture and Lévi-Strauss' treatment of Indian myth. The reason for this would be the similar position of the individual in both cases.

Crucially the consumer of popular culture confronts a structureless entity, in the creation of which he cannot and does not take part. This is apparently refutable, by citing cases where consumers seemingly transform (act on) items of popular culture. The first question of course is: does the individual consumer affect the structure? The answer to that is clearly no. But it might be argued that people whistle pop tunes, furnish their houses with items belonging to differing structures, wear clothes in an 'ungrammatical' manner, etc. Of course, the individual is perfectly capable of creating structure or structures; and no doubt may use an object of popular culture in the structures he is creating. It is as if I took a toy soldier from my child's toybox, and used him as a pawn on the chess board: I have left both structures totally intact. And if groups of people take items of clothing and wear them in ungrammatical combinations, they have used objects produced by popular culture and integrated them into new structures, where they now have a completely different value (i.e. wearing a dinner-suit from a jumble sale with a bush-hat and suede shoes, in a coffee lounge).

Thus Lévi-Strauss's treatment of myth is at best only a partial analogy to be used in the analysis of popular culture. If myth is in Lévi-Strauss' conception an objectification of universal psychological laws into one particular mode, then it is nevertheless the case that the psychological processes of the user of the myth are identical with those objectified in the myth. He is the consumer of a product of his own creation adapted to particular contextual necessities; and he constantly recreates this product in a number of differing forms. The consumer of popular culture on the other hand confronts a heavily transformed object, which is in no sense subject to his own creation: he is alienated from it. Language may furnish a useful example here: it seems to be the case that groups differing significantly use significantly (i.e. descriptively apparent) different forms of language. The most obvious example is class-language. The speaker of class language X is, in learning a language, a consumer initially; but once a speaker has learned language X (which exhibits, like other languages, universal laws), he also becomes a producer of language X. That is, he possesses the generative rules underlying forms of that language: the means of production. He is free to produce an infinite set of utterances in that language (all of which exhibit the rules of language X as well as the universal laws); he is furthermore capable of the same wilful variation with respect to language as the Amazonian Indian is with respect to myth. There is no break; consumer and producer are identical. With respect to language Y, however (the language of another class, let us say), this individual is a consumer only: he does not produce utterances in that language; moreover he is totally removed from all possibility of the 'wilfulness' open to the speaker of a language. He is not part of the process of creation.

As a hypothesis, this could be a crucial distinguishing characteristic of popular culture as against other forms of culture, in particular as against folk culture. In folk culture the relation between consumer and producer is that illustrated both in the situation of the Indian myths, and that of the speaker of a (class) language. The consumer and the producer are (potentially) indentical. The product is not alienated from the producer, or from the consumer: it demonstrates modes of structure which are common to both. Both have internalized the same set of rules: and both can function in either role. In discussions of folk culture the impression is sometimes given that the wilfulness, which both the producer of myths and of utterances display, is not possible. So forms of folk art are regarded as fixed, unchanging, showing, without modification, patterns reaching far back into history: patterns which the individual is unable to influence. This is of course false. The study of any given form of folk art will show significant changes in the surface structures over time. Anyone who seriously believes for example that corndollies produced in

1975 are identical with corndollies produced in 1875 or in 775 (let alone whatever form corndollies took in BC 775!) has been taken in rather seriously by the ideology of the stable structure. 'Wilfulness' is allowed as much to the acknowledged 'performer' of folk art, as it is to the speaker of language or the creator of myth.

In fact, the ideological basis of Saussure's view that the individual 'can never create nor modify (langauge) by himself' (a view held by Lévi-Strauss also) is not difficult to expose. Languages change. Forms of folk art change. Myths appear in differing forms throughout South America. What is the cause of the change, or the variety? Unless some mysterious process is at work in all these instances, it is the actions of individual speakers, folk artists, myth tellers, who, responsive to the demands of infinitely various situations (though not infinitely various situation types) use available forms in new contexts, or modify, very nearly imperceptibly, existing forms to meet the demands of new contexts. Of course, couched in an extreme form , no one would maintain that any one speaker can change the whole of any one language system. But if I heard yesterday *This material washes well* I might use today *That shirt doesn't wash at all well* (although there are many speakers of English who would regard this as ungrammatical: not within the scope permitted by the rules); and if I hear today *This studio records well* I could try tomorrow, at least semi-facetiously, *This room doesn't lecture well*. Given that I am operating in a structure where producer and consumer are (potentially) identical, and I am by general consent recognized as a competent member of that structure, I may influence that structure and bring about change. Of course there is inertia in the system; and the view of individuals may be that the structure has remained unchanged throughout history. That is, individuals may have a strong, though erroneous notion of the history of the system or the particular structure.

With popular culture on the other hand, I assume, as a working hypothesis the individual consumer remains consumer, and affects in no significant sense the structure of the entity. Abstention from consumption is his only option: and though this may have an effect, the effect is unfocused and in no way predictable: it does not determine the future structure of the entity. (Fashion might serve as a paradigm example here). Whereas folk culture is subject to gradual change, popular culture shows no development, it is marked by a lack of a sense of history: and by an overwhelming sense of the con- temporaneousness of its manifestations. It is marked by cyclical recurrence. The answer to the question: are pop songs of the twenties in any significant sense like the pop songs of the sixties, is yes: with this proviso, that we look at the same structural type, and treat content in the abstract manner outlined above. Then it is clear that one type of pop song presents the content: basic physiological rhythm, equality of participants, similarity to primitive form. And these characteristics are intimately connected with, or deriving from, the structural relations inherent in the two different forms: the disjunction of producer and consumer in one form, and the (potential) identity of producer and consumer in the other. One might borrow two structural terms from linguistics, and characterize the folk culture type as *intransitive* [either *John is shaving himself* or *John is shaving*] and the popular culture type as *transitive* [*John is amusing his children*, i.e. John (causer or agent) brings it about that his children (affected participant) are amused] . The two terms seem to characterize both the structural relations of items in the structure, and the nature of the two types of structure. The transitive type is fundamentally about control exercised by an external agent on an affected participant; the other is about action initiated by one participant, and, where there is an affected participant, he is identical with the one initiating the action.

The ideology of the stable structure has three main characteristics: (i) the homogeneity and stability of the structure, which is not the possession of the individual, but of the group; (ii) the equality of all participants in that structure due to the fact that they receive, equally, access to the structure, and (iii) the inability of the individual to modify the structure. That this is not inherently the nature of structures has been demonstrated with the examples of the *intransitive* type of structure, in which the individual plainly influences the structure, be it language, myth, or folk culture. It is the nature of the transitive type of structure, that the affected participant cannot, indeed, influence the structure.

The fundamental ideological stance inherent in structuralism (in both senses) is that it generalizes the relations existing within one structural type to all structural types. Under the guise of the equality of all participants in a structure in the face of the immutable structure it emasculates one type of participant in one type of structure, namely the consumer of popular culture.

As mentioned earlier, structuralism is confined to the analysis of entities seen as stable structures; structuralist analysis cannot deal with process. Thus an inherent defect in the methodology is at the same time a disabling ideological stance. Lévi-Strauss speaks of realities in process of change, and his view of the connection of myths also implies transformation, a process. However, what he considers are not the processes, but the states resulting from the processes. He too regards the individual as separated from and unable to influence the underlying structure of the myth, which he receives passively from the society whose property it is — immutably. It is therefore only by abandoning this disabling methodological/ ideological limitation to the stable structure that we see the two basic forms of structure: the structure in which the individual is potentially producer and consumer, the intransitive type (folk culture, Indian organization of myth, language, etc.), or on the other hand, the structure in which the generative categories are within the producer, but not within the consumer. Thus it seems that popular culture *presents* reality: the producer creates the object and presents it to the consumer who receives it in its finished form. (The syntactic form analogous to this structure is *Mary knits John a tie*: Mary knows how to knit, John simply passively receives the tie). Knowledge of the generative categories confers power; whether it be *cooking a meal for the husband*, or *running a power station for the country.*

If this analysis is correct, we might expect, as a further hypothesis, the content of the various forms of popular culture to attempt to present a picture opposite to that revealed here. In as much as consumers of popular culture occupy a disvalued place in the social structure, one would expect popular culture to present the consumer as highly valued. And just as structuralism presents all individuals as equally unable to alter the structure, though quite free to produce non-significant surface variations on the underlying forms, and just as it presents one particular structure as though it were the general form of all structure, so we might expect the contents of popular culture to be about creativity, equality, power. As a general hypothesis one would expect the contents of popular culture to be the opposites of the consumer's experience. But structuralism, as presently constituted, will not readily provide insight into the very ideological processes underlying it.

Bibliography

Barthes, R.   *Elements of Semiology*. London: Cape (1967); *Writing Degree Zero*. London: Cape (1967); *Mythologies*. London: Cape (1972).

Bierwisch, M.   'Strukturalismus: Geschichte, Probleme und Methoden', *Kursbuch*, 5. pp 77–152 (1966).

Chomsky, N.   *Syntactic Structures*. The Hague: Mouton (1957); *Aspects of the Theory of Syntax*. Cambridge: M.I.T. (1965).

Culler, J.   *Structuralist Poetics*. London: Routledge (1975).

Ehrmann, J.   *Structuralism*. New York: Doubleday (1970).

Fowler, R. G.   'The referential code and narrative authority'. To appear in *Language and Style* (1975).

Halliday, M. A. K.   'Categories of the theory of Grammar'. *Word* 17. 3, 1961. pp. 241–92.

Halliday, M. A. K.   'Anti-Languages', in *UEA Papers in Linguistics*, 1, 1976 (to appear in American *Anthropologist*).

Kress, G. R.   (ed.) *Halliday: System and Function in Language*. London: OUP. (1976).

Lévi-Strauss, C.   *The Raw and the Cooked*. London: Cape (1970); *The Savage Mind*. London: Weidenfeld (1972).

Saussure, F.   *Course in General Linguistics*. (tr. Wade Baskin) London: McGraw-Hill (1966).

6

Linguistics and Popular Culture

Robert Hodge

To talk about a link between linguistics and popular culture at this time can only be perverse or prophetic — perverse, since there is nothing to talk about beyond saying that this combination is a virgin field of study, prophetic, because this virgin could so easily be enflowered. The reasons for this state of affairs are, I think, important and worth discussing at some length. One reason is the problematic nature of 'popular culture'.[1] However, linguistics at present is so constituted that whatever is understood by popular culture, linguistics will contribute to its study only with great difficulty. This is due to a number of limiting assumptions which also make linguistics a far less important discipline in the humanities in general than it ought to be. So it is not possible to say how 'linguistics' can be useful in a study of popular culture without also indicating what basic assumptions will have to be modified or discarded, what basic reorientation effected, for this enterprise to succeed. But this sounds excessively negative. In fact, I want to suggest how easily linguistics could have a major role in this area of cultural research.[2]

There is one feature of popular culture which creates problems for a purely linguistic analysis. This is the inconvenient fact that so many forms of popular culture do not

[1] See the debate conducted in the present volume.

[2] The view of linguistics in what follows is argued at greater length in R. Hodge and G. Kress, 'Transformations, Models and Processes: towards a useable linguistics', *Journal of Literary Semantics* 1974, and the linguistics theory developed in our *Language as Ideology* (forthcoming). I hope the present discussion however will be self-explanatory.

communicate exclusively through language, words written
or spoken. Music is important in song (and even more
important in music), pictures in film and comics, performance
in theatre and so on. In response to this, linguistics might
limit itself to providing analyses of the linguistic component
of such forms, leaving it to other experts to fit the rest of the
jig-saw together. The danger of this procedure is that it begs
the very important question of the relation between the
linguistic and nonlinguistic elements, by assuming an invariable
additive relationship. But it might be the case that a song (to
take one instance) ought to be analysed not as words-plus-
music, but as a single complex communicative whole (with the
context of performance arguably also relevant to the understanding of this communicative whole.)

Another response to the importance of the nonverbal in
popular culture would be to extend the notion of 'language'
to include nonverbal forms of communication. Something
like this is envisaged by Saussure, often referred to as the father
of modern linguistics, when he placed linguistics proper among
the semiological sciences, seeing language as one (the most
important) of the systems of signs by which man com-
municates with his fellows. It is no accident that semiology
has proved available for the analysis of forms of popular
culture.[3] Unfortunately, however, the linguistics underlying
semiology is so rudimentary that it can provide little insight
into the linguistic qualities of forms of popular culture.
Linguistics gets lost in the semiological enterprise: what I
shall be advocating in this essay is the extension of linguistics
into all areas where 'language', or communicative acts, occur.

Linguistics as it has developed this century is a puzzling
combination of strengths and weaknesses. However, it does
not seem to me that these strengths and weaknesses are so
inseparable that the student of popular culture has to take
both or nothing. The limiting assumptions are detachable, or
easy to invert. To remove or modify these assumptions is not
to remove essential parts from a complex interlocking whole.
They are not a source of the power of any linguistic theory. On
the contrary, they all seem to act as brakes or governors,

---

[3] F. de Saussure *Course in General Linguistics* 1915, trans. W. Baskin (London
1959).

designed to prevent the linguistic car, vessel or rocket ship from going very far, very fast. However, I will not speculate here about the motivation for the built-in impotence which is a feature of modern linguistic theories.

This paradoxical combination of qualities can be seen particularly clearly in transformational generative grammar (TG), undoubtedly the dominant linguistic theory in England and the United States. This theory derives from the work of Noam Chomsky, and has been revised by Chomsky himself and re-revised by his followers. Linguists feel with some pride that the field is 'exploding' so fast now that no summary account could do justice to the current diversity of conflicting views.[4] This can then be used as an argument for caution in applying this otherwise most powerful of theories: any version of the theory may be obsolete or discredited by the time the work of applying it has been completed. This argument must seem a strong one in a culture where people change their cars every two years. However, I will not be trying to do justice to this diversity. Instead, I want to bring out what seems to me of permanent importance in Chomsky's work, the promising and powerful concepts which justify the dominant position of this linguistic theory in the contemporary scene and which make it, I would claim, a key discipline for the student of popular culture. Then I will try to drive with the brakes off.

There are a number of important concepts associated with this theory which contribute to its explanatory power. The first is generative grammar. 'Generative' here refers to the principle whereby a finite set of rules is used to generate a nonfinite set of utterances or descriptions of utterances. This allows Chomsky to insist on the infinite diversity of language, and the creativity of the language-user, while insisting at the same time that this diversity is rule-governed and can be described in a principled way. Associated with this concept is his account of the acquisition of language. Children are exposed to a very partial and imperfect sample of their native

---

[4] Chomsky's two most important statements of his theory are *Syntactic Structures* 1957 and *Aspects of the theory of Syntax* (Boston, Mass., Cambridge 1965). Although *Aspects* revises the earlier version, my summary account is often closer to the model of *Syntactic Structures*. As guides to the diversity of the contemporary linguistic scene, see J. Lyons (ed.) *New Horizons in linguistics* London 1970 or R. Fowler *Understanding Language* 1974.

language, he maintains, yet from this corpus they abstract the same rules, and are able then to produce new grammatical utterances, and can recognize the ungrammatical status of any ungrammatical utterances they may produce or hear.

This has important methodological implications for the student of popular culture. If the forms of popular culture are analysed in these terms, there is no need to attempt an exhaustive survey (which because of the limitations of time and energy will tend to be superficial). Any sample will do, as the starting point of enquiry, and intensive analytic scrutiny becomes legitimate and well-motivated. Of course, the under-lying rules will not be perceived directly, they will be hypothesized, and these hypotheses will always be tested against the rest of the corpus. This principle does not mean that the rest of the corpus can be ignored. What it does is to give an order to the enquiry which, Chomsky would claim, is natural to the human mind, since it is the strategy used by every language learner for his own language (and, if the analogy holds, the strategy by which anyone inward with some form of popular culture acquired his inwardness). A 'generative' account of this kind need not be reductive, either, since it neither attempts to categorize definitively, to sum up exhaustively, the full set of manifestations of a form, nor does it attempt to give undue emphasis to the typical. A generative account instead hypothesizes the principles which combine to generate all actual and possible 'grammatical' manifestations of the form, the rare and unique as well as the typical.

Chomsky makes an important division of the rules of a generative grammar, into rules of the base, and transformational rules, which act on structures generated by the base.[5] This leads to further economy of rules. It also allows a principled way of relating two superficially different forms, or distinguishing two superficially identical forms. The classic example Chomsky gives, in *Syntactic Structures*, is the active-passive relation. A passive like 'the ball was hit by the man', is clearly closely related to the active form, 'the man hit the ball', yet every word in its surface form is in a different position. The felt similarity is due to a common base structure according to Chomsky, the difference

---

[5] My account of Chomsky here follows *Syntactic Structures* rather than *Aspects*.

to a single transformational operation. Felt affinities and differences in forms of popular culture may prove susceptible to a description in transformational terms.

With this division of the rules of a grammar, it becomes possible to make a distinction between deep and surface structures of individual utterances. Underlying the surface structure of any sentence is its deep structure, consisting of base structures normally acted on by several transformations.

One important point Chomsky insists on is that sentences are interpreted in relation to their deep structure. This means that the surface form of an utterance is, so to speak, like a semi-transparent surface, beneath which the speaker or hearer apprehends the deep structure, whether or not he is conscious of doing so. The rules that have been internalized to constitute mastery of that language may be of formidable complexity, yet many of them have never entered consciousness, and knowledge of these rules is revealed only by the unerring capacity to produce only grammatical utterances, and to recognize the ungrammaticality of sentences which are not well-formed because they break one or more of these rules.

If 'mastery' of forms of popular culture works similarly, then two things follow. Just as the ability to speak even the most banal sentence is revealed by this kind of analysis to be a truly amazing achievement, so also with the production of the most ordinary specimen of any form of popular culture. The complexity uncovered by analysis will not then be felt as spurious, as the mere artefact of the theory (a suspicion which hangs over many analyses of popular culture that are not reductive). It will not invalidate the analysis in the least if the performer is unconscious of or inarticulate about what he 'knows': and what he 'knows' in this sense will probably go far beyond what any master of high culture is conscious of knowing.

This invocation of levels normally inaccessible to consciousness is not a piece of mystification either, since Chomsky also provides a strategy for arriving at these deep rules. The intuitions of a native speaker can be used as a precise check on hypotheses about the rules at work, since he can immediately recognize whether a new utterance, generated by a proposed rule, is in fact grammatical or acceptable. The kind of research that proceeded in these terms in the field of popular culture would be highly speculative and creative: and it could hope to uncover principles that have operated powerfully yet never been explicitly learnt.

But then, there are the brakes, the decelerative assumptions I mentioned earlier, which make the discipline of linguistics relatively safe as a minority subject in our academic institutions. Primary here is the insistence on the autonomy of linguistics. Saussure, the founding father, urged as the third of the three tasks which limit the scope of the subject, that it should seek 'to limit and define itself.'[6] Linguistics has done so. Although language is a social product, sociolinguistics is a haphazard enterprise which receives little intellectual sustenance from theoretical linguistics. Since popular culture is so intrinsically a social phenomenon, the kind of linguistics it draws on must be sociologically informed, able to work hand in hand with a sociology of popular culture.

For a professional linguist, working in an autonomous linguistics, the proper object of study is language, which naturally tends to be treated as autonomous itself. So Chomsky deals with grammars as theories about language, not with language as a theory or theories about the world. Such a linguistics will tend to formalism. Significantly, much of Chomsky's theory describes grammars, not speakers. Hence, the term 'generative' for Chomsky does not refer to speakers 'generating' utterances, but to the grammar, as a fictive person or machine, generating structural descriptions. Speakers do of course produce, or generate, utterances, and Chomsky would want there to be some relation between these two processes. But analysis in TG terms cannot proceed with any certainty, since the structures and transformations uncovered might have no psychological reality. Fortunately there is something one can do about this uncertainty: rely on the intuitions of native speakers to test and refine any proferred hypothesis.

Another important concept Chomsky introduces is his distinction between competence and performance. This is a simplifying assumption, which initially appears to be an enabling one, since it allows the linguist to abstract himself from the mess of actual linguistic phenomena. Competence refers to the knowledge of an ideal native speaker. Performance

[6] Saussure *op. cit.*, p. 6.

then refers to often imperfect utterances, which speakers, however, recognize are imperfect. But this distinction has its dangers. The notion of performance as a kind of incompetence, with the accidental becoming invisible in terms of the theory, must be problematic for a student of popular culture, since it treats spontaneous features of performance as irrelevant.

This assumption has the further danger that it can lead to the linguist ignoring social differences. The differences between university students and, say, blacks, or workers, can be seen as mere differences of performance between people who speak essentially the same language. If university students are then used as the most convenient source of native speakers, the description of the language will have assumed the homogeneity of the linguistic community. The student of popular culture must be more sensitive than this to differences of class within the same broad community. Reinforcing this tendency in Chomsky is his search for what he calls linguistic universals. If there are 'linguistic universals' fairly close to the surface of apparently different languages, if languages differ only through a set of transformations specific to each, then linguistically speaking we are all brothers beneath the skin. The notion of competence achieves the resolution of class differences at a methodological stroke: linguistic universals similarly achieve the brotherhood of man. These are admirable goals, but not if they give rise to a linguistics which is incapable of acknowledging cultural diversity or class conflict. It is, however, entirely consistent with a TG framework to emphasize diversity, different transformations acting on what could prove to be different base structures.

There is another linguistic tradition available to Anglo-American linguistics, associated with the names of Boas, Sapir and Whorf. This tradition is a most promising one for the student of popular culture, since it makes many of the connections that need making, between language and culture, and language and mind. Whorf's writings[7] are probably the most accessible and immediately relevant source for this tradition. He starts from the contention that language is the repository of the metaphysics and science of a community, the linguistic-

[7] Conveniently collected in *Language, Thought and Reality* ed. J. Carroll 1956.

cognitive habits through which the speakers of that community understand the world, the basis of perception and thought. He worked this out primarily by means of a contrast between the language of the Hopi Indians (a North American tribe) and what he contemptuously labels SAE — standard average European, for this purpose treated as an undifferentiated mass. He makes strong claims for the implicit science of the Hopi. They have a concept of space and time much closer to Einsteinian physics than SAE, which is still, linguistically, in the Newtonian dark ages. In Chomsky's terms, the competent speaker of SAE is a Newton (which is of course flattering) but the Hopi is an Einstein. Whorf is very persuasive in showing Newtonian assumptions underlying various SAE (particularly English) forms, and he is undoubtedly suggestive about Hopi.

A two-term opposition between Hopi and SAE is bound to be simplistic, but one attraction of it for the student of popular culture may be its possible resemblance to the opposition between popular and high culture (this being a parallel or analogy that has often motivated students of popular culture).[8] Whorf's account of Hopi splendidly champions what is usually regarded as the poor relation, so-called 'primitive' cultures. He may be providing terms for championing popular culture, as the poor relation in its own sphere.

One difference between Hopi and SAE language and culture concerns the medium of language itself. Hopi is an oral culture, SAE, certainly high SAE culture, assumes literacy. Along with this goes what may be termed a difference in senso-types. SAE is strongly spatial, visual and kinaesthetic, according to Whorf, constantly translating nonspatial phenomena into spatial terms. Hopi consciousness is organized more in terms of sound. So it may be the case that the difference between oral and literary modes of communication has a decisive effect on what can be communicated, thought and even perceived by speakers of a language.[9] This would be an extremely interesting conclusion for the student of popular culture, since it would account in a principled way for the affinity that has been sensed between 'primitive' and popular culture, especially in its more oral

[8] See e.g. S. Barbu in the present volume.

[9] Strongest support for this contention comes from J. Goody, and I. Watt 'The Consequences of Literacy', in *Literacy in Traditional Societies*, Cambridge 1968.

forms. Whorf is an important name in contemporary linguistics, but there is no neo-Whorfian school to challenge the hegemony of TG. Two thinkers, however, coincidentally both British, have made use of Whorf in ways that are of interest to the student of popular culture: M. A. K. Halliday and Basil Bernstein.

Bernstein sets the Whorfian opposition in class terms, within a single language.[10] He postulates two codes, restricted and elaborated. In a restricted code, found more among working class speakers, language is context-dependent, nonabstract and contributes to communal solidarity. The predominantly middle-class speakers of elaborated codes maintain individual roles, and their language is universalistic, abstract, formally complex, and can be self-reflexive. The terms of this opposition could be applied to the difference between popular and high culture. Bernstein argues that working-class children have limited access to elaborated codes, and hence, to the dominant culture which is transmitted in such codes. This is a kind of cultural deprivation at least, and may be (this is hotly debated) cognitive and linguistic deprivation as well.[11] This debate may have important implications for the student of popular culture. Where there is a close link between restricted codes and the forms of popular culture, then popular culture may be reinforcing nonviable forms of thought, perpetuating an obsolete 'science', and hence acting as an instrument of social repression. Even if restricted codes constitute merely an alternative 'science' superior in some respects to the dominant one (as Whorf claimed for Hopi), the question must still be asked: who wants a superior science and culture, if the real price is social repression and economic exploitation?

Halliday's work shows a strong Whorfian influence in his work on transitivity in English.[12] Forms of transitivity are the

---

[10] In 'Elaborated and Restricted Codes', In S. Lieberson *Explorations in Sociolinguistics* (1967).

[11] This view is contested by W. Labov from a TG framework in 'The Logic of non-standard English', *Georgetown Monographs on Language and Linguistics*, vol. 22, 1969. For the view that mass culture in capitalist societies is a means of social control, see H. Marcuse *One Dimensional Man* (London 1964).

[12] M. Halliday 'Notes on Transitivity and Theme', *Journal of Linguistics* 3 (1967) and 'Linguistic function and Literary Style', in *Literary style: a symposium* (5th edn, Oxford 1971).

main way of encoding units of causality, and are therefore one of the first places to look for a Whorfian connection between linguistic forms and 'scientific' models. A transitive (e.g. 'he hits the ball') encodes a transactive process, with an agent acting on an object. An intransitive ('he stands on the ground') represents the process as nontransactive, even if, as in the example given, 'ground' is there, in fact as much acted on as the ball. It is tempting to see intransitives as a less adequate means of representing causality, and hence, as the model for a more primitive science, or nonscience. However, both forms are so widely available in English that no form of linguistic determinism seems plausible. Predominant use of one or the other probably reflects rather than determines typical use of the underlying model.

Halliday also has interesting things to say on sound patterns of English.[13] He relates tone-groups, defined through pitch and stress, to information structure, and he points out that certain 'tunes' form part of the syntactic resources of English. Halliday does not derive this explicitly from Whorf, but Whorf's interest in *gestalt* psychology could be seen as foreshadowing such a development. As perception is organized in *gestalten* or fields round foci, so the intonation curves of the spoken language may represent cognitive fields with some immediacy and precision. This would establish a distinctively close link between language, thought and perception for oral modes. Also, music might conceivably come within the scope of linguistic description. Both these developments should be of great interest to the student of popular culture.

But the proof of the pudding is the eating. I want now to offer some speculative linguistic analyses, partly to show the value of the concepts I have sketched in, but also to give greater concreteness to the issues raised by the whole enterprise.

I will start with the kind of material which is most amenable to linguistic analyses, samples of written forms, dealing with different kinds of love, either different facets of a common culture, or distinct subcultures within a larger community. The following passage comes from *Mayfair* (vol. 4, no. 4, 1974), a popular British monthly. It comes near the climatic moment

---

[13] M. Halliday, *A Course in Spoken English* (London 1970).

of what is supposedly a confessional interview, with a lady who describes how she was unfaithful with John, the postman.

I was leaning with my hands on the table by this time and before I could straighten up, John had put two or three fingers right into me and was working me up terribly effectively, so effectively I remained where I was with my panties round my ankles and my rather generous bottom completely offered to his fingers. Then John took his other hand from my breasts and I looked down between my own thighs and watched him guide his rather delicious looking weapon beneath my bottom and between my thighs right to my pussy and I put my fingers through and held my lips apart for him and helped guide him into pussy. Then he started, bringing one hand back up to my breasts and the other helping him between my thighs and I leant on the table and the table shook and quivered and the drinks glasses rattled and banged and several of them fell to the floor and my whole body was trembling and swaying and jerking backwards and forwards and the dear boy pulled himself out before he climaxed and turned me round and asked me to stroke him gently until he was ready again and I suggested we go up to the bedroom and there we both undressed completely and climbed in and made love properly.

This seems to me a fairly typical example of the genre, but I will not attempt to substantiate that judgement, or show what it is typical of. Instead, I want to treat it as a fragment of a universe, the corpus from which to begin to derive the rules which generate that universe (to use Chomskyan categories) or which constitute the science and metaphysics of that universe (to see it in Whorfian terms) — whoever's universe, science, or metaphysic it may turn out to be.

First, basic to any putative science, is the concept of causality. Prominent in this passage is the large number of intransitives — vehicles of a nontransactive science — and reflexives, where the agent acts, but on himself or part of himself. To see the intrinsic limitations of nontransactive 'science', take the unobtrusive example 'I was leaning with my hands on the table.' With-phrases with intransitives are generally ambiguous in English, connected to the main action either instrumentally or more loosely. In this instance, the hands are probably instrumental — she is using her hands to lean on — but this is not certain. If she had said, 'I was leaning with my hands on my hips', we would assume a noninstrumental use, but again with some uncertainty. In the nontransactive mode there is no distinct notion of instrumentality available. In a transitive construction, with-phrases indicate instrumentality more unambiguously. For example, 'I supported my body with my hands.'

A defective model of causality is more striking in the third sentence ('Then he started. . . .'). Over the first five lines, ten intransitives are used to convey a sequence of events which are causally related. The effect of using intransitives throughout is to encapsulate the actions, expressing causality at most only through juxtaposition. So the table 'shook and quivered', and then, immediately afterwards in the sentence, the glasses 'rattled and banged', and then some of them 'fell'. It is as though these are all self-caused actions, which, however, followed each other. This science cannot make the distinction between *post hoc* and *propter hoc*, sequence and causation. Interestingly, the real cause for the disturbance to table and glasses is her 'trembling', etc., but this follows the cataclysm — it is as though somehow the fall of the glasses caused her to tremble. Newton's breakthrough, remember, came when he saw an apple fall, and asked why. This lady is pre-Newtonian. Nor is she capable of any kind of moral thinking that depends on perceiving the consequences of one's actions.

There are also a large number of self-reflexives, mainly actions on parts of one's own body. These appear to be the main field of transactive action in the passage. So the main transactive model has the self as sole agent, and the body, fragmented into individual parts (an oppressive number — 18 references to 9 specific parts) as the only objects that can be acted on purposively and transactively. One exception to this is that the penis or pussy can be the object of a transactive action, in which case it is often referred to as though it were the self ('right into me , 'helped guide him', 'pulled himself out', 'stroke him gently'), though a restrictive meaning is never absolutely certain. The primary model of the self clearly has a disembodied con-sciousness or will acting directly only on an assemblage of the parts of its body, but at certain moments, when sexual contact is achieved, another model can be employed, whereby the 'self' is identified with the genitals alone. 'Selves' make contact only as genitalia.

Except for this concentration of the self in the genitals, the passage shows what Whorf believed was an SAE characteristic — a meticulous precision about spatial relationships. The lady is confusingly specific about what part is where at any time. The parts are also assigned punctiliously to their owner, through possessive pronouns. But although conventionally we refer to these as 'possessives', what is involved with them is only one kind of possession, inalienable possession. These possessives here serve in fact to establish the boundaries of the two bodies. It is significant that possessives are not used of anything other than parts of the body. She talks of 'the table' and 'the drinks glasses', yet this is 'her' house, table, and glasses, according to some concepts of property-relations. (These are all her husband's, and therefore hers.) She clearly does not think of them like that, so it does not matter if they fall. What if they broke? We cannot be sure that they didn't.

A way of seeing this is to say that she seems to have only a nontransactive model of possession. Complex property-relations, involving minimally a possessor and object possessed, proprietary rights and modes of exchange, cannot be represented in terms of this simple model. In the interview as a whole she refers frequently and with pleasure to her opulent surroundings (her husband is some kind of executive). Again, mere proximity ambiguously represents more abstract relationships.

The lady's sense of temporal sequence is also interesting in the light of Whorf's strictures on SAE notions of time. According to Whorf, SAE tense-systems conceive of time unrolling like a scroll, and SAE in general spatializes time. Hopi does without tenses, and without our endemic spatial metaphors. The lady uses tenses, of course, like any grammatical SAE speaker. In fact she is generally very precise about the sequence of actions. In the first sentence, the pluperfect 'had put' carefully places that action in relation to 'before I could straighten up'. (The simple past, 'John put', would have been equally grammatical). However, in the orgasmic third sentence the sense of sequence is consistently blurred. The succession of 'ands' removes one kind of time-marker ('before', 'then', etc.), the order of the phrases no longer guarantees the order of events, and the past continuous is used instead of the simple past to indicate a diffused simultaneity. So something like Hopi atemporality is achieved for the orgasm, but achieved at the cost of near-deviance, suppression of linguistic devices which this speaker would normally use.

The language as described here has an equivocal relation to SAE and Hopi. In many respects it is totally ascientific, but it is ascientific in SAE ways. The consciousness that emerges is deeply self-alienated, incapable of a whole response, yet also in many ways primitive, pre-capitalist, with an infantile irresponsibility, and only rudimentary notions of ownership, predominantly employing a restricted code, to use Bernstein's categories, but as remorselessly explicit as any user of elaborated codes. Linguistics on its own cannot resolve these apparent contradictions. The analysis generates hypotheses rather than conclusions. One such hypothesis might be that this is no lady, but the fabrication of an anonymous feature-writer. The use of forms of nontransactive model seems controlled manipulation, since the story has always been worked out coherently in trans-active terms. Who is manipulating whom? Whose consciousness is this? Are the contradictions interclass or within the single class? These questions lead naturally into the sociology of popular culture, but not away from linguistics, because the answers to them should generate more questions about the language, which linguistics should enable to be formulated with greater precision.

The next passage I will look at comes from a 'Woman's Weekly' novelette, the final paragraphs of *A Time to Love* (London 1974) by Diana Noël.

He said nothing, just kept watching me, and a shock of realization brought my heart plunging sickeningly up into my throat, half-choking me. If I lost James now, if this canker in his mind was too deep-rooted to be exorcised by love, it would be far worse even than losing Geoff. It would be the end of everything for me. My voice was breathless as I tried to go on. 'James – oh, James my darling – what good is your conscience, your enforced loneliness doing to any of those people now, after all these years? But I – if you drag me down into your punishment too, I shall die. We've thirty – maybe forty – years ahead, my love, to be together, perhaps to have children and. . . .'

I couldn't say any more. Wearily, I leant against the side of the bed, grey despair crawling over me like a muddy tide. I couldn't get through to him.

Then strong hands were round my shoulders, pulling me towards him. 'Beth,' he said huskily. 'Beth.' Our first kiss, so fiercely tender, so passionate and yet so gentle told us what words could never say. The barrier was broken at last and we had come home, together, James and me.

Here Beth, a widow in her late thirties, gets her man, the attractive next-door neighbour. It is less easy to get at the causality in this passage, since the verbs tend to be heavily transformed, generally into passives or nouns, so in order to get some purchase on this complex, let us take the half-sentence 'and a shock . . .' There seem to be two transitives here, the two transactive agents being 'shock' and 'heart', the first action being the cause of the second. A well-developed sense of causality it would seem, in contrast to the *Mayfair* passage.

But shock is an emotional state, clearly a rather special kind of agent. This turns out to be a consistent rule of this universe: emotions or states, love, conscience, loneliness, despair, act powerfully in this world, as alien forces violently affecting the whole person. (There are no emotions or continuing states in the *Mayfair* world: only effects without affects.) In this particular sentence, the emotion acts on a single part, the 'heart', which seems to contravene this rule, but this heart defies physiology in a way that suggests that it may not be a physiological heart after all. 'Plunging' normally, though not invariably, is movement in a downwards direction, so this heart may be simultaneously plunging into the pit of Beth's stomach, and leaping into her throat. Outside this sentence there are only two parts of the body mentioned, the disembodied hands and her shoulders, a marked contrast to the cornucopia of organs in *Mayfair.*

But this account remains on the surface, a heavily transformed surface. For instance, 'shock of realization' will be understood as derived from, 'I realized x and felt shock'. Or was the shock simultaneous? Did the shock 'bring' her heart into her throat, or was that the physical manifestation of her shock? What seems to be happening here is that a partly unordered sequence of emotional events in the deep structure has been translated into an apparently tightly coherent sequence of violent pseudo-actions. (This would be the opposite to the *Mayfair* passage, where a coherent sequence is represented through an irrational surface order.) Psychophysical parallelism is in fact a general feature of this text. Beth often represents the intensity of emotional relationships in terms of proximity and effort — in spatial terms, which Whorf claims is typical of SAE. 'If I lost James', 'you drag me down', 'the barrier was broken'. This is mirrored on the physical plane by her leaning against the bed, and his pulling her towards him. The process may have some affinities with dream representation as described by Freud, whereby abstract relationships are translated into literal, spatial terms.[14]

The nominalization of 'realize' entailed the deletion of what she realized. This may be recoverable – 'if I lost James' – but it may go beyond that, deletion going with more thorough-going repression. In her speech there are two other transforms involving deletions; 'enforced' and 'punishment'. James seems to be the deleted subject of the enforcing. 'Punishment' derives from 'x punished y' where x is probably James again, but y is both James and Beth. So at the deep structure level there is a double accusation against James which has been deleted from the surface, but is still recoverable, still visible through the surface if he wants to see it.

Negation in various forms is an important transformation in this passage. There are a number of straightforward negatives: 'He said nothing', 'I couldn't say', etc. (Negation is notably absent from the *Mayfair* piece.) But as well as these, there are a variety of covert negatives. For instance, 'what good is your conscience' is a way of saying 'your conscience is no good', the question-transform functioning as a negative. Similarly with the if-sentences: 'If you drag me down' implies 'don't drag me down'. The complicated comparative 'too deep-rooted' realizes another negative, something like 'so deep-rooted that it cannot be exorcised'. 'Half-choking' perhaps realizes a kind of semi-negative: 'choking – not-choking'. The description of their first kiss perhaps contains two similarly constituted pairs: 'fiercely tender' is equivalent to 'fierce and not-fierce', as 'passionate yet gentle' is 'passionate yet not-passionate'.

So negation, overt or variously disguised, is an important structural principle in this passage.[15] It is also the main 'action' that can be performed in this world. He opens with a negatived action, 'said nothing', and this nearly destroys her. She responds by just not-making an accusation about his negativity, but this seems not to succeed. So she responds to his not-saying by her own not-saying, and by dramatically not-getting through she does in fact get through. In this grey world of negatives and withholdings from action, the unnegated sentence 'Then strong

---

[14] Cf. S. Freud *Interpretation of Dreams* 1900 (ed. J. Strachey, London 1955), Chapter VI, Section C.
[15] Cf. S. Freud 'Negation', *Collected Papers* V, 1950.

hands . . . ' comes through with startling force, body acting on body, breaking two of the primary laws of this universe.

One important methodological point is I think raised by this analysis. This story seems at first glance indistinguishable from hundreds of others, apparently a slight fantasy by a middle-aged, middle-class woman for others of her kind. Diana Noël has none of the virtues of a 'great' novelist of high culture, no particular wit, artistry, literary self-consciousness or wisdom. Yet the fantasy element in the story is easily detachable, to do with content not form. James is handsome (if 'mature'), still capable of love (though racked with guilt, a psychic cripple), and he happens to live next door. Otherwise the terms in which this universe is created impress as depressingly real, a complete science and metaphysic, a total set of cognitive strategies for coping (inadequately) with relevant experience. The normal judgement of 'high culture' on this then becomes more difficult to make. To despise a universe is to despise those whose universe it is (though judgement is possible even of universes). This may seem to make a method of analysis subvert a system of values, but what it does is rather to participate in a challenge to the basis of those values. High culture needs elites, great artists, and hence a principle for ranking writers and works. Two such principles are degree of consciousness and level of skill. A linguistic analysis of the kind I have engaged in can proceed without taking account of either. It becomes possible to compare Diana Noël with, say, Henry James, without an overpowering sense of James's superior craftsmanship and self-conscious technique constantly obtruding. This doesn't mean the end of all value judgements. Rather it allows prominence to other grounds for judgement, which do not of their nature establish an unbridgable gulf between high culture and popular culture, Dives and Lazarus.

I want now to push linguistic analysis into an area where communication involves more than words: in this case, pop music. Here (in a question-begging visual form) is a song of the 1960s, *You're Sixteen*, by Richard and Robert Sherman.

You come on like a dream, peaches and cream,
    Lips like strawberry wine,
You're sixteen, you're beautiful and you're mine.
    You're all ribbons and curls, ooh what a girl,
        Eyes that sparkle and shine.

You're sixteen, you're beautiful and you're mine.
     You're my baby, you're my pet,
     We fell in love on the night we met,
     You touched my hand, my heart went pop,
     Ooh when we kissed I could not stop.
You walked out of my dreams, and into my arms,
     Now you're my angel devine.
You're sixteen you're beautiful and you're mine.

We can begin by seeing what happens if we treat this as a normal piece of language, as if the musical setting had no significance. Such concern with causality as there is in the song is conveyed mainly through intransitives. 'You touched my hand' is the only transitive. It stands out in this song as much as James touching Beth. But the sentences are mostly equatives, expressing attributes ('you're sixteen') or comparisons (like a dream'). So the song comes across as a cluster of attributes and nouns (peaches as well as lips) round a structural 'you' who is given no referent. In contrast to the *Mayfair* piece, the parts of her body are not assigned to her through possessive pronouns. Possession belongs asymmetrically to the singer alone. Possession for him also includes her as well as his body. So he seems to have a slightly developed transactive possessive model, with however no notion of reciprocity.

But this kind of analysis is liable to seem pretentiously irrelevant in face of the manifestly inconsequential nature of the words of the song. The first line, for instance, could be dismissed as nonsense, a meaningless sequence of cue-words. 'Come on' is hard to interpret. What does she 'come on' to? Or does it have a sexual sense? The context does not reinforce this, but nor does it exclude it. 'Peaches and cream' is merely juxtaposed, and could go with 'come on', 'you', or 'dream'. Syntax normally acts as a filter, to allow only one relationship between the elements to apply. In this song syntax hardly acts at all to control relationships, to give a single structure. (There are fewer conjunctions in this song than *Mayfair* at its most orgasmic.) The order generally seems to have no relation to temporal sequence, and the singer seems to have a Hopi-like indifference to linear SAE time. For instance, if there is a sequential relation between the two phrases

You're my baby, you're my pet,
We fell in love on the night we met,

it has been inverted. In fact the 'right way' round feels unacceptable to me, 'ungrammatical' in terms of the grammar of this poem, precisely because it follows the temporal sequence. 'Now' in 'Now you're my angel devine' seems to break this rule, but in this context it is totally subverted. She walked out of his dreams, and now is his angel divine — back in his dreams again? This radical disengagement from SAE temporality and logic, which is not peculiar to this particular song, makes such a world a serious challenge, seriously alternative, to the modes of thought of contemporary practical life.

All this does not take account of its status as song. One hypothesis I want to suggest, following Halliday, is that the tune acts as a kind of syntax, expressing not logical relationships but relationships within a complex field.[16] The first two lines of the song then constitute a single field:
'You come ón like a dréám, peaches and créàm, lips like strawberry wine' (with 'You're sixteen . . .' perhaps dependent on the larger field). Here minor (/) and major (//) stresses are marked, showing upward and downward pitch-movement. If this gives a rudimentary map of the field, with rising pitch forward-looking, falling pitch backward looking, double stress the sign of the centre of a compound field (music notation would of course give a much more precise image of the shape of the field), then many of the syntactic problems we met earlier will be resolved. 'Dream' emerges as somewhere near the focus of the field, and the other units are related coherently but not logically. The field as organized aurally is much larger than the visual form of presentation suggests, and is capable of organizing material that would otherwise be unmanageably disparate. The tune is repeated later on, with a different content ('You walked out . . .') So a tune seems to act like a richly elaborated *gestalt*, which is capable of an abstract, independent existence, an empty complex field available for the precise organization or patterning of extremely diverse experience. Such patterning can dispense with the need for any other principle of organization, including logic.

Pop songs do not exist until they are performed. This is true of any act of communication. In response to this we can posit a series of models for the speech situation which we could

---

[16] My notation and interpretation here depart considerably from Halliday.

claim constitute part of the competence of a native speaker. The simplest such model would be the nontransactive Speaker (S) — Message (M) of a person talking to himself. A more transactive model would add a hearer (H) and an addressee (A). We need to invoke such models in order to explain what happens when for instance someone reads the text of this song (or this article):

$$S - M \quad \big\| \quad M - H/A$$
$$(Sf\text{–}Af) \quad \big\| \quad (Sf\text{–}Af)$$

Here Sf, Af stand for the fictional Speaker and Addressee of the song. The double-bar marks the gap between production and reception. The point is that in a silent reading, this gap is absolute. The actual speaker is more fictitious for the actual hearer than Sf, and the actual hearer is similarly unreal to S. Both halves of the process have become nontransactive in effect, except insofar as they are sustained by the basic transactive model. I have to put Ringo on the turntable again to reinforce, recreate, the primary transactive model.

When I listen to the record, the reconstituted model looks something this:

$$S - M - H$$
$$(Sf\text{–}Af)$$

Theoretically the hearer can relate to three roles, S, Sf, and Af, as well as remaining H. These roles are differentially available, however, with different songs and different hearers, so that the same song 'means' different things to different people. Af for instance is totally constituted round Sf's ego, existing only as possessed, dreamt, so it is hardly available to me. In a live performance, the options in the model alter. The S is palpably real, and the hearer can become an initiator (if only by screaming) thereby creating a weakly reciprocal transaction. So the sense that this is more adequate communication than is possible to someone reading silently is justified, even if the apparent content of the communication is nonsense. The act

of silent reading is sustained as a communicative act only by
the greater reality of the full speech-model. (Silent reading can
of course be meditative, i.e. nontransactive and not an act of
communication.)

This is only one area of nonverbal communication into which
linguistics might move. Another is the visual and kinaesthetic
(the distinctively SAE sensory modes, according to Whorf),
where I will say nothing, except to point out that actions can
realize transactive and nontransactive models as directly as
speech can. Nor do I want to generalize further about the forms
of popular culture I have discussed, since I ought to insist here
that I have been using a speculative development of linguistics
extremely speculatively. But to conclude in a vein of confident
prophesy, I believe that linguistics can and should have a
decisive contribution to make to the study of popular culture:
and if it does not, so much the worse for linguistics.

Postscript

I gave this piece to one literary critic, who reacted with representative scepticism: 'So what?' He wanted me to prove
unequivocally that linguistics analysis could reveal things never
dreamt of in literary criticism. Otherwise, he would continue
to believe that a literary critic, relying on mere intuition and a
finely-tuned sensibility, could conceivably see everything that
my analysis has brought out. There are of course vested interests
behind this kind of objection: literary criticism has at present a
dominant place in the curriculum, and literary critics naturally
would not like their claims to expertise to be discredited in any
way. Against such 'reasons', mere arguments are hardly likely
to prevail, since the literary critic is the judge in his own case.

But what is especially unfortunate about this objection is
that it shows a failure to understand the nature and needs of
current literary criticism. Literary criticism is a conglomerate
discipline. A literary critic can be an amateur linguistician, as
he can be an amateur sociologist, psychologist, historian, etc.
In some ways his amateurishness gives him an advantage over
academic professionals in these various fields, in that he can be
more independent of current institutional definitions of

subject and methodology. But amateurism also has its drawbacks. It encourages a genteel imprecision and aristocratic contempt for fact, and allows literary critics to be unworried by huge areas of ignorance. Perhaps a refounded literary criticism would be a far more serious matter. I would be delighted to think so. The boundaries between literary criticism, linguistics, sociology, etc., would then be impossible to fix: an outcome greatly to be desired.

At present the few literary critics who have tried to deal with forms of popular culture (Richard Hoggart, for instance to name one of the most notable examples) have been less interested in close analysis of language than would be possible even for a traditional literary critic. There is I think good reason for this. The linguistic theory underlying close verbal analysis in literary criticism (for 'New Critics' and others) is inimical to the kind of connection a Hoggart would want to make, and doesn't work well with the materials of popular culture. The inadequacy of the method of analysis is then felt to confirm the triviality of popular culture (like the masses, only significant for bulk, not quality). Literary critics interested in popular culture mistakenly accept this position, and react to it by avoiding close analysis. I think that what they really need is a refounded linguistics, whether or not they go to linguistics for it. I hope that what I have written here will help them to rethink their own practice, if it does no more.

7

Marxism and Popular Culture

David Craig

'Culture' has three distinct, overlapping meanings: the arts and
the media; or the lifestyle of a society as embodied in 'the
equipment which men make for themselves', to quote the terse
definition of the prehistorian Gordon Childe;[1] or the lifestyle
of the more recent societies whose way of life survives so fully
in records and memories that it can be studied in materials
much more various than 'equipment'. The social historian
Edward Thompson wrote recently: 'A critical area of any
Marxist analysis lies in the weighting of relations between
"social being" and "social consciousness". . . . The growing
interest in "popular culture" (using notations of culture
influenced by anthropological definitions) has placed increasing
weight on the second pole. In some accounts not only ideas
and value systems are seen as forms of social consciousness but
also traditional modes of work and new or old social relations.
Hence it becomes difficult to know what is *not* "culture".'
Thompson then discusses the work of John Foster on class
struggle in the industrial revolution and mentions that Foster
mistrusts findings 'not based upon measurable evidence:
attendances at church or chapel, incidence of transoccupational
marriage, membership of friendly societies, for example.'[2] The
range of this evidence is so wide that 'culture' comes to mean
the whole pattern of social habits. Popular culture would then
mean the social habits of the majority, the working people.

---

[1] V. Gordon Childe, *Man Makes Himself* (New York 1951) p. 33.
[2] E. P. Thompson, 'Testing class struggle', *Times Higher Education Supplement*,
8 March 1974.

Marxist writers on the popular media — songs, for example, or theatre in certain periods — have emphasized that these are working parts of a community living in specific historical conditions. This follows both from a political commitment to the mass of the people and from a historical-materialist principle: 'all history must be studied afresh, the conditions of existence of the different formations of society must be examined individually before the attempt is made to deduce from them the political, civil-law, aesthetic, philosophic, religious, etc., views corresponding to them.'[3] Marxist writers on the media move outwards from their formal properties to analyse that whole way of life — with its distinctive habitat, equipment, class system, and fabric of psychosocial impulses, beliefs, and fantasies — which called the art forms into being. In keeping with this, I will use 'popular culture' to mean the media most widely current in a society, with the implication that they are particularly direct and revealing evidence of how people were living.

According to the Marxist view, it is not just that the media 'reflect' any or every facet of social life, which is obvious, but that the work done by a social group to create the means of its livelihood, and the social relations it enters into through this productive activity, are the main forces that go to shape the media in which people create images of the world as they experience it and of themselves in it. Clearly such a theory has to be grounded in a huge range of material. For example, about 5,300 fiction titles are published each year in the United Kingdom. So far, what we have studied has tended to be a drastically reduced sample (often justified as a 'creaming off') from the whole mass of novels, or songs, or whatever. Marxist writers have not escaped the tendency to study the tastes of minorities, quite often of elite minorities, at the expense of the popular. Foremost among Marxist writings on culture are the studies of folksong made by George Thomson and A. L. Lloyd. This has not been, for some generations in this country, a mass medium. It was replaced by music hall, then by pop. But people never thought seriously about pop music until the last few years. As the film director

[3] Frederick Engels to C. Schmidt, 5 August 1890, Karl Marx and Frederick Engels, *Selected Correspondence* (Moscow undated), pp. 496—7.

Ken Russell put it recently:

If *Tommy*, instead of *The Knot Garden*, was put on at Covent Garden, it would do a lot to shake up the music world, because I think at the present moment too many composers are being supported by the Arts Council and producing work which is really of no interest except to a very, very small minority of people in this country and to themselves. I met some Hell's Angels who said: 'I'm glad you're making this rock film because at last we will have a film to go to that has got music in it that we like. We never hear music that we like.' I said, 'What do you do?' and one said: 'Well, I've worked for seven years in a pottery. I work from seven in the morning to seven at night. I have half a day off a week, that's Saturday from one o'clock to six o'clock,' and I said: 'Where do you go to then?' He said, 'Nowhere', and it's for the nowhere people, maybe, that we should start thinking.[4]

Media studies are now at last bidding fair to catch up with cultural change and pay attention to what most people see and read and hear. David Harker of the Manchester Polytechnic, studying the popular song of Tyneside in the eighteenth and nineteenth centuries, has collected over 6,000 songs and has included all the songs on sale or otherwise current, instead of picking and choosing from the material according to some specialized notion of what folksong ought to be — peasant, or oral, or non-industrial. Rachel Powell at the Centre for Contemporary Cultural Studies in Birmingham is one of a team who are examining 'a complete sample of picture usage and presentation in all the newspapers' and towards this are building a complete classified inventory of press photos.[5] John Berger and his co-authors in *Ways of Seeing* (1972) have studied pin-ups and advertisements along with oil paintings in order to explain the visual styles of European culture. This work is totally new and has still to complete its findings. Most of the writers chosen for discussion in this chapter formed their ideas by studying media from pre- or early-industrial societies, since the Marxist way of thinking about cultural issues has, so far, been most fully demonstrated there.

'Productive activity' means in the first place people at work. In a remarkable piece of reasoned speculation, the opening chapter of *The First Philosophers*, George Thomson argues that speech originated as a medium of communication between fellow workers without which they could not have organized

[4] *The Listener* 19 September 1974.
[5] Rachel Powell, 'Types and Variations of Newsphoto: report on work in progress', *Working Papers in Cultural Studies*, 3 (Birmingham Autumn 1972), p. 47.

the work that kept them alive, and that this is evident in the structure of our syntax and grammar. Germs of this theory are contained in an article Engels wrote a century ago, the fragment from an unfinished book on slavery which is called 'The Part Played by Labour in the Transition from Ape to Man'. Engels sketches the prehistoric evolution of the human hand and points out that it is 'not only the organ of labour, *it is also the product of labour.*' To carry out the tasks which the hand could manage once it was freed from weight-bearing, early humans had to make meaningful sounds: 'men in the making arrived at the point where *they had something to say* to one another. The need led to the creation of its organ; by modulation the undeveloped larynx of the ape was slowly but surely transformed for ever more developed modulation, and the organs of the mouth gradually learned to pronounce one articulate letter after another.' Such experience was stored in the expanding brain, linked as it was through the nervous system to the limbs and digits, which were adjusting themselves to ever more precise tasks. 'The reaction on labour and speech of the development of the brain and its attendant senses, of the increasing clarity of consciousness, power of abstraction and of judgement, gave an ever-renewed impulse to the further development of both labour and speech.'[6]

That does not yet directly explain why the media, the forms of human communication, are as they are. But it is only one step away. Thomson completes the theory (after checking it against the findings of recent prehistory and physiology) when he deduces the form of the sentence from the action of working: 'the sentence, in its elementary form of two terms, the one being incorporated in the other, or of three terms, the third mediating the action of the first upon the second, embodies in its structure the three elements of the labour process — the personal activity of the labourer, the subject of his labour, and its instruments.'[7]

Thomson knows that this is a speculation, impossible to verify. But it is not guesswork, it comes from a thorough analysis of the parts of speech. He starts by pointing out that

[6] Frederick Engels, *Dialectics of Nature* (Moscow 1954) pp. 229–234.
[7] George Thomson, *Studies in Ancient Greek Society*, II: *The First Philosophers* (London 1955), p. 41.

theorists of language now regard two parts of speech as fundamental, the noun and the verb. Morphemes, such as prefixes and prepositions, and interjections, such as 'Ssh' and 'Ouch', are not indispensable to articulate speech. In all languages the organic unit is the sentence. In English simple sentences are either nominal, two nouns linked by a copula, 'The stream is full' — or verbal, either two nouns linked by a verb or a noun with its verb, 'The stream floods the field' or 'The stream rises'. In each the core of the meaning can be given without the morpheme — 'Stream flood field' or 'Stream rise', which is the form of the simple sentence in many other languages. From this Thomson concludes: 'We are left with a sentence of two terms, connected either by simple juxtaposition or by a third term; and these two types of sentence correspond to the two types of musical form, binary and ternary. The distinction between the verbal sentence and the nominal sentence is reduced to this, that in the former our attention is concentrated on the action or process, in the latter on the state or result. The idea of change is inherent in both, but in the second it is implied rather than expressed.'

Thomson then joins this idea to the earlier stages of his argument. He has shown, with evidence from biology, zoology and physiology, that humans differentiated themselves from the most nearly kindred animals when they began to walk on the ground. The work done by the finely-articulated hand with its opposable thumb was controlled by the expanding brain. The motor organs of the hand and the organs of speech are controlled by neighbouring areas in the cortex: 'From this we may infer that the manual operations of early man were accompanied to a greater or lesser degree, in proportion to their difficulty, by a reflex action of the vocal organs. Later, in collective labour, these vocal movements were developed consciously as a means of directing the manual operations; and finally they emerged as an independent medium of communication, supplemented by reflex movements of the hands' [i.e. by gestures].

This 'medium' of communication' is then analysed according to Pavlov's theory of reflexes. Pavlov defines words as 'signals of signals'. The brain gets a signal from the finger that it is burnt, the finger is snatched away with an interjection express-

ing fear of pain or anger. All this is no different from the
reactions of many other animals. The person then defines the
cause of his reflex — 'Watch out! It's hot!' — in verbal signals
intelligible, and therefore useful, to fellow members of his
species. So Pavlov calls language the 'secondary signalling
system'. He writes: 'The word is for man just as much a real
conditioned response as all the other responses which he has in
common with the animals.' Thomson adds: 'This differs from
the other in that its characteristic stimulus is not an objective
natural phenomenon [heat] acting on the sense organs but an
artificial sound ['hot'] invested socially with a subjective
value.'

Thomson then discusses cooperation. The lengthy maturing
of the young human and the comparative defencelessness of our
bodies 'both necessitated and assisted the development of
collective labour, involving tools and speech'. A group of early
humans, whether a family or a 'tribe', would not have been
able to hunt efficiently together, to take decisions about where
to go for food, what food to store and how to share it, if they
had not been able to go beyond, say, the frightened and
frightening interjections which chimpanzee bands make as
they combine to throw sticks at a leopard. 'Thus, the three
characteristics we have distinguished — tools, speech, co-oper-
ation — are parts of a single process, the labour of production.
This process is distinctively human, and its organizing unit is
society.'[8] Finally, as we have seen, the sentence is analysed to
show how its structure embodies the elements of production:
the person's activity, the subject of his or her work, and the
things used in doing it.

It may seem incongruous on my part to count the sentence
among the media of popular culture. But wouldn't our idea of
human communication lack one of its main roots if we did not
understand how the unit of articulate speech was formed in both
its origin and its function? Thomson's chapter is a perfect
example of Marxist method in its tracing of the form of a
human activity (which could be the shape of towns or the
worship of a god) right back to its home in what we actually
do, and not to an invented abstraction such as the Hegelian
Idea or the Toynbeean 'challenge and response' in history.

[8] Thomson, *The First Philosophers*, pp. 22–35.

As the human life-style evolves, it becomes more and more complicated. Humans cease to roam and gather, they settle and grow things, settlements become cities, food surpluses accumulate, a class of managers and clerks develops to supervise the food-stores, systems of figuring and writing evolve to keep count of these supplies and to trade in them, and fundamental class distinctions are then reflected in the media, for example between the illiterate and the literate. Such complications mean that many stages come between a piece of work and its outcome in the way, say, of reward or trade. Activity is no longer limited to what is directly necessary for survival. Cults too become elaborate, and the old sympathetic magic to help the hunting, or the totemism which makes sacred some animal or plant from the habitat, evolves into worship of the god-king, administered by the high priest who controls the people's output in the temple granaries.[9]

From so complicated a system it follows that the forms of communication can no longer be as direct as they were when the sentence arose out of the labour process. The media now come to express reality through a series of removes. This does not invalidate the Marxist idea that culture grows up on a basis of productive activity. It does make it more difficult to trace the links which are there. This shows in the analysis which Thomson and Plekhanov make of song, dance, mime and music.

Plekhanov, Lenin's comrade in the early days of the Russian Social Democratic Party, was the first Marxist to write fully about popular culture. In 1899 he began a series of 'Letters without Address' which explore in rich anthropological detail the thesis that popular forms — in particular dance, chant, games, mime, ornament, pictures, and writing systems — have their source in production. In 1908 he published *Fundamental Problems of Marxism*: section 8 uses material overlapping with the 'Letters without Address' to argue that the evidence of popular culture in primitive societies provides 'unassailable proof of the soundness, one might say the inevitability, of the materialist conception of history.'[10] In the 'Letter' called 'Historical Materialism and Art' he had emphasized that 'the *direct*

---

[9] This sketch of social evolution is based on V. Gordon Childe, *What Happened in History* (London 1954), especially chapters 5–6.

dependence of art on techniques and the mode of production disappears with civilized peoples'[11] and in his final piece on the subject, 'Art and Social Life' (1912), he analyses French painting and literature of the nineteenth century, especially the 'art for art's sake' movement, and finds that this 'arises when they [artists] are in hopeless disaccord with the social environment in which they live.'[12] Here, however, he is inevitably using material that no longer belongs to popular culture — the novels of Huysmans and even Zola, the poems of Baudelaire. I say 'inevitably' because it is not possible for a truly popular mode to be in 'hopeless disaccord' with the environment. People are surely unlikely to absorb into their way of life a medium which runs clean against the grain of how they live. We shall see later that this is true even of the industrial folksong which protests most bitterly against the inhumanities of the factory system. The material Plekhanov has to use in 'Art and Social Life' is the printed work most admired by a minority of the middle class who owned many books. Plekhanov knew this perfectly well. In a striking aside in an essay he contributed to *Pravda* in 1905 he wrote that the revolutionary period in France 'far from stifled the aesthetic requirements of the people. Quite the contrary. The great social movements which made the people clearly aware of their worth gave a strong and unprecedented impetus to the development of these requirements. To be convinced of this one has only to visit the Paris "Musée Carnavalet" . . . . The numerous civic holidays, processions and celebrations of that time were the best and most convincing evidence in favour of the aesthetics of the *sans-culottes.* Not everybody takes this evidence into account however.'[13]

The evidence Plekhanov uses in working out his main theory of popular culture comes from the life of hunting and food-gathering tribes and it yields ideas more or less in agreement

[11] G. V. Plekhanov, *Art and Social Life* ed. Andrew Rothstein (Bombay 1953), p. 50.

[12] Plekhanov, *Art and Social Life*, p. 189.

[13] 'French Dramatic Literature and French Eighteenth Century Painting from the Sociological Standpoint' in *Art and Social Life*, pp. 174—5.

[10] G. V. Plekhanov, *Fundamental Problems of Marxism*, ed. D. Ryazanov (London 1929), p. 46.

with Thomson's in 'The Art of Poetry'.[14] Thomson's very full
references do not include the Plekhanov but both make
special use of Bücher's *Arbeit und Rhythmus*. Plekhanov's
main thesis is that a culture's forms and styles are necessary
if the society is to subsist — to feed itself and keep up morale.
For example, dealing with ornament he analyses the way in
which Red Indian men adorned themselves with bits of animals,
such as grizzly-bear claws, and African women wore iron
rings — as much as 36 pounds in weight — if their husbands
were rich. He concludes: '*That which is precious* seems
beautiful.' After studying the imitation and depiction of
animals in cultures such as the African Bushmen's and the
Brazilian Indians', he amplifies this point: 'the psychological
nature of the primitive hunter is the conditioning factors of
his general capacity to develop aesthetic tastes and concepts,
while the state of his productive forces, his hunting economy,
leads to the formation of his particular aesthetic tastes.' And
again: '*labour is older than art* and . . . in general *man first
looks on objects and phenomena from a utilitarian point of
view and only afterwards takes up an aesthetic attitude in his
relationship to them.*'[15]

In order to discuss Plekhanov and Thomson together, and
also to see whether or not their theory has overreached itself
in the directness of the link it posits between popular media
and work, I will discuss one main case, primitive or early
popular song. Thomson emphasizes that 'the three arts of
dancing, music and poetry began as one.'[16] Just as labour was
not yet divided (except between the sexes), so too the media
were still one. Plekhanov quotes Bücher, 'the secret of versification is to be found in productive activity,' and Wallaschek,
who classifies the subjects of early 'drama' as hunting, war and
the rowing of boats; among pastoral people, the behaviour of
domesticated animals; and among cultivators, the work of
farming, such as sowing, threshing, and vine-dressing.[17]

---

[14] This is chapter 14 of *Studies in Ancient Greek Society*, I: *The Prehistoric
Aegean* (London 1961); it is a slightly revised version of the first half of Thomson's
pamphlet *Marxism and Poetry* (London 1946).

[15] Plekhanov, *Art and Social Life*, pp. 26–7, 46, 102.

[16] Thomson, *The Prehistoric Aegean*, p. 451.

[17] K. Bücher, *Arbeit und Rhythmus* (Leipzig 1896) p. 342; R. Wallaschek, *Anfänge
der Tonkunst* (Leipzig 1903), p. 257; Plekhanov, *Fundamental Problems*, p. 48.

Plekhanov traces back the mime element in this manifold form to the actual mimicry which is necessary when, for example, an Eskimo hunts a seal: 'He crawls up to him on his belly; he tries to hold his head in the same way as the seal does.' And after more analysis, grounded in examples from many cultures, he concludes: 'As long as primitive man remains a hunter, his tendency to imitation, among other things, makes an artist and a sculptor of him. . . . He requires an ability to observe and manual skill. It is these very same qualities that he needs in order to be a hunter, too.'[18]

Thomson applies the same analysis and kindred evidence to the evolution of song. He cites Bücher's evidence of work-songs, for example spinning songs which actually help the wheel turn by marking the time of the spinner's foot on the treadle and also move through onto the plane of magic when the words become an incantation to powers that will bless or charm the work. He then analyses the components of versification − rhythm, stanza, rhyme, line, and refrain − and shows that they stem from utterance during work. Oarsmen use a two-syllabled cry to mark the time, first a preparatory signal and then the noise made at the point of effort as pent-up air is expelled, for example, 'O-op!' In heavier work like hauling boats, the space between such points lasts longer and the preparatory noises can grow, as in the Irish hauling cry, Ho-li-ho-hup! or the Russian E-uch-nyem! Noises can easily be replaced by articulate items, as in the English Heave-ho! Thomson comments: 'These two elements, variable and con-stant, which constitute the simple, disyllabic labour cry, can be recognized in the arsis and thesis of prosody, which denote properly the raising and lowering of the hand or foot in the dance.'[19]

If the conditions are right, the variable can be amplified, often in an improvising way, by the singing workman, as in a Thonga stone-breaking song:

Ba hi shani-sa, ehé!
Ba ku hi hlupha, ehé!
Ba nwa makhofi, ehé!
Ba nga hi nyiki, ehé!

[18] 'Labour, Play and Art' and 'Art and Utility (2)' in Art and Social Life, pp. 84, 149.
[19] Thomson, The Prehistoric Aegean, pp. 445−7.

They treat us badly, *ehé!*
They are hard on us, *ehé!*
They drink their coffee, *ehé!*
And give us none, *ehé!*[20]

Recent and familiar examples from our own culture are the shanties. Here a partial division of labour set in. The shantyman was a crew member who could stop his work on deck to make up lines which he sang in between the shorter and more conventional lines sung by the sailors, who needed most of their breath for raising the anchor or setting the sails. (It is said that the shantyman could get paid double, once by the captain to speed up his singing and make the work go, once by the sailors to slow down and give them an easier time of it.) So we have such fully-fledged versions of the old work-chant disyllable as the early nineteenth-century halyard shanty:

It was on a Black Baller I first served me time,
  Tibby way-hay, blow the man down,
And on a Black Baller I wasted me prime,
  O gimme some time to blow the man down.

Long before the shanty evolved, songs not linked with work came to be made on the same alternating pattern. The repeated chorus, sung by a whole community or subcommunity in unison,[21] was replaced by the refrain sung by the soloist him- or herself. This gives the structure of the ballad quatrain. It shows its source in the fact that the repeated second and fourth lines may have no logical link with the first and third lines that carry the story, for example, *The Cruel Mother*, in a version from a Perthshire singer:

She's taen oot her little pen-knife,
  Hey the rose an the linsey-o,
An she has twined them o their life,
  Doon by the greenwood sidey-o.

She's pit them neath a marble stane,
  Hey the rose an the linsey-o,
Thinkin tae gang a maiden hame,
  Doon by the greenwood sidey-o . . .

[20] Thomson, *The Prehistoric Aegean*, pp. 447—8.
[21] Still done in the Faeroe Islands in the old unified form including mime and dance: see William J. Entwhistle, *European Balladry* (1951), p. 35.

Thomson points out that even ballads without a refrain preserve the original rhythmic structure 'which rests on a continual alternation of thesis and antithesis, announcement and responsion'. Each couplet or musical phrase contains two figures and each stanza or musical sentence contains two phrases. 'The members of each pair are complementary, similar yet different. This is what musicologists call binary form.' His conclusion is that 'the first step towards poetry properly so called was the elimination of the dance. . . . In song, the poetry is the content of the music, the music is the form of the poetry.'[22]

This analysis is fundamental. It explains one of the main and most long established forms of human expression by tracing it to its root in work — the activity without which we cannot survive. The great bulk of poetry is still in songs (nowadays in pop) and songs still have rhymes and stanzas and a metrical pulse.

There remains a basic point in the Marxist case here which is disputable. Thomson says that the source of the unified art of dancing-music-poetry was 'the rhythmical movement of human bodies engaged in collective labour'. How do we know? Thomson's and Plekhanov's examples all had to come from material which had survived long enough to be collected. They are from primitive cultures in historic times. No doubt they are very like the materials of the prehistoric stages of cultural evolution, just as the shamans and animal friezes still painted or carved in soapstone and whalebone by Eskimos on the north-east shore of Hudson's Bay are very like the cave art of the Old Stone Age in France and Spain.[23] But although the prehistoric and the modern-primitive are alike, they are not the same, and the time span is so long that it leaves plenty of room for the cultural needs and functions served by seemingly similar media to have altered. Alan Bush, the composer, has recently wondered whether the earliest music was not work songs but ritual chants. He quotes von Hornbostel, the leading modern expert on primitive music, as arguing that 'primitive

[22] Thomson, *Prehistoric Aegean*, pp. 450—51.

[23] James Houston, 'Living Art of the Eskimos', *The Observer*, 11 October 1972; Peter J. Ucko and Andrée Rosenfeld, *Palaeolithic Cave Art* (1967), e.g. figures 22, 47, 61, 89.

work songs, while among the earliest musical forms which man created, were preceded by totemistic dance songs, sung by tribes of nomadic food-gatherers, who had not reached the stage of hunting, agriculture or any form of communal labour.' And again: 'Their expeditions to gather food are often individual, and are in any case so little organized that they do not require the rehearsal practice of the hunting tribes, which rehearsals are, as we know, organized musically by means of songs, expressive of the processes of hunting.'

Any such theory is partly speculative, as Alan Bush allows, and it also depends on the 'general anthropological theory that food-gathering tribes preceded hunting and agricultural tribes'.[24] This no longer seems likely. Finds in Africa have shown that Australopithecines ate plenty of meat, and by the time *Homo erectus* had evolved, planned hunting had become fairly skilful: for example, the ambushing and killing of large baboon hordes, which has left a complete fossil picture at Olorgesailie in southwest Kenya.[25] And this was half a million years ago, which was presumably at or before the beginnings of musical utterance. Furthermore, food-gathering and hunting can not be sharply separated, since in palaeolithic times 'tools were not yet specialized as with us to specific ends, but the same roughly-chipped flint served all purposes from dispatching a tiger to scraping the hairs off his hide or digging up roots.'[26] So the same people both gathered and hunted. From that age the richest tangible evidence of popular culture to have survived are the paintings, carvings, and sculptures from the walls, floors, and roofs of caves in the Dordogne and upper Garonne in southern France and near the northern coast of Spain. These seem to show a similar fusion of art media and social function. Ucko and Rosenfeld analyse minutely a great number of paintings and reliefs and rethink the current theories about them, to try and see what cave art was used for. Their conclusions are all provisional or mixed. 'The choice of animals represented may either be due, in part at least, to actual environmental conditions . . . or to the art being a record of

---

[24] Alan Bush, 'What Does Music Express?': *Marxism Today* (April 1964), p. 123, and letter to me, 30 April 1965.

[25] Edmund White and Dale Brown, *The First Men* (Amsterdam, 1973), pp. 67–8.

[26] Childe, *What Happened in History*, p. 31.

myths or symbolism.' And again: 'some representations were the work of children. . . some were used in acts of sympathetic magic . . . some were illustrations of myths and traditions.'[27] Notice that these functions merge with each other. Children would draw animals they had seen, whether alive or dragged home for meat by their parents; sympathetic magic would be used to help the hunt; and the myths would concern such things as totemic ancestors, expressing a reverence for certain animals, whether common locally or not, and also the valued foodstuffs, for example the Pygmies' elephant-hunting songs.[28]

What we are looking into, in the cave art and in the dancing-music-poetry of Thomson's theory, is a state of culture where all the media are bound up with the life-supporting activities of the people. In contrast our culture splits the forms apart, and so far from work, art and magic being fused, there could not be a greater difference between the factory work we do through the day, the disco we dance at in the evenings and the church we stay away from on Sundays. The older integrated state is defined by the Austrian Marxist Ernst Fischer. He has quoted a sorcerer's song from eastern New Guinea, calling on a hornbill to bring disease upon an enemy: 'The original magic gradually became differentiated into religion, science and art. The function of mime altered imperceptibly: from imitation intended to bestow magic power it came to replace blood sacrifice by enacted ceremonies . . . when certain Australian aboriginal tribes appear to prepare for an act of blood vengeance while, in fact, appeasing the dead by means of mime, this is already a transition to drama and to the work of art.' Similarly Thomson writes, after describing totemistic increase ceremonies used by Australian nomads: 'The original object of such performances was probably actual practice in the behaviour of the species, whose habits had to be studied before it could be caught. Later, with the improvement of technique, this function was superseded by that of a magical rehearsal. . . . Magic rests on the principle that by creating the illusion that you control reality you can actually control it.'[29]

[27] Ucko and Rosenfeld, *Palaeolithic Cave Art,* pp. 234, 239.
[28] C. M. Bowra, *Primitive Song* (London 1962), pp. 44–5.
[29] Ernst Fischer, 'The Origins of Art' *The Necessity of Art* (London 1963), pp. 34–6; Thomson, 'Totemism,' *The Prehistoric Aegean,* p. 38.

In such cases we can see how the distinction between early work songs and ritual chants disappears: they were one and the same. This is confirmed by the cave art. Ucko and Rosenfeld discuss the point also raised by Plekhanov: why was it that hunting peoples excelled in drawing animals and drew them to the exclusion of nearly all other subjects? They write: 'either animals were the predominant concern of Palaeolithic artists for something like fertility or hunting magic for food-animals' or else it was because of their 'role as "background" for actual human participation (as "actors") during which "props" may have been brought into the caves for any given occasion (for example, actual vegetation).'[30] Again there is no need to draw a sharp line between rite and art. This early 'theatre', as Ucko and Rosenfeld call it, seems to have been, not a specialized entertainment in the way of modern cinema or football, but a kind of communal exercise that grew out of work and fed back into it.

I suggested before that the separating of the media from productive functions did not sever the links but only made them harder to trace. This must be tested against media from modern times. What link could there be between, for example, the style of oil painting, especially portraits, and the productive function of the class who commissioned or bought them? John Berger writes: 'The function of portrait painting was to underwrite and idealize a chosen social role of the sitter. It was not to present him as "an individual" but, rather, as an individual monarch, bishop, landowner, merchant and so on. Each role had its accepted qualities and its acceptable limit of discrepancy. (A monarch or a pope could be far more idiosyncratic than a mere gentleman or courtier.) The role was emphasized by pose, gesture, clothes and background.' This is borne out through an analysis of the painterly qualities of many pictures, in particular Holbein's *The Ambassadors*: 'What distinguishes oil painting from any other form of painting is its special ability to render the tangibility, the texture, the lustre, the solidity of what it depicts. . . . Every square inch of the surface of this painting, whilst remaining purely visual, appeals to, importunes, the sense of touch. . . . Except for the faces and hands, there is not a surface in this picture which does not make one aware of

[30] Ucko and Rosenfeld, *Palaeolithic Cave Art*, p. 228.

how it has been elaborately worked over — by weavers, embroiderers, carpet-makers. . . . Thus painting itself had to be able to demonstrate the desirability of what money could buy.' This does not only apply to a nonpopular medium, the portraiture of the dominant rich. On the nude, Berger says, after comparing a pin-up from a girlie magazine and *La Grande Odalisque* by Ingres: 'Is not the expression remarkably similar in each case? It is the expression of a woman responding with calculated charm to the man whom she imagines looking at her — although she doesn't know him. . . . It is true that sometimes a painting [more rarely a pin-up, more often a sexy advertisement] includes a male lover. But the woman's attention is very rarely directed towards him. Often she looks away from him or she looks out of the picture towards the one who considers himself her true lover — the spectator-owner.'[31]

This is a good example of Marxist method: once the medium or the work has been known or perceived as sensitively as possible, the question can be put to it (and the way of formulating the question will have suggested itself), what productive use does it (directly or indirectly) serve? what is the social function ingrained in its style? how does the medium image the class experience of the people it appeals to? I will conclude my review of Marxist work on these matters by considering a medium, industrial song, whose very existence would be unknown outside the pit villages and old cotton towns had it not been for the collecting, singing, and analysing work of Marxists such as Ewan MacColl and A. L. Lloyd. In 1951, to mark the Festival of Britain, Lloyd collected miners' songs partly by appealing through the National Coal Board magazine, *Coal.* Sixty-seven were published with sixteen tunes in *Come All Ye Bold Miners* (1952). In 1954 MacColl published a songbook of industrial songs with the Workers' Music Association, called *The Shuttle and Cage*, including pieces from the railways, coalfields, building sites, and old pit and weaving villages. In 1956 and 1958 he issued two ten-inch records with Topic, *Shuttle and Cage* and *Second Shift*, sung by himself, three quarters of the material being traditional: that is, made up for

[31] John Berger, 'The Changing View of Man in the Portrait' in *Selected Essays and Articles: The Look of Things* (London 1972) pp. 37–8; *Ways of Seeing* (London 1972) pp. 88–90; 55–6.

the community whose life was imaged in the songs and not for a national network. In 1963 Lloyd organized a twelve-inch Topic record, *The Iron Muse*, which aimed at being a representative sample of industrial songs and instrumental music; the leaflet of notes was the first detailed study of this medium.[32] This was followed by two full studies: in 1967, Lloyd's chapter 'The Industrial Songs' in his *Folk Song in England*, and in 1973 my chapter 'Songs of the Bleak Age' in *The Real Foundations: Literature and Social Change*.

The approaches in these books are similar enough, though independently written, for them to be discussed as one. Both writers see industrial song as the distinctive voice of a new class, the proletariat. The medium evolved as this class 'gradually isolated itself from the peasantry to form its own culture.' The essence of the relation between class and medium was that the songs were 'made and sung by men who are identical with their audience in standing, in occupation, in attitude to life and in daily experience.' Class struggle had been heated and sharpened by the socialization of labour in factories. The style of the songs articulates this:

Consolation, a most powerful element of rustic lyrics, was giving way to exposition, complaint, exhortation even. In a short time, the first concern of the song-makers was no longer to create a stylized backcloth for some emotional fantasy; rather it was to set out the facts of working men's lives in all their nudity and to appeal that something be done to set wrongs right. . . . It seems that as the working people became fully industrialized — doing one job only, under intensively disciplined conditions, and living off this alone — the iron entered into their souls (for all that material standards of living often improved) and it could not be got out again without a struggle, both grim and invigorating, which itself became a potent influence in their song-making.[33]

The main seedbeds of the songs were the trades and areas that were giving the lead in mechanization, in the growth of cities and in the militant organization of working people to struggle for political and social rights. In his classic social

[32] The three other basic recordings of this material are: *The Elliots of Birtley: A Musical Portrait of a Durham Mining Family*, ed. Ewan MacColl and Peggy Seeger (Folkways, New York, 1956); *American Industrial Ballads*, ed. Irwin Silber, sung by Pete Seeger (Folkways, New York, 1956); and *Tommy Armstrong of Tyneside* (Topic, 1965).

[33] Lloyd, *Folk Song in England* (London 1969 ed.), pp. 319, 368, 324; Craig, *The Real Foundations* (London 1973), p. 63.

history Edward Thompson counts the handloom weavers among the groups whose 'experience seems most to colour the social consciousness of the working class in the first half of the century', whereas 'the miners and metal workers do not make their influence fully felt until later in the century.'[34] Textile workers had been striving to organize themselves throughout the eighteenth century. 'Artisans who organized so early must have had amongst them an unusually high proportion of men with minds able to seize upon and see through to the marrow of any vital new matter.' From this group sprang the classic songs of changing English experience, *The Weaver and the Factory Maid*, often published on broadsides in Manchester in the 1820s, and *Jone o' Grinfilt Junior*. *The Weaver* ends:

How can you say it's a pleasant bed
When nowt lies there but a factory maid?
A factory lass although she be,
Blest is the man that enjoys she.

Oh, pleasant thoughts come to my mind
As I turned down the sheets so fine
And I seen her two breasts standing so
Like two white hills all covered with snow.

Where are the girls? I'll tell you plain,
The girls have gone to weave by steam,
And if you'd find 'em you must rise at dawn
And trudge to the mill in the early morn.

This is 'the acme of folk poetry in that it is both down-to-earth and tender. . . . During the century after the date of that song it was not possible for an artist to move with ease across the gamut of his experience'[35] — the implication is that it is in this anonymous song, circulated on cheap sheets, that the watershed between the wholeheartedness of the preVictorian mentality and the repression of the Victorian is most strikingly marked. It must be enough to say about the other classic song of the time, *Jone o' Grinfilt Junior* — called *The Oldham Weaver* by Elizabeth Gaskell in *Mary Barton* — that it is a flawlessly poised and lifelike story of hunger, hardship and

[34] E. P. Thompson, *The Making of the English Working Class* (London 1963), p. 212 n.
[35] Craig, *Real Foundations*, pp. 64–6.

resistance. It belonged at the centre of popular taste. Its prototype, *Jone o' Grinfilt*, was said to be the best selling song in country Lancashire; further versions followed to 'celebrate' the New Poor Law, the Chartist movement and the Crimean War; and a shortened, and saddened, last form of it could still be got in one of the old industrial villages above Oldham as recently as 1953.[36]

The historical aspect of this analysis is continued through an account of the miners' song culture. Its deep lyric roots put forth a great body of song in the epoch of the strike wave in the mid-1840s which tore 'the miners of the north of England forever from the intellectual death in which they had hitherto lain; they have left their sleep, are alert to defend their interests, and have entered the movement of civilization.'[37] Engels is defining the qualities at work in a political movement. They also apply perfectly, in that movement from 'intellectual death' to 'alertness' and 'civilization', to the *self-expression* achieved in the songs.

To take the full measure of the Marxist analysis, it ought to be noted that it is not a matter of searching for the materials that inertly 'reflect' whatever was happening at the time or that neatly confirm some thesis. The significance of the media — that is, the fullness, accuracy and nuance of the insight they offer into the balance of psychosocial forces in their place and time — cannot be understood unless the analysis of them is as sensitively directed by personal taste as it is grounded in historical information. When the writers refer to the 'richness in lyrical value' of the mill and coalfield songs, or judge that they make up 'a *tradition* and one that images contemporary life more effectively than the main art poetry of the same phase,'[38] they are invoking criteria and going by a taste that must be justified in the general cogency of the criticism being made — in the aptness and rightness of it as it comes over to the reader. If you find, after listening to the songs, that they are not powerful but inexpressive, then you will not agree with

[36] Lloyd, *Folk Song in England*, pp. 324—7; Craig, *Real Foundations* pp. 71—2; *Ballads and Songs of Lancashire*, ed. John Harland, rev. T. T. Wilkinson (1882 ed.), pp. 162, 164—5, 173—5; MacColl, *Shuttle and Cage*, side 1, track 6, and n.

[37] Fredrik Engels, *The Condition of the Working Class in England in 1844*: K. Marx and F. Engels, *On Britain* (Moscow 1953), p. 293.

[38] Lloyd, *Folk Song in England*, p. 331; Craig, *Real Foundations*, p. 71.

Lloyd that they are valuable if you want 'to find what labouring people were feeling at important moments.'[39] Just because the taste in question is popular taste it does not mean that the only criteria to be used are sales, box-office returns, and viewing figures. The bread-and-butter media, which have been beneath academic notice for generations, are creative — they are efforts to compose a vision of what it is to be alive in a place and time, and they must be interpreted accordingly.

From time to time Marxists have developed important new work on the popular cultural bases. George Thomson's study of Greek tragedy (in *Aeschylus and Athens*, 1941 and 1946) led to productions of the ancient plays which he did in old amphitheatres in Greece during the 1960s. MacColl, with his wife, Peggy Seeger, and the then BBC producer Charles Parker, made seven radio ballads between 1958 and 1964 which presented various walks of life, usually based on a trade, through the unaltered words of the people belonging there, recorded on tape and spliced in with songs based on the idiom of industrial and country folksongs.[40] Hamish Henderson, the folksong collector, has reached deeper into the wellsprings of the people's singing than any other collector in Britain and he has also made songs, some of his own, some that are composites of traditional items, which have gone back into the repertories of the travelling people and others of the main song carriers in the folk networks.

In each case these Marxist artists and thinkers are working in the spirit of the axiom Luther followed when he was preaching, translating the Bible and writing hymns: 'Watch the people's mouth'. Brecht invokes this saying in his essay, 'On Rhymeless Verse with Irregular Rhythms'. To my mind it is the most important single piece in which a Marxist writer explains his ideas about popular culture. In the middle 1920s Brecht had been chafing at the damping and stereotyping effect which 'the oily smoothness of the usual five-foot iambic metre' had had upon theatre poetry. He started to syncopate his lines,

---

[39] Lloyd, *Folk Song in England*, p. 344.

[40] Four of the radio ballads are on Argo Records; the significance of their form is discussed by Parker in 'The Radio Ballads': *New Society*, 14 November 1963; and their style is analysed in my 'Growing Points of Literature', *The Real Foundations*, pp. 301—2.

not just as 'a protest against the smoothness and harmony of conventional poetry' but as 'an attempt to show human dealings as contradictory, fiercely fought over, full of violence.' He wanted his poetry to move with the runs and checks and stresses that belonged to the life it was evoking. The models he needed in working out new rhythms came from shouts he heard in the Berlin streets, during a workers' march on Christmas Eve through a well-to-do part of town and by a man selling booklets on the pavement, and from printed advertising slogans. He quotes the political slogans, which were shouted in unison: *Wir haben Hunger* — (We're hungry), and *Helft euch selber, wählt Thälmann* (Help yourselves: vote for Thälmann). He then scans them to show how their rhythms help to keep the voices together and to drive their message home.[41]

'Watch the people's mouth' could serve as the motto of all the work that has been discussed in this chapter. The socially tragic aspect of it lies in the division of society into classes. This places between the various parts of the culture barriers which can scarcely be crossed. The poems and plays Brecht wrote in the idiom of the people are not known to most Germans. Parker's radio ballads went out theoretically to everybody, but on a minority channel, the Third Programme, and though they reached a maximum audience of 230,000 (for *Singing the Fishing*), the series was presently axed by the BBC management. Marxism is a revolutionary theory, and it cannot bear its full fruits, whether political or cultural, until a revolution takes place.

[41] First published in *Das Wört* (Moscow 1939): *Brecht on Theatre*, ed. John Willett (1964), pp. 115—19

2 Images

8

As We See Ourselves

Bill Owen

Sunday afternoon we get it together. I cook the steaks and
my wife makes the salad.

Togetherness really exists in our family. My daughter and I operate the lunch room at the Valley Inn. My sons work part-time with their dad, hanging sheetrock. And my eldest two sons work at the Gulf gas station on P St. We have 7 cars and 2 motorcycles in our family.

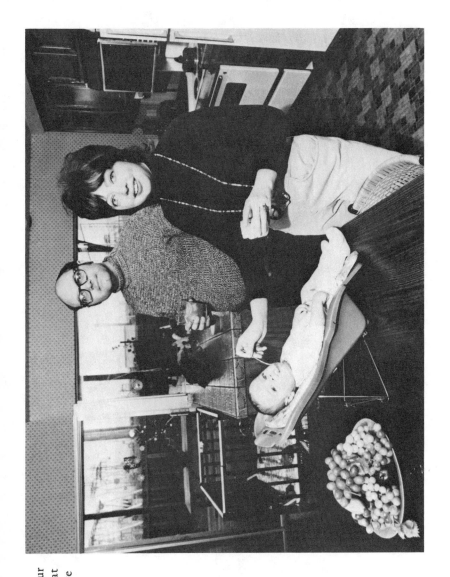

We're really happy. Our kids are healthy, we eat good food and we have a really nice home.

Our eighth grade graduation dance was really far out. We spent over $160 on crepe paper, stars and decorations. There was an arched entrance with flowers, a white picket fence, a fountain with real water and a black light. We have live music and a buffet with chicken, turkey, ham, salad, dessert and punch. We had a ball. You only graduate from the eighth grade once.

To be president of the Livermore *Juniors* is a great honour. It is also a terrific responsibility. We have only fifty-six members but carry out over seventy service projects each year. I have nine committees for these projects, and the responsibility falls on the president's shoulders.

At the dedication of Foothill High School, the Principal, Vice Principal, Superintendent of Schools and President of the School Board each prepared a speech. The ceremony took one hour and fifteen minutes.

The *Companions of the Forest of America* teaches devotion to the home, respect for other people's religious beliefs, loyalty to the American flag and obedience to God's commandments. Our motto is 'Sociability, Sincerity and Constancy.' Many good and lasting friendships are formed through membership in the Companions of the Forest of America.

The *Masons* is the oldest fraternal organization in the world. We believe in God, Brotherhood and Charity. We stick together and stay middle-of-the road. As a Mason you are never down and out. There is always a brother to help you.

I enjoy giving a Tupperware party in my home. It gives me a chance to talk to my friends. But really, Tupperware is a homemaker's dream, you save time and money because your food keeps longer.

This is my second marriage and Ken's third. This time it's for keeps. We were both looking for someone to be together with all the time. Now we're together at work and at home.

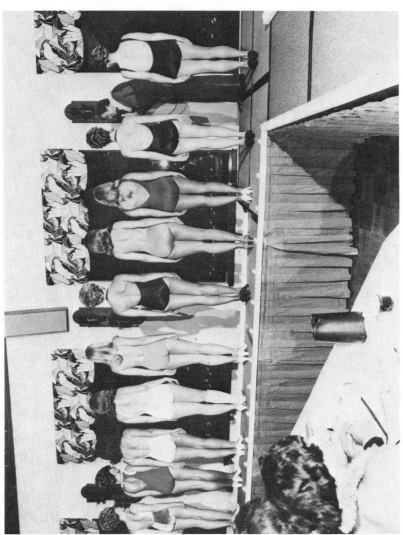

A lot of people say we're
chunks of meat, like
cattle, but we're not.
We're all individuals with
dreams and aspirations
like everybody else..
Being a beauty contest-
ant has taught me about
myself, other people,
poise and public speak-
ing. If I had to do it over
again, I would.

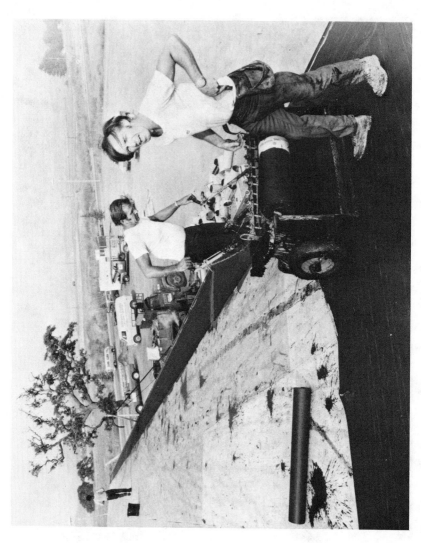

Build up roffing is super hard work. A 'hot man' is really a commercial roffer. We're members of the United Slate, Tile and Composition Roffers Union Local #81. A good 'hot man' can make $80 to $100 per day. That's if he gets any overtime.

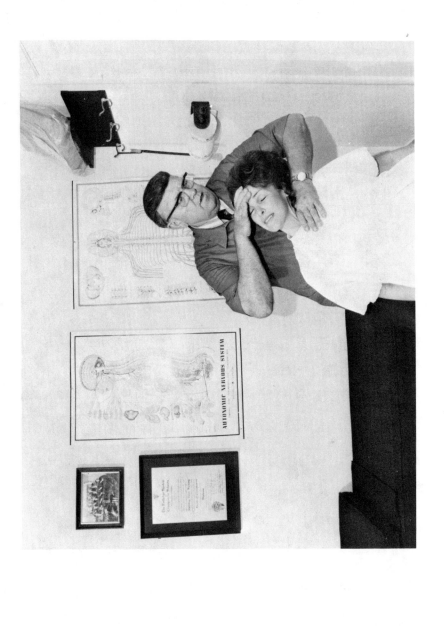

Before I got into the grave digging business I was a body and fender man. My job is more than grave digging. It is maintenance and planning. It's filling a need.

3 Examinations

9

Screen Violence: Emotional Structure and Ideological Function in 'A Clockwork Orange'

Thomas Elsaesser

No discussion of the cinema as part of popular culture seems able to avoid the question of violence and sex in the movies. In recent years the view has often been expressed that violence is becoming increasingly 'gratuitous', 'explicit', 'pornographic', and that this is bound to have an effect on public morals. From the scientific point of view the assertion is difficult to prove, since it is by no means evident that the relation between violence and morality is one of inverse proportionality, even if one were to accept — though I don't think one can — that either of these entities is in any sense quantitative. Victorian melodramas (or for that matter, the novels of Dickens) show a certain reciprocity of sex, violence and morality (what one might call the Nancy/Sykes syndrome), but the salient feature there is surely the opportunity which violence affords for strong effects, for the *mise-en-scène* of a spectacular poetic justice, itself the expression of a profound doubt not only about the efficacious working of social justice and the nature of good and evil, but also about the kind of psychic forces, the dialectics of sado-masochism which crime and punishment bring into play. On no account does it seem possible to argue that violence is synonymous with immorality, however much guardians of public taste wish to contain the debate within these terms.

Insofar as one can speak at all of 'popular culture' today in relation to the cinema, one has to face the possibility that one is dealing with an extensive and no doubt complex institution of socialization and social control (i.e. an apparatus which manipulates consciousness), generated and maintained by concrete economic interests. Whether popular culture in the technological media is, as has often been asserted, entirely programmed so as to rehearse and internalize the behavioural norms and psychic patterns necessary to reconcile reluctant individuals to their roles in the productive processes is perhaps an open question. Such a view assumes too much intentionality and design arising out of the diversity of individual interests and motives among those working in the media, nor does it adequately explain the fact that popularity is such an unpredictable quality. That the cinema is nonetheless locked very securely into the division of work and leisure which is shaping and adapting most manifestations of culture to the restrictive categories of entertainment is indisputable, and so is the fact that entertainment is itself an industry, organized according to the laws of the commodity market, where demand and consumption are stimulated, if necessary, by creating new needs rather than fulfilling existing ones. In this context, the primary need which the cinema promises to fulfil is to codify an experience of reality which is directly sensual: it offers the world as an emotional spectacle. Especially since it began to compete with television, which also provides visual representations of the real, but with a much lower degree of affective involvement, the cinema has had to stake its chances for survival on emotional intensity and as such partakes fully in the manipulation and exploitation of desire, the senses and of aesthetic emotions which one associates with advertising. As long as the popular cinema remains commercial, it will continue to be bound up with a particular rhetoric where objects and people become fetishes, and where desire produces fixations, convertible into commodities for the benefit of consumption.

If the consumer society has occasionally been defined as the commercial exploitation of false needs, then the commercial cinema could be called the aesthetic exploitation of false consciousness. Without intending to go into the usefulness or limits of the latter concept, it should be said that as far as the cinema goes, too little emphasis has been given to the emotional structure subtending this consciousness, usually defined in ideological and political terms alone. Freud has attempted to explain how such a structure might be constituted, though not, alas, with reference to the cinema, and only intermittently with an eye to the general aesthetic implications. Yet even so, his theories of affectivity suggest that the kind of emotional intensity provided by the popular cinema, the plenitude of emotional signification in action and gesture — in short, the dramatic spectacle — could well be of a neurotic kind and reveal compulsive mechanisms through which are repeated a ritualistic fixation of psychic energy in the way reality is apprehended, and where a narcissistic fascination with an imaginary self-image allows an alienated subjectivity to experience itself vicariously as object.

On the other hand, the language of strong emotions, coded as violence, comedy and eroticism continually reformulates social and psychic conflicts in a way that modern literature, with its declared aversion to emotionality in art, has long ceased to do. These conflicts which the commercial cinema reflects are not always easy to decode. For one thing, a specific film moulds itself around economic interests and conditions of production as much as it has to mould itself around the presumptive demands and expectations of its envisaged audience. The cinema has a place in contemporary 'popular culture' as long as it remains financially profitable. Its attractiveness as an industry lies in the rapidity with which the capital invested can return profits, its precariousness in the fact that the high stakes are accompanied by high risks: what the investors speculate with is an elusive factor — popularity. The attractiveness for the consumer is the promise a film gives of entertainment, and that means filling a time euphemistically called 'leisure' with a kind of emotional nutrient which can be consumed without effort or exertion, mental or physical. A good movie, the advertisement tells the prospective spectator, is 'packed': with action, thrills, glamour, suspense. The persistence of the appeal to plenitude points to a corresponding lack elsewhere. It predicates and subsumes an emotionally empty time from which it promises relief. To put it differently: a film is an emotional experience structurally related to what it is not, e.g. work, everyday reality; but because of its representational realism, its photographic illusionism it, also posits a high mimetic convergence with an identifiable external reality. It is both an imitation of life as a tissue of appearances and its negation as a psychically meaningful experience. In the shift between the two levels lies a manipulative power, but also a potential truth value. The emotions generated are both real and false, a negation of one reality, and a massively orchestrated affirmation of another. These relate to each other in a complementary and indeed compensatory way, which means that the manipulative processes (e.g. assuming identity and analogy where there is difference and contradiction) in order to take place at all, have to leave visible the very dynamics and structures they are attempting to steer in a particular direction. Every Smirnoff ad refers to a recognizably undesirable reality prior to the shattering effect. In just the same way a movie allows one to see, sometimes only in X-ray negative, but at other times quite deliberately (and herein lies the subversive dimension of the best Hollywood films, for instance) not only the reality it subsumes, but also the processes of transformation by which it generates out of an absence the illusion of a presence, out of a lack the sense of plenitude.

In what way, then, might violence, considered as an aesthetic spectacle and a form of extreme emotional plenitude, serve the purpose of social control, in the way that representations of sexuality have become an instrument of manipulation in advertising? What is it, if anything, that screen violence could attempt to sell?

Fortunately there exists a film which raises the problem of violence and social control explicitly as one of its themes.

A Clockwork Orange, directed by Stanley Kubrick in 1972, is based on the novel of the same title by Anthony Burgess, first published in 1962. Apart from seeming to confront in a critical spirit certain topical concerns such as hooliganism, mugging, the Welfare State, sex, drugs, police brutality and corruption in politics, the film — notwithstanding these forbiddingly 'serious' issues — has the inestimable advantage of having been a popular success, and (aided by a general debate about sex and violence, obscenity and law and order) of having been profusely commented on by the press. The timing was not entirely fortuitous: *A Clockwork Orange* received its very full coverage by the daily and weekly papers, the specialized magazines and the trade journals after a carefully planned prerelease publicity campaign which got under way well before the first day of shooting. For a commercial film, the range of the reviews was unusual — from a story in *Time* magazine and a review of the film by Anthony Burgess himself in *The Listener* to the coincidental publication of a monograph on the director and (apart from the obligatory reissue of the novel by Penguin) the publication of the film as an almost shot-by-shot comic strip version — the media were giving maximum support to Kubrick's strategic advance.

Can *A Clockwork Orange* serve as a model case for analysing the relation between emotional structure and ideological function in a popular movie? In many ways the film proved extremely baffling to critics and audiences alike. Was it a conservative film advocating a law-and-order stance against the permissiveness of the Welfare State? Was it a radical film celebrating the anarchic and subversive side of violence? Was it a proto-fascist film? Was its ethos a liberal-humanist one? Was Kubrick detached and 'objective'? Was it a satire, and if so, of what? Was it realistic, a fantasy or science fiction? Did it show a 'dehumanized society' in which the individual has to take a stand, if necessary, by resorting to violence, or were the hero and his gang 'demented laboratory rats'? These views and many more were expressed verbally and in print and they could hardly have been more contradictory. Surely, if a film is so confusing and equivocal in what it says on important issues, this must detract from its credibility? It would seem not, for the odd fact emerged that it was almost universally praised, and as the box-office returns proved to Kubrick, he had yet again hit the jackpot. How can a film full of 'gratuitous' violence, 'sadistic' rape, 'pornographic' drawings, physical and mental cruelty, be enjoyable to an educated audience, who, without a trace of cynicism, were apparently prepared to stand up and applaud, even if for their life they could not make up their minds what it was about? Not normally at a loss for a moral judgement when it comes to assessing the 'intentions' of a film, the reviewers in this case were happy to shift to an area where they felt on firmer ground: Kubrick's craftmanship, his technical virtuosity: 'justly deserves his reputation as the cinema's greatest perfectionist'; 'can select lighting and lenses with invincible authority'; 'not a single point is missed or miscalculated . . . each camera-movement and cut is exact and correct'; 'the whole thing works, yes, with the absolute precision of clockwork,' etc. What, one may rightly wonder, has all this to do with the issue of sex and violence that brought the film notoriety? The censor spelled it out: 'in his [i.e. the censor's] judgement the use of music, stylization and other skills of the director succeeded in distancing audiences from the violence, which includes a gang fight, several scenes of beating up, and murder and rape, and keeping the effect within tolerable limits.'[1] The aesthetic apparatus surrounding the film, one is given to understand makes it acceptable: presentation and packaging give the commodity respectability.

If 'stylization' and 'distancing' made *A Clockwork Orange* unobjectionable to the censor and pleasing, even enjoyable, to watch for the larger audiences, this explains less than it is supposed to do, and in fact poses real questions: what has happened to the fact that it is by all accounts a disturbing film, what has happened to its message about violence in society, and what exactly does it mean to say that 'the director succeeds in distancing audiences from the violence', what is this magic wall that protects them from possible harm? If one reads the reviews, one notices that, clearly, a shift has occurred between the emotional reaction to the film, the elucidation of the ostensible subject and the value judgement in which the whole was then couched. Unsettled by the experience, uncertain about what the film had to say, confused by the director's attitude, reviewers nonetheless enjoyed it, an enjoyment rationalized into eloquent, but in the context quite irrelevant, raptures about' correct camera-movements', 'authoritative lighting', and 'perfect timing'. The suggestion offers itself that here one has an example of either conscious or unconscious displacement, affecting potentially very

[1] I am indebted for the quotations and for first suggesting the idea of writing about *A Clockwork Orange* to an article entitled 'Strawdogs, A Clockwork Orange and the Critics', by Charles Barr, *Screen* VVI 13, 2, summer 1972, pp. 17–32.

disturbing psychic material, and that the film itself invites this kind of rationalization. Could it be, for instance, that the reviewers, much impressed that the film dealt with serious issues, were in fact grateful for its ambiguous attitude, and for Kubrick having had the tact to raise these issues without pretending to answer them? For if he had spelled out his views, or if critics had been less ready to be manipulated, might they not have felt obliged to disagree and thus be disagreeably impressed by their own ability to take pleasure in violent scenes?

One would want to go a step further and hazard the hypothesis that the film was successful precisely because it suggested to the spectator that he was having his cake and eating it. Could this constitute an ideological function? Raise controversial topics, acknowledge the existence of a political and social reality, but provide an emotional structure which somehow admits of a pleasing resolution which one cannot fault because one cannot get it firmly enough into one's grip. Is this the recipe for a successful and popular movie? And what role does violence play in this?

The reply is not easy to give. It involves a careful tracing of the way the film tailors itself to fit the spectator's expectations and his emotional reactions. In other words, it involves an analysis, however sketchy, of Kubrick's emotive rhetoric, which is no less than a close look indeed at his technical 'virtuosity', but also a look at the specific situation of the viewer vis-à-vis the screen. It is enough to remember how different watching a film is from reading a book, looking at pictures, going to the theatre or even watching television. Only in the cinema is attention so tightly focused on the limited and circumscribed area which is the screen. The continuous flow of images makes a film primarily an experience of organized time rather than space, but one in which a segment of time is marked off by strong discontinuities at either end (lights down —projection time — lights up): a form of closure, in other words, which is the more intense because the filmic sequence is irreversible. Unlike television, on the other hand, there is no domestic setting, no familiar surroundings or additional source of light to neutralize the spell a film casts on its audience. Under this spell, the spectator is willy-nilly a

voyeur, and what is more, he is a passive recipient, fed and
wanting to be fed with images. A film for mass audiences,
i.e. a cinema based exclusively on the dramatization of conflict
and tension in spectacular form, makes out of the spectators
a captive audience by creating, as it were, a circuit of emotional
involvement, where the representation of movement and
physical action combines with a visual and aural assault on the
senses: the cinema, in this way, is by its very nature an
aggressive medium. For in so far as an audience judges a film
to be 'good', it actively seeks the captivity, the engrossment
that comes from being subject to an articulation and experience
of time over which one has no control. Switched into the will
of another being, the audience's awareness is at every moment
controlled by the movement and angle of the camera, and the
steady cadence of 24 frames a second. No possibility of going
back to an earlier passage or skipping another, no possibility of
a discursive, reflexive experience, no off-button to press or
switching to another channel. *A Clockwork Orange* provides a
graphic illustration of the position of the spectator: under the
Ludovico treatment the hero is strapped into a cinema seat,
straight-jacketed like a lunatic, and clamps are put on his eye-
lids to stop him shutting his eyes or averting his gaze. This, in
effect is what a film does to its audience. Not with clamps and
straight-jacket, for sure, but with what one might call the
psychological equivalent of aggressive coercion. The irony here
is that the audience pays and demands that their eyes and ears
be 'riveted' and 'glued' to the screen.

If pleasure can be derived from subjection to emotional
pressure and coercion, then the circuit established between
screen and audience is one of exchange, taking place in an
atmosphere charged with 'static'. The spectator, passive and
almost supine, enclosed in a womblike space, isolated and
insulated from others by darkness and a comfortable seat,
necessarily projects the correlative of his state of dependency
onto the screen in the form of psychic energy — whether this
be as expectation, anticipation, daydreaming and a general
relaxation of control and defense mechanisms, or more
aggressively as a manifestation of impatience, boredom or in
extreme cases, a voyeuristic fixation on obsessional fantasies.
The film, by means of action, conflict and drama in turn

provides a narrative sequence whereby this energy can be managed, articulated and focused, thus containing it, and channelling it into projection by way of a unilinear but two-way flow. In other words, regardless of subject matter, any film designed for a mass audience cannot avoid entering into this energy circuit whose exigencies have a determining influence on the formal organization of the narrative, the camera-movements, the editing, the kind of action and conflicts depicted and lastly, on the meaning and function of 'violence': the same scene has a completely different effect, and therefore meaning, depending on whether it complies with or obstructs, as it were, the direction of the flow 'inside' the circuit at any given moment.

Within this field of force, created out of expectation and familiarity, suspense and its release, surprise and gratification, the emotional contact with the main protagonist is of crucial importance because it provides the initial vector of responses. Much time is spent in a film on mapping the framework of orientation, and where it is not an actual or potential 'couple' sharing equally the audience's attention, a careful line of identification is build up with the central hero. There are countless ways in which this can be done effectively, and in this respect, the hero of *A Clockwork Orange* is doubly privileged: not only does Alex dominate by being continuously on screen and thus providing the narrative logic by which action and plot progress from one scene to the next, he is also present by means of a first-person narrative, a sort of running commentary, in which he confidentially and conspiratorially addresses the spectator in mock-heroic terms such as 'oh my brothers' and 'your humble narrator'. He is enlisting a subtle degree of jovial complicity that overtly appears to acknowledge his dependence on the audience's approval, while also efficiently ensuring the reverse, namely their desire to be led in their responses by his judgements and values. This double role — that of visually continuous presence and primary, organizing consciousness — is made necessary in *A Clockwork Orange* by the nature of the chief protagonist, who is of course a rather nasty piece of work, a young hooligan lacking precisely what one would normally regard as 'values'. The director (following the footsteps of the author) has to make sure, therefore, that the spectator is and stays interested, and he does so by showing the hero's awareness as obviously deficient, 'inferior' to that of the spectator, so that across the gap the mechanism of identification can energize itself. The careless assumption of superiority which lulls the spectator into a deceptively relaxed stance will eventually be turned against him with a vengeance and this is part of another strategy intended to enforce complicity. Identification in the cinema is always a process which involves, besides recognition and confirmation of familiar stances and experiences, a fixation of affect, of a libidinous or aggressive nature, at a stage where it produces inhibition, anxiety and guilt, itself the result of a partial recognition whose blockage is overcompensated.

Kubrick's skill is lavished on finding a cinematic form, half-way between social realism and the strip cartoon, whereby this process is given full play, so that identification can develop both by focusing energy (empathy, recognition) and by dispersing it (laughter, incongruity). Some of the passages in the film — notably the scenes of gang warfare or the night-ride through the countryside — are reminiscent of slapstick comedy, a genre well known for the way it turns aggression and inhibition to comic effect. Because the confrontation between Alex's Droogs and Billy-boy's gang is orchestrated with the overture from Rossini's *The Thieving Magpie*, and the preceding 'gang-bang' is 'staged' in a derelict music-hall theatre, the 'distanciation' of which so many critics approved is retrieved by the parodistic implications which, in scenes such as these that are much too overtly aggressive for direct emotional participation, allow a release of aggression through laugher, the latter lowering, if only momentarily, the spectator's psychic defences. To return once more to the Smirnoff ads: the potentially hostile disbelief in the shattering transformation which the girl from the local library or the typing pool is supposed to experience after drinking the stuff is overcompensated in the laughter provoked by the very incongruity and improbability of what the prospective customer is asked to 'swallow'. Thus, aggression, or tendentiousness played for laughs, far from alienating the mechanisms of identification, reinforces them.

The scene in which the relaxed identification jackknifes

and freezes the laughter comes when Alex rapes the wife of the writer while doing the song-and-dance routine from Gene Kelly's *Singin' in the Rain*. The apparently incongruous disjuncture between action and song, image and sound is pushed to an extreme where an uncanny recognition obtrudes itself on the spectator who suddenly discovers an unexpected congruence. The scene delves deeply into the nature of cinematic participation and the latent aggression which it can mobilize with impunity: what happens is that before one's eyes an act of brutal violence and sadism is fitted over and made to 'rhyme' with a musical number connoting a fancy-free assertion of erotic longing and vitalist *joie de vivre*. Kubrick is able to exploit the undefined, polyvalent nature of the emotion which the moving image generates, by running, as it were, two parallel cinematic contexts along the same track, or rather, short-circuiting two lines, both charged with emotional energy. What this demonstrates, I think, is the structure of the emotional circuit mentioned earlier, where the dynamics of love and violence, aggression and vitality are oddly aligned, for in effect they seem to share a common trajectory towards energy-projection and what Freud called cathexis. Primarily an articulation of musical or rhythmic elements, this pattern of energy not only comprises the soundtrack proper, but also speech, gesture, movement — including the movements of the camera. All aspects of the filmic process are therefore potential lines of energy which the narrative, by its selection or stylization, either discards or 'realizes' in the course of the action.

One of the significant implications of this would seem to be the probability, on one level at least, that a musical or a melodrama is as 'violent' as a gangster movie or any other kind of action picture; that besides the violence *on* the screen there exists the violence *of* the screen (or between screen and audience) and that of the two, the latter would seem the more 'insidious', if one were to argue in the language of the sex and violence debate. At all events, there appears to be an evident analogy between violent and erotic expenditure of affect, in the way it is portrayed in the cinema, and the intensity of that expenditure is most commonly scored by a musical or rhythmic notation that carries the kind of emotionality specific to film (and possibly opera). What makes the scene quoted somewhat special is not only the extremity of the contrast, but the fact that the effect is thematized in the film itself: normally a movie's emotional line is conveyed by the music on the soundtrack either in a manner made unobtrusive by convention (when a love scene gets the inevitable string accompaniment) or as a form of parody in order to force a distanciation (the Rossini overture mentioned above); here, however, it is the hero himself who cynically parodies the facile emotionality of film music. The theme, played in another key, so to speak, is provided by Alex's fondness, indeed passionate devotion to classical music, especially Beethoven's Ninth Symphony. What in the book is possibly intended as a satire on the fate of 'high culture', by pointing up the relation between violent music and violent action, i.e. what might be called the 'fascist' side of romantic and Wagnerian music, with its suspect cult of dionysiac frenzy (latterly Ken Russell's particular pitch), this the film apostrophizes with a possible critique of cinematic language as a language of manipulated emotions, as the medium of dynamism that essentially exploits sex and violence, eroticism and aggression because they are the two faces of emotionality.

But is it in fact a critique? As so often with this film, one must be careful not to mistake the intelligence of its maker for a sign of his integrity. The sick humour of the musical rape, while affording in retrospect an unusually transparent insight into the cinema's rhetoric, is actually used to tie the spectator in a kind of double bind to the hero: while Alex's violence is stylized into libidinal self-expression and his destructiveness becomes a manifestation of a self-assertion that promises a subversive, anarcho-individualist liberation, the spectator cannot help identifying — not with the victims themselves — but with their situation, the brutal and apparently unmotivated intrusion into 'innocent' and 'peaceful' people's homes by a gang of vandals and hooligans. After all, the latent fears of such an intrusion provide the basis for a good many horror movies, where the thrill consists in being made to identify with the threatened victims (though there as well, empathy is often deftly split between *belle* and *bête* — King Kong, Frankenstein, and even Dracula). In *A Clockwork Orange* the spectator is allowed to overcompensate by distanciation and parody for an identification with the victims which the film both invites and denies. This cuts considerably deeper than simple identification with either hero or victim, and one imagines that even the most hardened viewer will scarcely be able to protect himself from such a direct raid on his unconscious. One thinks of the crisis of identification deliberately provoked in early surrealist films such as Buñuel's *L'Age D'Or* (1930), where a somewhat similar orgy of libidinal aggressiveness was rehearsed in order to confront the audience head-on with scandal and gratuity. Alex, however, is despite his violence cautiously programmed not to confront, but to accommodate contradictory fantasies and projections: embodiment of a fun-and-consumption hedonism, he is also an urban guerilla ravaging bourgeois homes; he is anti-intellectual, but has a passion for Beethoven and a respect for classic art; he is a born leader, virile and ruthless, but sensitive to the point of sentimentality. A working-class tough with a touch of Billy Liar, Alex is a composite figure, whose authority is helped considerably by the rugged but friendly masculinity of Malcolm MacDowell (of *If . . .*) and the rollicking picaresque narrative reminiscent of Albert Finney's hey-day as Tom Jones: all in all a recognizable stereotype — the subversive stance in British culture that because of its pathological individualism wants to have nothing to do with politics.

The credibility of such a hero stands or falls with the type and calibre of his antagonists. Here again, the film is carefully calculated, and a kind of defamatory aesthetics ensures that moral emotions are neutralized. A massive appeal is made to photogenic contrasts between attraction and repulsion. Any sympathy one might have, for instance, with the writer who is forced to watch his wife being raped while his mouth is sellotaped and gagged with a golfball is cancelled by the grotesque physical ugliness of his protruding eyes, his salivating mouth, his grunts and shrieks, all of which connote a blubbering, impotent rage, in comic contrast to the phallic mask, the jockstrap, the grace and ease, the good-humoured cool displayed by Alex. Kubrick shoots the scene so that he keeps the writer's face, distorted by the wide-angle lens, in close-up, to balance the impact of the rape occurring in the middle distance. From the start, the wife is made disagreeable by an upper-class, domineering voice, and with her expensive-looking woollen jumpsuit which she wears without underwear or modesty, she suggests a degree of sexual licentiousness which easily mobilizes (along with envy and class antagonism) frustration and sadistic rage against the life-style of the bourgeois-intellectual jet-set. Such encouragement as the spectator receives to indulge his antipathies is directed towards helping him to rationalize his voyeuristic pleasures. The illicit thought that she is justly served has scarcely been repressed when it is allowed to re-emerge more strongly in the presentation of the catlady, Alex's subsequent target. Kubrick cunningly assembles a host of subliminal prejudices which connote phoney-ness: the pictures on the walls and the giant white plastic phallus spell pseudo-culture, or more exactly, an attempt to pass off 'pornographic' material as 'art' (which, once registered as 'pseud', allows the spectator-voyeur to enjoy it as pornography). The health-farm trendiness is played off against her vulgarities of speech, and when talking to the police on the 'phone the tone and idiom of the landed gentry only exacerbate a feeling of closed, slightly nauseous and suffocating intimacy produced by the presence of the cats, stereotyped symbols for a feline, and therefore aggressive feminity.

One may object that the scene is harmless because it is tongue-in-cheek. But this is to underrate the purpose of caricature in the film, which is quite specific: it allows a powerful discharge of aggressiveness and resentment against the catlady to mask itself and find an outlet when the hero strikes out against her. The attack may seem gratuitous and unprovoked on the surface of the plot, but more than one spectator will experience Alex's behaviour as the retaliation to a threat, implicit only, but substantiated subliminally by the sexual and social overtones which decor, voice, demeanour connote. Far from alienating and interrupting the mechanism of identification the scene seals a guilty complicity of the audience with the action. It is perhaps the most aggressive and sadistic moment in the film, and because of that, Kubrick has constructed it with great care. The rape-murder of the unfortunate victim with her own cherished sculpture is filmed as a montage sequence based on a series of substitutions. Instead of showing a continuous action scene (as in the scene with the writer and his wife) or building up eye-level, medium-shot 'realism' (of the kind Peckinpah uses in *his* rape-scene in *The*

Straw Dogs), Kubrick, when not resorting to extreme wide-angle shots at close range, substitutes a chain of 'metaphoric' images, made up of segments, close-ups and cut-outs from the pictures on the wall — pop art representations of female breasts, genitalia and a masturbation scene. On one level, this substitution, which on the soundtrack is accompanied by electronic music hovering between a scream of pain and of lust, detracts from and obliterates the physicality of the situation by transposing it into a different realm and medium, that of paint, the canvas and the comic-strip. The film, at this crucial point, seems to flinch from its own explicitness and veer towards the formal or abstract play of aggression and violence reminiscent of a Tom & Jerry cartoon. However, this on closer inspection is a strategic measure: the montage of nonrealist fragments into the flow of the action tells a story that is thematically relevant and graphically explicit. It reiterates in pictorial form the message which the preceding passages simply connoted: that the catlady gets what she deserves and probably gratifies a masturbatory fantasy. Kubrick simply flashes on a close-up from the painting of a woman masturbating. This is by no means subtle, except that the scene is over in a matter of seconds, though not before one registers a shot which shows a mouth that is also the female genitalia surrounded by two rows of teeth. The insert can only be explained as an appeal to the male spectators unconscious. In a situation, where any manifestation of overt hostility would be severely censored by feelings of guilt, the film has to aid the spectator in maintaining his identification with the hero, and the subliminal shot of the genital dentures mobilizes a latent psychosis by terrorizing him with the anxiety of a castration fantasy, which allows aggression and destructive rage — sadistic impulses, in short — to flow without an inhibiting check, disguised as they now are as a defensive reflex against — this time on the psychic level — a hallucinated image of aggressive, voracious female sexuality. In other words, while in terms of the plot Alex is a vicious, sadistic, unmotivated sex-maniac and killer, the inner lining of the plot, so to speak, by the actual construction of the pictorial sequence spells an inverse story, in which the victim is made to appear as the real aggressor, while Alex seems justified, having as it were, acted in psychic self-defence. This secondary message, subliminally but visually received, would seem to undermine the primary moral response and one could assume the spectator to be not a little confused, having to cope with conflicting psychic impulses emanating from an emotionally intense experience where aggression, anxiety and guilt are locked together in an archetypally traumatizing situation.

Having produced this trauma, Alex no longer needs to carry the spectator's identification on the basis of a mixed dose of aggression, inhibition and aesthetically transposed release of emotional energy. From the moment he is knocked over the eyes with a milk bottle by one of his Droogs and abandoned to the police, the dynamic symbol of phallic power, retributive vengeance and unstoppable individualism is changed into a Christ-figure embarked on an odyssey of suffering and victimization.

For while in the first part he realizes the aggressive fantasies of the working-class Billy Liars or the frustrated public-school boys from *If . . .* , he now corresponds to the emotional reality of their sense of failure. Alex's stations of the cross begin with the betrayal by his disciples and end with his Golgotha in the upstairs room of a country house, when Mr Alexander torments him with Beethoven's Ninth Symphony into attempting suicide. After his fall from the window, he metaphorically rises from the dead in hospital, and finally ascends, transfigured, 'cured', into the heaven of total instinctual gratification. There is no need to enumerate in detail the frequent references, verbal and visual, to Christ; suffice it to say that the other crucial montage of pictorial rather than filmic elements combines a ferocious-looking Beethoven, a picture of a naked woman, a Christ off the cross duplicated and cut so as to suggest him moving in step with the music, his clenched fist raised in the black power salute, with intermittent close-ups of a crown of thorns on his blood-stained head. Orchestrated by the full volume of the final movement of the Ninth, the scene is a conveniently itemized collage of the main emotional states that the film attempts to merge: aggression, sex, music, exultation and physical pain.

In the context of the steadily escalating violence to which Alex is subjected during the second part — from homosexual probation officer, sadistic police detective, authoritarian prison guard, repressed and unctuous prison chaplain (a character to

whom Burgess in the book had given a more complex and
mitigating role than Kubrick allows him) to brainwashing
scientists and doctors of foreign extraction, two-faced liberal
intellectuals and smoothly cynical politicians — it is perhaps
important to point out that the film, though it explicitly
excludes the hero from any political awareness, unmistakably
suggests to the spectator the political character of his oppres-
sors and tormentors. Alex's antagonists, like his victims,
though more crudely, are virtually without exception
physically unattractive or repulsive, emotionally repressed,
crazy, vindictive, pathologically violent if given half a chance,
and prepared to abuse institutional power for personal ends.
Not only are they caricatures designed to arouse the spectator's
easy antipathy, they are cast as stereotypes whose appearance
can be greeted with the laughter of malicious recognition.
This works out to the benefit of the hero, the only 'human' in
a world of grotesque and monstrous adversaries. Against the
corporate violence of institutions, Alex's simply private,
individualist violence takes on another redeeming feature.

The *mise en scène* in the second part takes account of the
changed rapport of forces. For whereas Kubrick stylizes the
violent behaviour of his hero by a strategy that substitutes,
disperses and masks consequences, his victimization at the
hands of 'society' is undistanced, in fact, calculated to yield
a maximum of 'realism' and verisimilitude and to spare the
spectator nothing of Alex's emotional agonies and physical
suffering. To an aestheticized, formal, abstract representation
of violence in the first part corresponds a visceral 'gut-level'
involvement in the second. Gone is the stylish cool, a blood-and-
tear-stained masochism takes over. To give two examples:
much is made of the clamps applied to Alex's eyes as instruments of torture. Physically, they are, one assumes,
uncomfortable rather than painful, but because the spectator,
himself in a voyeuristic position, is understandably sensitive
about his eyes — a phenomenon which Bunuel had exploited
in the notorious eye-slitting sequence of *Un Chien Andalou*
(1928) — Kubrick can create an equivalent to physical pain
which every spectator feels in his nerve-ends as he watches.
Who, in these circumstances would not give Alex undivided
and keen sympathy? A similar attack on perhaps equally

sensitive parts of the body (when Alex snips with a pair of scissors at Mrs Alexander's nipples) is comically distanced by the pop-art effect of the round holes cut in her red suit, while the consequences, as we are later told but never shown, are of course lethal to the lady. A similar example of Kubrick's two-tier realism is the scene in which another of Alex's victims is given his come-uppance: the old Irish dosser whom the Droogs beat up under the arches, recognizes Alex when the latter is no longer in a position to defend himself. Here a comparison of the *mise en scène* is again instructive; while the scene under the arches is filmed either in long-shot as a montage of shadow and light, or in close-up with Alex's smiling face iridescent in a shower of backlighting, the revenge of the dosser and his cronies is a sheer unending series of close-ups, consisting of nothing but popping eyes and toothless mouths, distorted by fiendish grimaces of impotent anger and pent-up frustration. To underline the message of geriatric ugliness, Alex philosophizes on the sound track about 'old age having a bash at youth'. Here the function of the close-ups and the wide-angle lens (as in previous scenes), is to arouse revulsion on aesthetic rather than moral grounds; the light-and-shadow show of the original beating, followed by a cut to an elaborate stucco ceiling and Rossini's music, removes the spectator as far as possible from any physical immediacy or sense of moral ugliness.

The evidence adduced so far suggests that Kubrick's *mise en scène* is guided by one overriding principle: to maintain identification between hero and spectator at all cost. If this requires distanciation, modernist techniques of collage and pop-art, devices borrowed from slapstick comedy and the animated cartoon — so be it; but then again, if a more old-fashioned realism is called for that gets the spectator in the gut rather than appealing to his head, Kubrick is prepared to put up with what might otherwise appear a serious stylistic inconsistency. Clearly, what the critics admired when they talked about 'distancing', etc., was Kubrick's subservience to the needs of the spectator, in whom the voyeur is in turn gratified, exposed and justified: aggression and guilt, anxiety and frustration which an audience brings to a film that deals with so many powerful psychic fantasies, are carefully balanced and manipulated in terms of involvement and indifference, humour and empathy, cynicism and sentimentality.

Towards this end works a remarkable device in the novel: the hero's language, a form of teenage slang called 'nadsat', which Kubrick takes over. But in the film the distancing effect is much attenuated when compared with the book, where our perception of the violence that takes place is largely transmitted in nadsat. Two features are significant. First, the Russian origin of many of the words which gives them, when pronounced in English, the appearance of diminutives, of belonging to a kind of baby-talk: gooly, itty, lewdies, malenky. This is emphasized where the root word is English: baddiwad, jammiwam, guttiwuts, eggiweg. Secondly, the areas of experience where nadsat is most inventive describe the human body and its functions: rooker=arm, groodies=breasts, rot=mouth, litso=face, krovvy=blood, sharries=buttocks, etc. A sentence where Alex describes his encounter with the catlady, for instance, runs like this: 'you could viddy her veiny mottled litso going purplewurple where I'd landed the old noga.' The associations provoked by the words distract from the reality of the action, and the effect is a highly euphemistic language about the reality of physical violence. The film has to show this violence and therefore cannot rely on these pleasant circumlocutions, but not wishing to forego such an instrument of manipulation, Kubrick, as indicated, invents his own pop-art picturegrammes and uses them as inserts. Baby-talk is replaced by the strip cartoon.

One may wonder why persistence of identification and the delicate handling of visualization are apparently such crucial strategies. The answer lies in the nature of the psychic material that the film is attempting to bring into play, though it is not altogether easy to follow the relation between the overt plot and the covert fantasies it sets in motion. What would be needed is a sequential account of the narrative situations and a typology of the functions they codify, clearly a task that cannot be undertaken here. Even a casual glance, however, indicates what is central on a thematic as well as an emotional level: fear of being powerless and paralysed in a hostile, aggressive world, where the reasons and motives for violence are hidden, if not wholly unknowable, and where disaster can strike out of the blue and no place is secure. This is thematized in complementary fashion: in Alex's raids on 'real people's houses', as the catlady puts it, and in the Ludovico treatment, the effect of which is to induce a sickness caused by one's own aggression, entailing loss of control over one's bodily movements and the consequent hazard of victimization without the ability to defend oneself and hit back. Whatever their justification in real life, both are fears that the spectator can readily identify with on the basis of his specific experience as part of a cinema audience: they correspond to his vulnerability and passivity. For this reason, dependency and helplessness, however, can also give rise to a pleasurable fantasy associated with the security of a prenatal state. On the face of it, the film would seem to leave no scope for portraying this attractive prospect. But the scene in hospital with Alex up to his chin in plaster and spoon-fed by nurse, parents, doctor and ministerial visitors pictures rather convincingly a child's fantasy-fulfilment of just such a return to maternal dependence, made particularly satisfying by the fact that it is Alex's tormentors who have to look after him and beg his forgiveness. Clearly, here is the stuff that fairy-tales are made of, and the film skilfully plays on the ambivalence of this fantasy in an earlier scene, when Alex, reduced to a lamentable sight by his former droogs turned policemen, is carried over the same threshold of Mr Alexander's 'Home' where he had previously forced his entry. Extreme aggression and extreme helplessness are thus graphically correlated, and the desire to regress would seem to demand compensatory fantasies of power – of the kind that Alex's 'horrorshow ultra-violence' amply gratifies. In this context, the otherwise curious espiode involving Alex's parents takes on special significance, for here the fantasy of dependence, of 'home', is actualized in its traumatic aspects, when the boy-hero is excused from becoming adult and independent by showing the mother guilty of withdrawing her love, a guilt symbolized by sibling rivalry, for the lodger has obviously been adopted as the parents' true son and as the Oedipal lover of the mother. Because it is one of the funniest scenes in the movie one might overlook its psychic function: it sanctions and motivates retroactively Alex's savage rage against those who have 'homes', and explains his ambivalent attitude to the long list of father-figures which the film parades.

Thus, while the overt logic of the plot argues in terms of 'you have done wrong, therefore we punish you' ('Violence is a very horrible thing. That's what you're learning now. Your body is learning it.' — 'You've made others suffer. It's only right that you should suffer proper.'), the logic of the central fantasy reverses this order into 'I have been unloved, abandoned, robbed of my home and identity, therefore I have every right to avenge myself, by being in turn violent and helpless.' It is the latter logic that the film in its emotional structure exemplifies, and another reason why the audience seems prepared to forgive Alex any amount of violence. In this sense, the order of the narrative sequence reverses the logic of the fantasies. Cause and effect are inverted and what appears gratuitous is motivated, and vice versa. This is made plausible by the neat circularity which the end bestows on the film as a whole. On the level of the fantasies, the contradiction between loss of control and the need for security, between destructive aggression and affirmation of libido, has been resolved in terms of a sado-masochist bind, where the punishment that the hero metes out to the 'real people' and the victimization he is subject to in return are accepted as inevitable and recurrent phases of a circular movement. What is being carefully eliminated is the third term: who punishes the father-figures, the law, the monstrous guardians of society? With this question conveniently erased, the spectator is encouraged to project his aggression and introject his guilt-feelings, his desire for instinctual gratification and his fears about the consequences. In other words, where the plot installs a triumphantly ironic ending, the fantasies seem to confirm a (neurotic) internalization of conflicting demands.

This points directly to the nature of the political theme with which Burgess is concerned. Faithfully preserved by Kubrick in the film, the novel is focused on the argument about individual freedom and the dangerous forces that encroach upon it. However, the moral centre of the story is not represented by a character (in the book, at least, Mr Alexander and the prison chaplain together formulate an intentionally inadequate version of it; the film dispenses with that), but is, instead, displaced and distorted. Extreme variants of individualism, whether aggressive like Alex's or defensive like that of the people barricaded in their various 'homes', are pitted against each other or confronted with equally extreme forms of social control, interventionism and behaviourist social engineering. What is posited as an argument is that if libidinous individualism and post-Freudian laissez-faire has its way, social anarchy ensues, and the state will show its totalitarian fangs. In fact, as it emerges, the argument about the double invasion of privacy cleverly runs together several normally opposed ideological stances: it combines liberal misgivings about state control and state intervention with conservative demands for a strong government of law and order, while casting doubt in general on the viability of parliamentary democracy and its executive institutions. Or, to put it another way, superimposed on an Orwellian nightmare is a Graham Greene story about Christ and redemption in the slums, the whole designed to recall the idiom of a Marcuse making up to East End skinheads for having a bash at 'the system'. What seems probable in this ideological *jeu d'esprit* is that the target is the Welfare State and the idea of technology as a form of social planning — both associated in Britain with the brand of socialism which the Labour government tried to practice in the 1960s.

That the film is not a serious political analysis is clear, nor does it pretend to offer one. On the other hand, neither is it as innocently above politics as some critics have asserted. The most charitable thing one can say is that neither Burgess nor Kubrick go out of their way to avoid confusion. This does not mean they are neutral or objective: what is offered, is a successful blend of prejudices culled from various points of the political spectrum whose common denominator is frustration — which perhaps explains why all the political options that the film presents seem equally undesirable, thereby locking the argument on the rational, discursive level into a series of contradictions: if you want to live for pleasure you have to put up with aggression, one man's meat is another man's poison; if you want a safe home, you have to accept Big Brother; if you want technology, you have to put up with mad scientists; if you want total individualism, you have to accept the law of the jungle; if you want the Welfare State, don't complain about hooligans and layabouts; etc. The reasoning may be primitive, but once one accepts the either/or logic underlying it, it is hard to disagree with, or rather, the very structure of the film makes it impossible to do so.

For the 'violence', it now appears, has its chief function not in the way it constitutes one of the ostensible subjects of the film (it accepts violence as 'given'), nor in order to produce a sense of the physicality of violence (only the masochistic side is allowed to 'bite'), but to provide the kinetic energy that supplies the narrative with a narrowly dualistic logic, and imposes it as natural and inevitable. Violence is an emotional form of reasoning, one that because of its emphatic nature brooks little argument, eliminates the nuances, excludes the middle term and progresses by sharpening the issues into confrontation and opposition. Thus, the movie gives emotional resonance and authority to what may well be casuistry and jesuitical logic. As a rhetorical device physical violence, just like real-life violence, stops further discussion and shifts the debate onto another terrain. It acts as a means of displacement — here into the realm of the psychic. This has to be borne in mind when one considers the way the plot is essentially didactic. Unlike the conventional realist narrative, where the initial situation progressively unfolds its ramifications, which the plot explores and organizes, *A Clockwork Orange* is satirical in structure, aggressive, working by juxtaposition, analogy and exaggeration — except that it shrouds its satirical bias elaborately in paradox and a balancing 'objectivity', i.e. the ideological aesthetic underpinning the realist mode of fictional discourse. What the plot symmetry accomplishes for Kubrick is to reiterate an apparently moral dilemma, not by varying the terms and examining implications, but by reinforcing the contradictions. It suggests causal connections where on the face of it there is only a purely formal play of repetition and reversal (the Irish dosser recognizing Alex, the droogs reappearing as policemen, Alex falling into Mr Alexander's hands, etc.) which may yield irony of a sort, but which, in the absence of a point of view organizing the narrative perspective (in the book, a conservative Catholic eschatology) takes on the portents of a somehow significant poetic justice, whose manipulative pay-off is entirely on the subliminal, unconscious level.

Confronted with the 'choice' between the amoral, hedonistic, libidinous terrorism of Alex, and the totalitarian, institutional terrorism of brainwashing scientists, the spectator, in an instantly ideological reflex, sides with the 'individual' against the 'system', and opts for Alex, as being the lesser of two evils, even though the film gleefully points out that this is jumping from the frying-pan into the fire. The truth is, he is given no alternative, for what he has been persuaded to accept as an emergency situation is clearly a vicious circle, made to appear so by the verbal and visual rhetoric which avant-garde art and literature has put in the hands of advertising agencies, and their cinematic disciples.

The spectator is thus being tossed about between two kinds of violence which, instead of breaking up the ideological nexus and dismantling the false inevitability implied, merely welds them together more compactly. To opt for Alex at the end means to be plunged headlong into the psychic fantasies which he symbolizes, for the triumph of the hero deals the final blow to the spectator: betrayed of any real insight, baffled by his own conflicting attitudes, he is confirmed in his suspicion that whatever his own fantasies of power or aspirations to freedom, he had better keep them to himself rather than try and live them out. Quite logically, Alex's 'cure' is represented by an image which within the film itself has the status of a private fantasy: in what looks like a vast bed of feathers Alex is seen cavorting with a naked lady, to the approving applause of elegantly dressed bystanders while in 'reality' he is still helpless and passive in his plaster casts. Along with the hero, the spectator is encouraged to indulge in a purely personal world of the imagination, which in actual terms spells adaptation to the powers that be, just as Alex, in his 'new understanding' with his friend, the Minister, has learnt that it is to his advantage to go along with the system rather than oppose it. What looks superficially like a scandalously immoral ending conceals a very conformist message. Incited by the narrative structure which promises rebellion, but carried along by the persistence of identification to share a neurotic ambivalence,

the liberation that the spectator is given points only in the
direction of internalizing regressive experiences: the aesthetics
of fun-and-consumption, masochistic dependence, infantile
helplessness — with the compensatory fantasies of total,
apocalyptic destruction. Why then, if it insinuates so much
hysteria, has the film nonetheless such an undeniable appeal?

Why is it popular? In one sense, the question presents no
particular problem. The audience brings to the film a very real
fund of dissatisfaction and boredom (precisely the defensive
but peremptory insistence that all they want is 'entertainment')
which the spectacle acknowledges, and on which indeed it
cannot but speculate. This dissatisfaction is mobilized by a
mixture of cynicism and sentimentality. In the film's cynicism
the spectator recognizes the negative experiences, the failures
and disappointments of his own everyday life; a hostile impulse
is allowed to avenge itself on a hated and incomprehensible
world. On the other hand, the sentimentality enshrines and
reinstates those feelings, hopes and wish-fulfilling dreams whose
impossibility and failure the cynicism confirms. This in itself
is a vicious circle, but one that gives pleasure because of the
way it validates the spectator's personal experience ('yes, I
know, that's how it is') — a validation that functions as an
important criterion of realism in the cinema: it 'feels' true to
life (i.e. to one's negative response). Whether the strategy is one
of acting out recognizable sentiments and homegrown ambitions
in exotic locations or high places (the formula of a certain
type of melodrama and adventure of film of the '40s and '50s)
in which case the cynicism is replaced by the accents of a
tragic pathos — which, too, is a sign of spectatorial self-pity,
or whether it offers more overtly aggressive power fantasies,
as in the gangster film of the film *noir*, the compensatory
relation between affirmation and negation, dreams of self-
fulfilment and the certain knowledge of failure, impenitent
optimism and soft-core pessimism persists, and is reactivated
every time. *Love Story* and *The Wild Bunch*, nostalgia movies
and brutal cop thrillers, codify the same substratum of
exasperated longing forever cheated. In this sense, the
emotional structure of *A Clockwork Orange* gratifies a complex

set of fantasies, whose neurotic core is experienced subliminally as realistic, because it exploits the latent moral and emotional nihilism of its audience. It confirms a life of frustration, guilt-feelings and discontent, it justifies a cynical and pessimistic apathy. One does well to insist on the 'realistic' dimension of the popular movie, since critics of popular culture have for too long talked about 'soap operas', the 'dream factory', etc., as if what characterized 'entertainment' was its unreality, its lack of realism: this would seem a grave error. The realism to be found in the popular cinema is a negative one, is in fact an emotionally coded protest against life as it is lived, and therein lies its potential for liberation and its manipulative power.

A Clockwork Orange contains both, and it entertains because the fantasies it stimulates and nourishes are, as I have tried to show, essentially regressive, pleading against rationality and inquiry and for the security of immobility, for the passive enjoyment of maternal dependence, while bottled up inside is the rage for chaos and destruction. The film, despite its 'violence' relaxes and entertains because it posits Oedipal situations (relating to the law, the father, the system — all clearly guilty though never punished) but resolves them in an 'oral' mode of parasitic dependence: it collapses complex situations into dualistic patterns, and thereby relieves anxiety. As such, this might almost be a definition of 'entertainment'. The general strategy, therefore, does not distinguish A Clockwork Orange from countless other films, except that because of the explicitness of the aggression, the insistence on victimization it gives particularly full scope to the contradictory impulses inherent in the sado-masochistic bind. Thus it gets much closer to the sources of taboos and provides a correspondingly greater pleasure when these ambivalences are successfully managed and translated into formal-dynamic terms. Less apparent is the tendency towards neurosis and infantilism that it aggravates, and thus reinstates as a recurrent need, an addiction.

What does distinguish A Clockwork Orange and makes its popularity both more problematic and significant is the way the ideological aspects are brought to the surface. It boldly seems to confront overtly political and controversial material, in a spirited, authorative manner. Yet its language of violence

effectively depoliticizes the issues by switching back to a
rhetoric of affect and overdetermination, which on the level of
formal elaboration shapes and sustains an aesthetics of
ambiguity and whimsical paradox. In a movie appearing as a
social and political satire this can only mean that the impulse
to reveal is short-circuited, and replaced by a chain of dis-
placements. The authoritative tone — the 'unflagging pace' of
which one reviewer spoke — gives a semblance of commotion
and energetic development, but this simply serves to disguise
the fact that everything stays in place, or as the phrase goes,
the 'status quo' is maintained, though as one can see, this does,
nowadays, take some effort: in short, it requires 'violence'. To
a forcibly dictated narrative logic of an either/or dualism that
paralyses the intellect (though it pleases the senses with the
neat formal patterns it generates out of heterogeneous
material) corresponds a dense ideological smokescreen. The
function of this exercise is to provide an emotional grid where
frustration is allowed to surface and to be accommodated in
the fictional narrative, only to be the more efficiently displaced
into areas where the real contradictions resolve themselves in
witty incongruities and ironic parallels.

In order to do this successfully, the aesthetic strategies
themselves must be sources of pleasure. And so it is not
surprising to see why critics laud Kubrick's craftmanship, his
precision, his perfectionism because it is precisely the neat
technocratic functioning of the machine, the sharp economy
of the aesthetic apparatus, the chrome-and-plastic polish of
Kubrick's (di-)stance which ensures that the form by itself will
give pleasure. The futuristic trappings of modernity appeal to a
functionalist, technicist imagination which flatters the dominant
cool. The concentration on surfaces and outlines — achieved by
the tactical use of the wide-angle lens — gives a crystalline
hardness which is itself aggressive since it has sealed itself off
from contact by an emphatic construction of symmetry and
order — though as has been seen, this clearness of outline is
ultimately in the service of ambiguity and evasion. The film,
emotionally very provocative, designed to get under the
spectator's skin and to mobilize his unconscious, gives itself
the formal appearance of objectivity, autonomy and the pure
aesthetic perfection of closure. This 'object'-ness, because of

its intense psychic component, is actually an estranged subjectivity and mirrors the situation of the fetishist; the film thus makes the spectator experience himself as a voyeur, an omnipresent, distanced master of the spectacle, seeing but not seen, although in this position of privilege and apparent power, he is the spectator of his own victimization, to which he consents by allowing Alex to become the agent of his own alienation. Many a spectator will experience Alex's violence not as gratuitous, though he may be hard put to verbalize the exact nature of his response. What the audience greets with the laughter of recognition are the hostile, aggressive impulses, which relieve self-hatred and constitute an admission of impotence — social and emotional — in a universe that has long ago accepted the individual's expendability. Not surprisingly, *A Clockwork Orange* gratifies the negative self-image of a despairing, bankrupt liberalism.

What remains is the contact which the film makes with the real, the positive dimension, so to speak, of its negative realism. In order to manipulate the spectator successfully, as has been said, it needs to pay attention to his sense of the real. And so, beneath the massive distortions, one can see the outlines of another reality, the kind of reality which the film's ideology is attempting to disguise. For this we have to return to the political argument of both book and film. One of the crucial aspects of the problem of individual freedom is its operation in the economic sphere, the freedom to contract one's labour force, and by extension, personal energy and initiative. Now, Alex and his droogs are depicted as nonproductive member of society, they are the parasites which the Welfare State is so often accused of having created. Nonetheless, they possess almost total economic freedom, because they rob, steal, rape and appropriate according to need and whim. What is odd about them is that they do this neither for purposes of self-enrichment or accumulation, nor are they apparently motivated by greed, hatred, the profit motive, or lust for political or social power. They do it simply to increase their spending power in the fun-and-consumption game. Their violence is scandalous because it seems gratuitous, but it seems gratuitous because none of the motives accepted by bourgeois society (i.e. greed, etc., which it recognizes in the members of its own class and has found ways of making ideologically and emotionally plausible) are present. On the other hand, because of the ruthless logic of their fun-morality Alex and his droogs exhibit the behaviour of the ideal consumer from the point of view of the producer: indeed they are a parodistic mirror image of the affluent society and its most successful members, for they enjoy an apparently unlimited supply of fast cars, hi-fi equipment, records, fashionable gear, women, drugs, drink, kicks — in other words, all the things which the ordinary person works for so hard and is persuaded by advertising to make the measure of his achievement in the general pursuit of happiness. Except that of course, Alex and his friends don't work for it, but accede to this consumer's paradise by the simple expedient of 'violence' and 'crime'.

The film sets 'violence' at the place in the logical chain where the spectator knows there to be the day-to-day drudgery of a probably meaningless job. The 'gratuity' of the violence in this perspective is outrageous, because it suggests that most forbidden of subjects — the gratuitousness of one's work and the reality of one's exploitation. Perhaps it is here that one can see most clearly through a likely chink in the film's ideological armour: an added attraction of the film might lie in the way it momentarily illumines the screen of consciousness with the promise of real liberation, only then to foreclose it the more definitely. The real spectacle of violence — the job, the factory, the office, the family — is blanked out in the film, and into the blank is flashed the individual, anarchic physical violence of the hooligan, and the story-book nightmare violence of mad scientists and totalitarian politics. The panic fear of the physical assault on the one hand, and the equally panic fear of autocratic-technocratic state is mobilized to occult the emotional violence of the nuclear family, the economic violence of monopoly capitalism, the technological violence of production-line labour, the aesthetic violence of consumer terrorism.

This way, the manifestations of frustrated aggression and anxiety are taken into the film as acknowledged, but inexplicably 'given' facts, while their social and economic sources are carefully masked, indeed the causality gap is overcompensated by a violence, a form of direct physical aggression (rape, mugging, breaking and entering) which is particularly heavily censored, tabooed and fraught with guilt-feelings. In other words, the language of violence in the film does not indicate the warning signals of a conscience-stricken critical intelligence (as in some playwrights, e.g. Edward Bond), it is, in *A Clockwork Orange*, employed to induce a moral shock, a crisis in which the central proposition about liberation is abstracted and shifted towards regressive substitutes of the fun-and-games type, while the use of violence, the analysis of its social function (we know that the Labour government doesn't use the Ludovico treatment, so there is no analytic thrust in *that* piece of satire) is screened from those areas where it actually operates every day, and where violent means bring about real changes instead of merely imaginary ones. The spectator, constantly tempted to vent aggression and incited to an orgy of destruction, is remorselessly directed towards targets (women, the old, the defenseless, the economically weak), who are *de facto* in our society objects of victimization, but of a victimization that goes ideologically unacknowledged and is invested with feelings of guilt and shame.

The violence of *A Clockwork Orange* has spilled more ink than blood. On the face deemed subversive and dangerous to the fabric of the nation by apostles of 'morality', and hailed by liberal intellectuals as the triumph of style over subject, it turns out on closer inspection to be a perfect means of terrorizing the spectator into adaptation and docility, by once more tabooing the possible image of his own liberation. He is being programmed to put up with the real violence he suffers in his waking life, to internalize it, and to resign himself to it as inescapable. Perhaps one might say that 'violence' in *A Clockwork Orange*, and one needs to resist generalization on this, rather than tempting the spectator to sadism is finally more efficient by turning victims into masochists.

10

The Dilemma of the Communicators

Stuart Hood

Professional communicators are middlemen and men in the middle — mediators who discharge their role on a number of different levels. Thus in the field of broadcast journalism they mediate between individuals, whether they be public figures or private citizens, and the radio or television audience; in a wider sense they perform the same function where organized social groups — political parties, trade unions, employers' federations, churches and so on — are concerned. As representatives and short- or long-term employees of broadcasting institutions they mediate between these organizations and the society which has created them in that their activity as communicators must be an interpretation of, and consonant with, the proclaimed policies of their employers. In a more general sense, they mediate between society (conceived of as the global audience for their broadcasts) and the broadcasting institution itself, as part of that necessary process of self-reflexion through which a society creates and sustains its own image and reinforces its own ideology. To be a middleman in any of the senses set out above is an uncomfortable situation, but one which appears ineluctable. Perhaps it is the essential nature of the task of communicating in the mass media of radio and television (the press, I believe, faces other problems) to confront the communicators with a number of dilemmas which are in part political, in part moral, in part concerned with those limitations on expression which any society places on what may be said or presented by these media — in short, with questions of 'taste'. It is noticeable that, when professional broadcasters from different social systems meet, they tend to discuss in much the same terms the same problems and express the same frustrations and doubts — a fact which is less the demonstration of some convergence theory than a demonstration of the similarity between the restraints society, any society, imposes on its mass media.

Naturally the areas in which the specific problems faced by the communicators arise must overlap, for 'taste', moral judgements and political decisions are not totally distinct and a judgement in one area will be influenced by considerations derived from other apparently remote factors. There are, however, certain situations familiar to those who work in the documentary and news fields in particular which present the programme maker — usually a producer, director or reporter — with difficulties which he must frequently overcome alone and without much time for reflection. One such problem is concerned with the relationship the programme maker develops with the individuals or groups of individuals who provide the raw material on which he works by selection and editing. The problem most often discussed concerns his activities as a mediator whose announced aim is to transmit, on edited film or tape or on both together, to a mass audience his view of what is interesting, 'relevant', or important in what these men or women have expressed to him — his view of what is worth showing of the material his camera has been able to record of their appearance, expressions, modes of behaviour, their dress and the surroundings in which they live and work.

There is the question, for instance, of how far one should go in helping a subject to frame his or her thoughts in a sufficiently coherent form for them to be recorded and reproduced, given the fact that both materials (tape, film) and time (the director's, the camera crew's and the subject's) are necessarily limited. The difficulty arises because the subject may be strongly affected by the amount of equipment brought into a familiar environment for filming, by the physical discomfort of the lights, by the number of persons in the crew, by the overwhelming presence of the camera or microphone. In such circumstances, the subject may prove incapable of repeating relatively simple formulations arrived at in the preliminary discussions conducted before the irruption of the recording crew. The degree of inter-

vention in such cases goes far beyond any simple parallel to the
Heisenberg principle, which covers the scientist's intervention
in the physical world. The kind of question that arises is — to
quote a specific instance from my own experience — how far it
is legitimate to help an inarticulate, depressed woman in the
slums of south London to formulate her interesting and very
relevant (to the subject of the programme) views on the
behaviour of the police where working-class adolescents are
concerned? Totally intimidated by the camera, she had to be
prompted throughout and coached to repeat phrases and
sentences which she had undoubtedly formulated in ordinary
conversation but was now incapable of repeating spontaneously.
What was recorded on film was 'true'; the real truth, however,
was her silence when the shot was called and the camera and
sound recorder began to turn.

There is a further social and human problem with which
makers of documentary programmes are familiar. It is posed
by the curiously close relationship they may develop with the
subjects of a particular programme and their necessary involvement even as outsiders (mediators) in the circumstances of their
subject's lives and fates. Although he may not always be conscious of it, the programme maker arrives with the authority
and prestige of the medium he works in and the organization
he represents behind him. It was not unnatural, for instance,
that the woman in the south London slum should have come,
in the course of several days involvement, to believe that I
might be able to help her by persuading her landlord to give
her other accommodation than the damp-ridden flat she occupied.
The communicator, however, is not primarily concerned with
resolving the problems of the subject but with communicating
the facts of the case or those relevant to the programme in
hand to his audience. He is, in this sense, parasitic on his
subjects whom he, in a literal sense, exploits and then abandons,
having merely by exploring their problems and listening to their
woes, aroused expectations which in the nature of things — that
is to say the constraints of his work situation and the social
structures within which he operates — he is unable to fulfil.
His task completed, shooting over, he will move on to other
areas of interest. Exceptions to this pattern are rare. Nor is the
organization for which he works concerned in the solution of

such problems. Indeed it is likely to consider that the discussion
of how to solve them within the framework of the programme
is unacceptable for political and policy reasons. It is not difficult
to imagine a society, however, in which the examination of
social problems went hand-in-hand with attempts to remedy them.
This presupposes a social system which would permit the mass
media to discuss solutions on the air and to urge the social
services, for example, to take the necessary action by direct
communication with these institutions. The problem is largely
determined by the defined function of the mass media in a
given society — the role it has been allotted. Political realism,
however, must suggest that in any society there will be areas in
which the proposal of solutions by the mass media which have
no real constituency, will encounter resistance by the institutions
involved; the role of the mass media is therefore likely to
remain more or less circumscribed. This appears to be the true
reason for the difference between the type of investigative
journalism which the press in liberal democracies is permitted
to carry out, within certain limits, and the more restricted type
of inquiry which is possible on radio or television. A 'public'
medium is by definition a restricted one; its role is noninter-
ventionist.

The difficulties encountered in the editing process, which
involves active mediation between the subject of the programme
and the audience, are usually experienced by programme
makers in what they define as 'sensitive' areas. 'Sensitive' areas
are those where the activities of the broadcasting institutions
bring them into contact with the dominant forces in society —
economic interests, political parties, ideological groups. These
are the very forces which have set up and which finance and
control the broadcasting institutions, constraining their
freedoms by methods which vary in sophistication and
intricacy but are always and necessarily operative. The institutions have over the course of time, partly empirically and
partly as the result of conscious deliberation, evolved codes,
which are not usually formally defined, for discussing the
activities of those dominant interests. These codes, which
are obviously elaborated on the premise that the dominant
institutions of society are open only to minor criticism, relate
to both the language and terminology which may be used in

describing the policies and functions of these institutions, and the images which may be used in presenting them in pictorial terms. Thus, to give an obvious example, in the West it is inconceivable that a serious programme would be allowed to employ terms drawn from the Marxist tradition: only those acceptable to the dominant political and economic theories of a capitalist society would be used. In consequence, it is unthinkable that the Chancellor of the Exchequer should be cross-examined by a Marxist economist whatever his eminence in his field. It is important to note that these codes are not evolved by the broadcasting institutions in isolation nor do they depend entirely on the fact that the executives of these organiz- ations have an understanding, based on class and education, of the limits of the codes. The codes are evolved by a process of involving the complicity of representatives of the dominant interests, who, when they take part in radio or television programmes, define the terms in which a particular subject may be discussed and constrain the communicators to adopt the same terms.

When the programme makers come to mediate between their subjects and the audience the same codes become operative, those who use them firmly believing that when applying them they are making commonsense or even instructive judge- ments. At the moment of recording, whether on film or tape, the codes define the form of the questions, the language in which they are couched, and the propositions underlying the questions. During the editing process they are applied to determine what portions of the material (replies to questions during an interview, statements to camera, conversations) are interesting and germane to the theme, and which must be suppressed as 'uninteresting' a term which frequently means impermissible in their formulation or in their terms of reference because they are not those of the dominant codes. It is a growing awareness of how the codes are applied that has led trade unionists in situations of confrontation — strikes, picket lines, sit-ins — to refuse to appear before cameras to be interviewed. Whether Marxist or not, they know that their praxis, which determines what they have to say about their conditions and aspirations, is unlikely to provide answers that fit the codes of the communicators, who, for their part, are baffled by answers which they cannot 'read' and which they dismiss as strange, unintelligible and wayward. The code of the working class does not coincide with the class-determined code of the communicators, whose mediation becomes ineffective or distorting.

The communicators may, however, encounter difficulties in another direction. They arise, as Stuart Hall has pointed out in a recent paper, when there is a clash between the hegemonic code and the professional code, the latter being the code that governs the conventions the programme makers have elaborated in the development of the capabilities of the media and which 'applies criteria . . . of a technico-practical nature'.[1] Using these criteria, the professionals make certain judgements about the efficacy of their mediation and the methods that should be used to interest the audience and its attention. In general, the assumption is that a programme should have a dramatic shape — a beginning, a middle and an end — together with points of tension and resolution. When applied to the behaviour of groups in society, these criteria may lead to the attempt to create or to simulate confrontations from which derives the sensationalism and trivialization, of which the communicators are so often accused. If the procedures of the communicators — working within a specific tradition and a specific convention to which there are, naturally, alternatives — run counter to the interests of the dominant groups (politicians, clergy and economic interests), then the organizations responsible come under pressure and criticism. The situation is even more serious in those instances when the communicators deliberately break the codes because they believe that the results will be amusing, startling or critical. It was one of the strengths of the BBC's 'satirical' programmes, beginning with *That Was the Week That Was*, that they broke both the accepted codes of visual representation and the accepted codes of language, presenting establishment figures in unacceptable visual forms and discussing their activities in unacceptable linguistic terms.

Conservatively minded politicians from within the consensus attribute such breaking of the codes to political radicalism at work within the broadcasting organizations. The process is

[1] Stuart Hall, *The Television Discourse*, Education and Culture no. 25, The Council for Cultural Cooperation of the Council of Europe.

actually an expression of what Colin Seymour-Ure, discussing the role of *Private Eye* (several of whose contributors were active in the satirical programmes) has called, 'the politics of the Fool'; the Fool, he points out, has a love/hate relationship to the King and is basically supportive of the King's dignity and power.[2] In spite of the complaints and cries of outrage that greeted the satirical programmes, the fact that they were broadcast at all was a sign of the confidence of sections of the dominant groups (including the communicators) that the social fabric was strong enough to accept the breaking of the codes without suffering any real harm.

The broadcasting organizations, I have suggested, are engaged in an activity that allows a society to examine its own image and to strengthen its assumptions about itself. In this sense the communicators are engaged in the business of elaborating and developing the ideology of that society or of the dominant elements in it. As we have seen, when discussing the role of the programme maker in the fields of news and documentary programmes, the communicators, for the most part, themselves accept that ideology and require no instruction on how to interpret it to society. The producer of light entertainment or drama is equally sure of his procedures; if he were not he would find himself in constant difficulty, unable to determine what jokes, allusions, what dramatic situations (and what resolutions of them) can be safely — in terms of general acceptability — placed before the mass audience. It is noteworthy in this connection that the main opponents of satirical programmes within the BBC were executives and producers in light entertainment — men who could interpret with the utmost precision the limits of 'taste' and whose guiding principle was (and is) the depoliticization of all situations. They are unaware that depoliticizing is in itself a political act and would argue that the guying of working men and trade unions is permissible and nonpolitical because their programmes are 'only entertainment'. Yet it is in entertainment programmes and dramatic programmes at the level of straightforward narrative — serials and series on radio and television — that the audience is most frequently and most assiduously invited to reflect on the nature of society and

[2] Colin Seymour-Ure, *The Political Impact of the Mass Media* (London 1974).

to approve it. It is here that the clichés of sexual and familial relationships and of relationships between communities are reproduced for approval or disapproval. It is here that the rewards of our society and the taboos it operates are most clearly set out. The outcry over the 'kitchen sink' drama in the early 1960s was less due to the quality of the plays, which was uneven, than to the fact that the characters portrayed in them so frequently denied the aims and values of society.

There are situations, however, when what begins as a case of breaking the codes becomes transformed with time to a restatement of the codes in new terms acceptable to important interests. An interesting example to study is that of the BBC's police series which began with *Z Cars* and developed into *Softly Softly* and *Task Force*. The original concept was that of a series of dramatic programmes which would discard the codes used in the anodyne *Dixon of Dock Green* and, in doing so, make a statement about the life and activities of the police more consonant with the experience ordinary people and, in particular, working-class people have of them. The first programme was badly received by the authorities. The chief constable who had collaborated closely and had given extensive facilities for the filming of the opening programme was made aware of Home Office disapproval; he himself was deeply disturbed by what he saw on the screen. The first programme showed, for instance, a policeman smoking on duty and another quarrelling with his wife. These were unacceptable representations of the policeman as he figured in the minds of high police officials. Curiously his lieutenants, perhaps more closley in touch with the realities of the situation and certainly more aware of the possibilities offered by the programmes, were enthusiastic for the concept, which came to enjoy the enthusiastic support and approval of the police force as a whole. The most probable interpretation of this change of heart is that the police came to understand that the portrayal of policemen on the beat and in police stations as determined, tough, and not beyond using subterfuge, was a flattering one. *Z Cars* and its successors validated police behaviour in a period when the methods of Dixon were no longer — if they ever were — the norm. The police series, in which the police themselves continue to participate with enthusiasm, have legitimated the toughness of their behaviour and rendered it acceptable.

It is because they are obliged to operate in areas where social forces of real power come into play, that the task of the communicator is at times difficult and — in extreme circumstances — dangerous. They are liable to come under intense pressures not only from forces outside their organizations but from within, from the upper echelons of the organizations and the bodies that control them such as boards of governors, advisory councils, etc. External pressures are frequently resented and resisted in the name of professional independence or in terms of the defence of the broadcasting institutions, which — in the more extreme formulations of the theory — are thought of as being part of an independent estate of the realm and as such able to treat with government or opposition on equal terms. The institutions are seen, that is to say, as the custodians and protectors of a version of truth, objectively arrived at, to which politicians and other groups do not have access. From this it is an easy step to claiming that they are socially and politically neutral within society. The BBC, in particular, proclaims its independence in these terms, basing its argument on the somewhat tenuous grounds that the licence revenue is an independent source of income and, as such, guarantees the independence of the institution. This sophistical argument obscures the fact that the BBC, like any other mass media organization, must be subject to political restraints, must respect the political consensus obtaining in society, must not permit its programme makers to break the hegemonic code — or only in 'nonsensitive' areas — although it may, from time to time, allow a strictly rationed dose of dissenting opinion to shore up its claim that it is able to act without constraint.

To complain that the great organs of broadcasting are not free, or that the spectrum of opinion exposed by them is limited, is a liberal confusion. Such is the nature of central, state-founded, state-sanctioned broadcasting organizations. There are those who argue that it is possible to imagine broadcasting systems based on alternative methods of distribution of the signal, centred on small social units rather than the country at large, democratically controlled, equipped with less complicated, less expensive equipment. It is certainly true that examples from Canada of the responses of ordinary people to a camera crew whose code is congruent with their own demonstrate that the problems of mediation which confront the organizational communicator can be overcome in some cases. The same holds good of interviews which have been conducted by a politically sympathetic video crew in this country during strikes. The quality of the response of the men and women interviewed is totally different from what one might see on a television screen at home. But is is a form of utopianism to believe that portapacks and cable television will necessarily introduce some sort of democratic communication. Local power interests are not necessarily less powerful than national ones – they are indeed often part of larger national interests. The restraints on the communicators are – except in cases where programmes are shown only on closed circuit to small groups – likely to be as real and as acute as in the national situation. Communication is a social activity; the communicator undertakes a social function from which he cannot escape.

What follows from this view is the belief that those who choose to work in the mass media of radio and television and to be employed by the great broadcasting institutions must be prepared to accept the dominant codes of the society which founded these institutions and controls them. Provided the communicators accept the dominant codes of the institutions and the society they may be allowed, if they are fortunate and the political climate is favourable, a certain degree of creative freedom – that is, a certain freedom of choice as to how they work within the professional code; but they will not be allowed to challenge the dominant code or the social assumptions on which it is ultimately based. A challenge to these assumptions is impossible within the established institutions. At most there exists the possibility of a certain desultory sniping at occasional targets. If there are exceptions to this rule they are provided by the opportunities which occur in times of social change or of revolution, when the constraints may be loosened and the codes can therefore be broken – not safely, for the consequences are dangerous, but certainly broken. One historic example is the part played by Czech radio and television in 1968 during the Russian invasion. Indeed the 'guerilla' action – as it was called – whereby transmission of radio and television

reports continued even after the tanks were in the streets of
Prague was the logical continuation of a process which had begun
more circumspectly a couple of years previously, when the mass
media were able, with the connivance of their chief executives,
to present to the mass audience politicians and spokesmen who
were not acceptable to the Establishment, were indeed opposed
to it in varying degrees, but were able by exposure on the media
to win support from the public at large. Such a situation is
possible only in a situation where there is a certain balance of
power within the dominant groups of a society and the issue
has not been decided. With the failure of the Prague spring and
with the Russian invasion the possibility of a *fronde* within the
mass media disappeared and those responsible faced jail or exile.
The question of the role of the mass media in times of social
and political change is one to which the media sociologists have
given little attention, preferring to devote their time to studies
of the reinforcing role of the mass media at general elections.
We have, therefore, still to wait for a true assessment of the
role of the BBC in the General Strike of 1926 (or as a propaganda
weapon on the home front during the war), although in the
former case Reith's statement that in 1926 the BBC 'was on
the side of the government too' is a clear rebuttal of the legend
that it was in 1926 that the BBC asserted its political independence. There is no study, to my knowledge, of the precise role
played by the mass media in Czechoslovakia nor of their
function in Allende's Chile. The fact that the Chilean junta was
quick to seize the university television stations and to
persecute their staffs indicates that they were politically
important.

The argument is, then, that in most societies at most times
in their history the communicator plays a restricted role, which
is not to say that his role is unimportant, only that his freedom
of action is limited by strong social and political forces. Within
a strictly authoritarian system the limits will be extremely
narrow. The moment authoritarian control is relaxed the communicator will find himself forced to make delicate political
judgements which are inseparable from his task as mediator.
The case of Polish television provides an example. After the
Szczecin riots, high government and party officials appeared
before the television studios to answer questions from viewers,

which were phoned in to the television organization. These calls, as is normal, were monitored before being passed on to the politicians, the decision as to which should be passed on and which blocked being made by the head of programmes who had to exercise political and social judgements as to what questions were of interest to the audience and what questions were acceptable to the politicians. It is a situation that presents itself in television studios throughout the world. If there are difficulties in this form of mediation it is because of divergent attitudes towards information. The communicator will instinctively wish to communicate; that is presumably why he chose the profession in the first place. The politician may have what seem to him to be a number of good reasons to communicate only partially, only on certain subjects, or not at all. It may be that there is within any society a tension between those who wish to communicate and those who wish or require to preserve confidentiality or secrecy. Within an ideally democratic system this tension would no doubt disappear, it being the concern of the rulers to communicate with the ruled to the maximum degree and of the communicators to further the process by the dissemination of issues, their discussion, examination and criticism, from which would come new formulations of policy. Until such time as such a society exists, those who cannot accept the dominant codes of their society will be well advised to resign themselves to working elsewhere than in the mass media.

11

On the Social Significance of Television Comedy

Sinclair Goodlad

For the student of culture, television comedy is a subject of immense interest and importance. In the United Kingdom, it is not uncommon for one person in three over the age of 5 to watch a comedy programme on television. What is the social significance of the immense investment of time and resources involved? Is television comedy an expressive aspect of culture, reflecting our perception of contrasted social norms and values? Or is it rather an instrumental aspect of culture, one dimension in a complex social construction of reality? Most likely, it is both. But, can one say anything more precise? Can sociology, which seeks to relate culture to social structure, enrich understanding of popular television any more fruitfully than interpretative 'literary' criticism? The purpose of this essay is to indicate some of the practical difficulties involved in studying television comedy if one wishes to maintain a balance between empirical observation and theory, and, in particular, by examining the uses and abuses of content analysis, to suggest how television comedy may usefully be approached.

Comedy is part of the wider field of humour, and the study of humour is a field in which theories abound. Patricia Keith-Spiegel[1] has provided a convenient classifactory summary of the principal theories which include:

1   *Biological, instinct, and evolution theories* — which main-

---

[1] Patricia Keith-Spiegel, 'Early Conceptions of Humour: Varieties and Issues', chapter 1 in J. H. Goldstein and P. E. McGhee, eds., *The Psychology of Humor* (London 1972) pp. 5–13.

tain that laughter and humour serve some utilitarian purpose —
for example, being 'good for the body' because it stabilizes
blood pressure, oxygenates the blood, massages the vital organs,
stimulates circulation, facilitates digestion, etc. The theories in
this category suggest that humour is a vestige of adaptive
behaviour.

2   *Superiority theories* — which hold that the roots of
laughter lie in our triumph over other people or circumstances.
These theories propose that we experience elation when we
compare ourselves favourably to others — as being less stupid,
ugly, unfortunate, weak, etc. Hobbes's definition of laughter
as a kind of 'sudden glory' which we enjoy primarily by
observing the infirmities of others and comparing them with
the 'imminency' in ourselves, is the most famous: Ludovici's
theorizing is perhaps the most elaborate.

3   *Incongruity theories* — which say that humour arises from
disjointed, ill-suited pairings of ideas or situations or the
representation of ideas or situations which diverge from the
usual custom. Of these, Bergson's opinion on the basic cause of
humour as 'something mechanical encrusted on the living' is the
best known.

4   *Surprise theories* — Keith-Spiegel comments that 'the
elements of 'surprise', 'shock', 'suddenness', or 'unexpectedness'
have been regarded by many theorists as *necessary* (though not
necessarily *sufficient*) conditions for the humour experience.
There is some similarity between the concepts of surprise and
incongruity in that both involve instantaneous breaking up of
the routine course of thought or action. It is, therefore, not
unusual to find many theorists utilizing a blend of surprise and
incongruity theory in explanatory concepts.' She notes that
one advantage of incorporating surprise into a theory is that of
being able to account for the decline in appreciation involved
in repeated exposures to the same situation or joke.

5   *Ambivalence theories* — which hold that laughter results
when an individual simultaneously experiences incompatible
emotions or feelings. Among clashing feelings or emotions which
may resolve themselves through laughter, Keith-Spiegel lists:
love modified by hate (Greig), mania alternating with depression

(Winterstein), superiority fused with limitation (Dessoir), playful chaos mixed with seriousness (Knox), sympathy and animosity (Gregory), and conflict engendered by blocking the behaviour associated with an instinctive drive (Menon). The difference between these theories and incongruity theories, she suggests, is that incongruity theories tend to stress ideas or perceptions whereas ambivalence theories stress emotions or feelings.

6   *Release and relief theories* — such as that of Kline which maintains that 'the tension accompanying thought occasionally exceeds the capacity for controlled thinking causing a wave of emotion. Sometimes this leads to humorous experiences which serve the useful purpose of alleviating the strain involved in sustained attention.'

7   *Configurational theories* — which suggest that humour is experienced when elements originally seen as unrelated suddenly fall into place in the individual's consciousness. In Keith-Spiegel's view the difference between these and incongruity theories is that in incongruity theories, it is the perception of 'disjointedness' that somehow amuses, whereas in configurational theories, it is the 'falling into place' or sudden 'insight' that gives amusement. Configurational theories, she suggests, either anticipate or reflect the broader theoretical model of *gestalt* psychology.

8   *Psychoanalytic theories* — of which the most famous is that of Freud. As Keith-Spiegel writes, 'Freud contended that the ludicrous always represents a saving in the expenditure of psychic energy. When energy built up for occupation in certain psychic channels (cathexis) is not or cannot be utilized (owing to the censoring action of the super ego), it may be pleasurably discharged in laughter.'

To be of value to the sociologist, such theories, stressing as they do the psychodynamics of humour, must be evaluated by a methodology which can relate the intellectual content of humour to social structure. The psychologist or psychiatrist may be interested in humour for what it tells of the *individual's* preoccupations and perceptions; but the sociologist must examine forms of humour which can yield information on the systematic linking of ideas and *institutions*. Comedy is of particular interest to sociologists because comedy is institutionalized humour. Comedy contrasts social norms and values in conditions of public performance. But, comedy is an extraordinarily widespread social phenomenon ranging from the sophisticated comedy of Moliére to the vulgar knockabout of the Whitehall farces. Clearly, some comedy is highly idiosyncratic, having a specialized authorship and a limited appeal. As a testing ground for theory and methodology which might ultimately encompass all forms of comedy, it is, therefore, prudent to begin with a form of comedy which is widely diffused in society and which is popular — in the sense of enjoying mass appeal. Television comedy meets these requirements.

Television-watching is the single most widespread and time-consuming leisure activity of United Kingdom citizens.[2] And television comedy is among the most popular types of television fare. In 1973, for example, productions of the following television comedies were among those watched by more than 20 per cent of the UK population over the age of 5: 'Father Dear Father', 'Whatever Happened to the Likely Lads?', 'Nearest and Dearest', 'Monty Python's Flying Circus', 'Whoops Baghdad', 'Steptoe and Son'. More than 30 per cent of the population watched productions of the following programmes: 'Morecambe and Wise', 'The Benny Hill Show', 'The Dick Emery Show', 'Some Mothers Do 'Ave 'Em', 'Love Thy Neighbour'. And on Christmas Day 1973, 45 per cent of the UK population over the age of 5 watched Mike Yarwood, and 49 per cent watched Morecambe and Wise — figures only equalled by the 'Eurovision Song Contest,' 'Miss World', and the royal wedding of Princess Anne.[3] From these figures, there can be no doubt that television comedy is a form of comedy eminently suited for analysis.

A precise classification of content is obviously a prerequisite in any sociological analysis seeking to relate an item of culture to social structure. This is the fundamental aspect of methodology upon which theory may be erected — for a theory is only

[2] See, for example, Kenneth Roberts, *Leisure* (London 1970) p. 16. Also James Curran and Jeremy Tunstall 'Mass media and leisure' chapter 14 in Michael Smith, Stanley Parker and Cyril Smith eds., *Leisure and Society in Britain* (London 1973).

[3] For this information, I am indebted to Miss Joan Robinson, Audience Research Department, British Broadcasting Corporation.

as good as the methodology it implies. Uses and gratifications research, for example (a widely practised and respected form of functional analysis), is plagued with the difficulty of describing the cultural phenomena which are supposed to provide uses and gratifications to given audiences. If the sociological study of culture is to claim the status of an exact science, its descriptive language must be unambiguous — for systematic description is the alpha and omega of science. By examining the strengths and weaknesses of the methodology (in this case content analysis) we may approach a type of theory appropriate to cultural analysis.

The first problem in content analysis is to decide what units to examine. In studying television comedy, does one concentrate on complete shows? individual jokes? sketches? single lines in sketches? or what? Before any type of uses and gratifications or other such research can be carried out, this problem must be confronted. Audiences may derive satisfaction from the periodicity of complete shows, or the familiarity of form, quite apart from any of the detailed intellectual content. The analyst must be sensitive not only to content, but also to the form through which content is presented. When one examines a typical scheme of content analysis, the formidable complexity of the enterprise becomes apparent.

In 'An experimental study of comedy',[4] E. G. Gabbard identified seven comic devices which are commonly used in comedy in association with five elements. The devices are: overstatement; reversal; impropriety; substitution; double-meaning; understatement; repetition. Each comic device may be found in association with any one or more of the following elements: idea; characteristic; emotion; sound; sight. Gabbard's scheme of analysis provides, that is to say, 35 separate categories of form which the analyst can apply to a complete show, to an individual joke or sketch in the show, to a single line of dialogue, to the spectacle of somebody curiously dressed, and so on. Any one of these devices or elements could be significantly related to the social characteristics of the audience which appreciated it.

But, Gabbard's framework of content analysis dealing with form does not, of course, refer to subject-matter — what is said.

[4] E. G. Gabbard, *An experimental study of comedy* PhD. Dissertation, University of Iowa, 1954. University Microfilms 10–212.

Let us combine for purposes of argument, Gabbard's framework with the well-known framework of 'what is said' categories propounded by J. Cartwright[5] in chapter 10 of *Research Methods in the Behavioural Sciences*. Cartwright directs the content analyst's attention to the following ten categories: (1) subject matter — what is it about? (2) direction — is treatment favourable or unfavourable to subject? (3) standard — on what basis is the classification of direction made? (4) values — what goals are explicitly or implicitly revealed? (5) methods — what means or actions are used to reach goals? (6) traits — what characteristics of persons are revealed? (7) actor — who initiates actions? (8) authority — in whose name are statements made? (9) origin — what is the place of origin of the communication? (10) target — to whom is it particularly directed? For good measure, one might add two more categories concerning 'how it is said' proposed by Cartwright: (11) form of statement — what is the grammatical, syntactical, or other form of the unit of analysis? (12) intensity — how much strength or excitement value does the communication have?

The combination of Gabbard's framework dealing with form and Cartwright's framework dealing with both form and content, offers the analyst a grid of 420 possible types of observation to be applied to every unit. The more sophisticated the humour, the more complicated becomes the problem of analysis — for economy is an artistic virtue, as Arthur Koestler, for example, has noted.[6] Several possible 'meanings' may be telescoped into a single idea, sight, or any other element, and one must be able to describe what meanings are available before one can explain why a given meaning is preferred by a member of the audience.

The next major difficulty in content analysis is that the definition of categories must be worked out *before* a particular comedy is studied. At first sight, this may seem a trivial requirement — a necessary precondition for any 'scientific' procedure in which two observers must be put in the position of simultaneously making the same observation. But, how does one decide in advance the categories of subject matter to be noted? Comedy can be *about* practically anything. Too narrow a list

[5] L. Festinger and D. Katz eds., *Research Methods in the Behavioural Sciences* (New York 1953).
[6] Arthur Koestler, *The Act of Creation* (London 1964) p. 82.

of subject-matter codings can be limiting: too wide a list of codings can prevent instant coding. And *instant* coding by the content analyst is critically important particularly with comedy, for surprise, as we have seen above, is often a crucial element in humour. Surprise is inevitably destroyed by the second viewing of a television comedy. If content analysis is to reveal anything, the analyst must put himself in a position to see and hear what the original viewer saw and heard — otherwise he will be analysing something different from the cultural phenomenon he is seeking to explain.

But, on whose terms is the content defined? To take one trivial example: with how much intensity does a viewer perceive Dick Emery's portrayal of his standard flamboyant homosexual? Or again, when Mike Yarwood overstates the characteristic of Edward Heath's laughing shoulders, is his treatment favourable or unfavourable to the subject? Or again, is the impropriety of idea of a 'Ministry of Silly Walks' in 'Monty Python's Flying Circus' *about* anything? Is it perceived by the viewer as a savage attack on the Civil Service? Or is it merely a playful caprice relying for effect on the values believed to be held in Civil Service departments? If content analysis is to be in any way 'objective', the perception of the analyst must be impeccable. It seems that one is trapped by a sort of Catch 22 of cultural analysis: that to perceive all necessary facets of a joke one must share the culture in which the joke is propounded; but to detach oneself sufficiently to describe the joke, one must leave the culture and observe from without. If one shares the culture of the joke, one is likely to be as amused and involved as anyone else; if one does not share that culture, one may miss finer points of the joke. Deliberately to put oneself outside the culture obliterates the necessary perception. (One may say in passing that analysts of humour are nearly always scorned by the 'common man' — precisely because, to be analytic, they stand aside, negating the taken-for-granted components of the culture which allow a joke to work. Humour, for most people, is a serious business.)

These 'internal' difficulties of content analysis point to the related difficulty in experimental work of finding out what the *audience* perceives. Projective techniques themselves depend on content analysis, and, as we have seen, content analysis is plagued by inter-subjectivity: one is trapped in a vicious circle. Again, humour is used mainly in *social contexts*: what sort of social context is the mass communication of television comedy? Controlled studies of the psychodynamics of humour have been notoriously unsuccessful, and many experiments with luckless graduate students in psychology departments have shown the appalling difficulty of controlling all the variables which may make up the humour situation. Even more unsuccessful have been attempts to describe the social dynamics of humour situations — where only the broadest outlines can be proposed with any certainty. To get anywhere near the true 'meaning' of humour as communicated in television comedy, one would be faced with an impossibly complex task not only of content analysis, but also of describing the social conditions of perception of the humour. The more sophisticated the categories of analysis, the further one gets from the cultural phenomenon one is trying to apprehend. Just as magnification of a newspaper photograph confronts one with an incomprehensible blur of black and white dots, so content analysis is in danger of replacing an intuitively grasped whole with a congeries of bewildering detail.

The main justification for studying television comedy is that in a very real sense it represents 'popular' culture which contains 'common denominator' aspects of culture which coexist with whatever idiosyncratic aspects define more specialized subgroups in society. But, because television comedy is mediated by a broadcasting institution, it may tell us nothing at all about the norms and values of the society in which it is believed to be popular. That is to say, if our interest is in the significance of the norms and values embodied in comedy, we should perhaps look not at content, but at *omissions* — what is excluded and why. As 'expressive culture', television comedy may reveal only the popularity of norms and values which survive the policies of supervisors and controllers, and the obsessions and idiosyncrasies of production and performance personnel.

Empiricist sociology, aspiring to the rigour of exact science, would, then, demand unambiguous description of communication content to which the social structures determining transmission and reception can be systematically related. But, if as I have suggested such rigour of 'scientific' analysis is unhelpful in the study of television comedy, so too is solipsism — the appeal to the discriminating powers of self-congratulatory coteries whose interpretations of 'meaning' are not backed by any coherent framework of observation other than a hidden curriculum of ideological values.

The eighth of the sixteen meanings of 'meaning' reviewed by C. K. Ogden and I. A. Richards[7] is 'the place of anything in a system'. Sociology's contribution to cultural analysis is not, I suggest, to be found in 'factor analysis' or any other of the strategies of brute empiricism. Rather it is in the supplying of theory which 'locates' television comedy as an aspect of culture and which can use content analysis as a tool without being obliterated by it. Interpretative literary criticism has usually tried to enrich a reader's perception of *possible* meanings in a literary text, without necessarily trying to *prove* that any particular meaning suggested is definitive. In like manner, and without making inflated claims of superior insight, symbolic interactionist sociology can point to layers of meaning which deepen one's understanding of a popular art form like television comedy.

The symbolic interactionist view of comedy can be simply stated. Social institutions are regular patternings of roles; roles are defined through symbolic interactions; and comedy is a major form through which roles are defined. Offering one such view of comedy, H. D. Duncan[8] has written that 'A social order *defines* itself through disorder as well as order. Impropriety sets limits; they begin the moment of negation where the positive content of a role ends. Without such limits a role cannot take form.' Duncan's view of the significance of comic disorder is echoed and developed in depth in Mary Douglas's analysis of concepts of pollution and taboo in *Purity and Danger*. 'Reflection on dirt involves reflection on the relation of order to disorder, being to non-being, form to formlessness, life to death. Wherever ideas of dirt are highly structured their analysis discloses a play upon such profound themes.'[9] And again, 'we

[7] C. K. Ogden and I. A. Richards, *The Meaning of Meaning* (tenth edn, London 1956) p. 186.

[8] H. D. Duncan, *Communication and Social Order* (New York 1962) p. 281.

[9] Mary Douglas, *Purity and Danger: An analysis of concepts of pollution and taboo* (London 1966) pp. 5—6.

can recognize in our own notions of dirt that we are using a kind of omnibus compendium which includes all the rejected elements of ordered systems.'[10] It is not insignificant that the word 'dirt' is often unthinkingly applied to the blasphemies and obscenities of Alf Garnett in the television comedy series 'Till Death Us Do Part' and to the innuendoes of Frankie Howerd. Clearly, 'dirt' is precisely what this type of television comedy is supposed to be! And in signalling 'dirt' such television comedies are relying on a structuring of our perceptions, a consensus about system and disorder which enables us to 'enjoy' the sense of superiority or incongruity, the surprise, the ambivalence, or the release which psychodynamic theory insists upon.

Mary Douglas has herself carried the analysis of humour to very sophisticated lengths in 'The Social Control of Cognition: Some Factors in Joke Perception.' She argues that the joke is an attack on control.

> 'My hypothesis is that a joke is seen and allowed when it offers a symbolic pattern of a social pattern occurring at the same time. As I see it, all jokes are expressive of the social situation in which they occur. The one social condition necessary for a joke to be enjoyed is that the social group in which it is received should develop the formal characteristics of a "told" joke: that is, a dominant pattern of relations is challenged by another. If there is no joke in the social structure, no other joking can appear.'[11]

Arguing that a standard rite is 'a symbolic act which draws its meaning from a cluster of standard symbols,' she suggests essentially that a joke is an anti-rite. Where rites assert hierarchy and order, jokes have the opposite effect, destroying hierarchy and order, denigrating and devaluing the dominant values. Laughter and jokes, she maintains, since they attack classification and hierarchy, are 'obviously apt symbols for expressing community in this sense of unhierarchised, undifferentiated social relations.'

Mary Douglas argues that 'a joke confronts one relevant structure by another less clearly relevant, one well-differentiated view by a less coherent one, a system of control by another independent one to which it does not apply.'[12] The main thrust

[10] *Ibid.*, p. 35.
[11] Mary Douglas, 'The Social Control of Cognition: Some Factors in Joke Perception' *Man* 1968, vol. 3, pp. 361–76, p. 366.
[12] *Ibid.*, p. 371.

of her analysis is to urge that joking cannot be understood without reference to social structure. Her distinction between joking and obscenity is particularly revealing in this respect:

> Abomination is an act or event which contradicts the basic categories of experience and in doing so threatens both the order of reason and the order of society. A joke does nothing of the sort. It represents a temporary suspension of the social structure or rather it makes a little disturbance in which the particular structuring of society becomes less relevant than another. But the strength of its attack is entirely restricted by the consensus on which it depends for recognition.[13]

To work at all, comedy depends upon consensus about values and norms. Without a clear intuition of order, one cannot apprehend disorder: normality is defined by reference to abnormality. It is tempting to see television comedy as a celebration of socially constructed reality — not just of social reality, but of *all* reality. P. L. Berger and T. Luckmann,[14] the chief proponents of the theory of the social construction of reality, have been criticized (for example by Peter Hamilton in 'Knowledge and Social Structure'[15]) on the grounds that as a sociology of knowledge their theory is clearly non-empirical. Is it, therefore, of no value in elucidating the social significance of television comedy? The answer will depend upon one's understanding of the meaning of 'meaning'. In my judgement, an additional layer of meaning may be said to have been disclosed when an interpretation of observable phenomena is given which is internally consistent, which fits the facts, and which by doing so proves itself upon one's pulses. Television comedy most likely both reflects *and* controls our perception of reality.

Our perception of what is 'normal' is socially determined and must be repeatedly reinforced by symbolic interaction with our social and physical environment. Confirmation of our perceptions is satisfying; disconfirmation is disturbing — often to the point of mental collapse. In the routine exchanges and stereotyped behaviours of television comedy, our perception of the world is reflected and at the same time controlled. Any social certainties offer a springboard to the comedian. Language,

---

[13] *Ibid.*, pp. 371–2.
[14] P. L. Berger and T. Luckmann, *The Social Construction of Reality* (London 1966).
[15] P. Hamilton, *Knowledge and Social Structure* (London 1974) p. 145.

the primary constructor of reality, is an endless source of
fascination, particularly to children who delight in puns and
verbal quibbles to test their apprehension of the normal:not
surprisingly, elementary playing with words is a prominent
feature of much television comedy. Again, we confirm our
perception of the physical world by systematic and predictable
interaction with it: the total failure of Frank Spencer in 'Some
Mothers Do 'Ave 'Em' to interact successfully with the physical
world is a delightful reminder of the many ways in which our
modest technological achievements succeed by contrast with
his disasters. To ageing adults, 'Monty Python's Flying Circus'
is often irritating and sometimes 'meaningless': its main following is among young people — perhaps deliberately rejecting the
greyly ordered world of their parents, but also more likely
showing an assumed sophistication by apparent unconcern at
manifestations which negate all forms of order. For any closed
group, there is a special delight in demonstrating mastery by
use of jargon and codes: Mike Yarwood, like a cartoonist who
relies on *gestalt* to conjure an entire world with a few squiggles,
flatters his audience's self-esteem by simultaneously creating a
world of well-known politicians with a few tricks of disguise
and ready-made gestures, and indicating that these 'significant
others' are non-threatening because reduceable to the matey
social world which viewers know Mike Yarwood to represent.
Frankie Howerd, leering from a papier mâché Pompei or
Baghdad, suggests a whole world of sexual sophistication with
a few nods, grunts and winks. All these examples of television
comedy presuppose a taken-for-granted 'normal' world of
sights, sounds, and social proprieties as rigid as a carapace.

The standardized techniques of television by which this
elemental world is maintained may themselves be part of the
shield against terror. As sometimes may be seen in 'Steptoe and
Son', the absurd and the *Absurd* are closely related. Indeed,
Peter Cook and Dudley Moore have made a speciality of showing
the skull beneath the skin — of letting language not merely fail
to sustain a social world but run the danger of dissolving it
completely. It would be quite wrong to distinguish television
comedy too rigorously from other forms of fiction: in the
social definition of the normal, there is a continuum from
funny ha-ha to funny peculiar. Television fictions, be they

comedies, one-shot plays, drama series or serials — may (as I have argued at length elsewhere[16]) usefully be interpreted as the ritual rehearsal of social values.

Whether television fictions serve simply to express, or rather to control, our values, we may never know. Content analysis, modestly used, represents a worthwhile attempt to be systematic in the description of cultural artefacts. But, just as Heisenberg, through his 'uncertainty principle', drew attention to the limitations of observation in physics, so one must stress the theoretical impossibility of ever achieving a definitive description of the interaction of culture and social structure.

What I have tried to suggest in this essay is that the cultural significance of television comedy may be approached through sociological theory which is internally consistent and which does not violate observable facts. Analysts of the media are today posting back to the writings of Ferdinand de Saussure and Charles Sanders Peirce hoping there to find the foundations for a scientific study of culture. However, in my judgement, some of the difficulties inherent in the conventional content analysis which flourished in the 1950s and 1960s are likely to plague semiology. Obviously, television comedy relies upon signs: but, can anyone say with certainty what the system is?

Harold Macmillan once said that a politician was for ever poised on a knife-edge between a platitude and an indiscretion. In like manner, the student of popular culture teeters between cliché and gibberish. Empiricist content analysis leans towards the former; the 'lit. crit.' approach, applied to intellectual trivia and seeking Unique Insights, leans towards the latter. However, social theory provides a reason for being interested in television comedy; interpretative criticism, informed by such theory, offers a method by which *some* of the social significations of television comedy may be exposed.

---

[16] J. S. R. Goodlad, *A Sociology of Popular Drama* (London 1971).

12

Blue-eyed Blues: The Impact of Blues on European Popular Culture

Paul Oliver

A couple of hours spent listening to Radio One can provide some measure of the influence of the blues on popular music, and hence popular culture, in Europe. Pop music *is* popular culture to the youth of Europe; it is the focus of social activity, the source of language and styles of dress, the symbol and the expression of youth culture mores. So switch on, and count the bars of the stanzas of each item being played; a large proportion of the numbers will fall into a twelve-bar verse structure. Whatever their content, whoever sings the vocals, they are indebted to the blues for their form. Punch the buttons on the TV set until a pop/rock show comes up, or go down to the local teenage disco, or better, visit the Rainbow Room (or some such name) when a rock group is playing — through the tangle of go-going dancers and waving arms, discerned in flashes under the strobe lights, the lead guitar and the Fender bass players will be playing their instruments at crotch level. The sliding hands on the guitar necks may seem obscene, the wailing, howling sounds of the brass ring on the steel strings amplified, fed back, wa-waed through the amplifiers at chest-throbbing volume, distorted and pained; the growling, screeching or mike-biting vocals sensual and aggressive. They are. And they owe their sounds above all else, to the influence of the blues.

To the influence, in fact, of a music as old as a life-time: the form, the vocal style, the guitar technique were first observed over seventy years ago in rural black communities of Mississippi. Not amplified of course, nor very similar in other respects, for the blues as a folk music has had a history of evolution and change during that period; but there are recognizable links between the music of the Delta and that of the rock temples of the Mersey or the Rhine. At another level they can be detected in the rapport that the musicians establish with their dancing audiences and the means by which they achieve it, and in the importance of the music they sing and play in centralizing the cultural identity of the group.

But why the blues, and why at the present time? By what process did the music of cottonfield sharecroppers in Arkansas or ghetto street cleaners in St Louis, or steel workers in Gary, Indiana, become adopted by teenage secretaries in Frankfurt or art students in Leeds? The answers lie, at least in part, in the nature of the blues itself, and the means whereby European youth became aware of it.

Blues is not one music, but many, bound together by shared structural characteristics, technical mannerisms, rhythmic and melodic motifs, instrumental and vocal qualities of timbre and expression, and persistent thematic devices. Stylistic features differentiate Mississippi blues from those from Texas or Georgia, combinations of instruments and a brash urbanism may distinguish the blues of Chicago in the 'fifties from the Southern blues of a couple of decades earlier. Vaudeville singers in the twenties sang blues that would be just recognizable to the rock and roll generation. These elements can be identified and they can be copied. But to black Americans, such imitation is not blues. 'Blues is *our* music,' they say (or said, for Soul is now).

'All Negroes like blues. Why? Because they was born with the blues,' said the much recorded Leadbelly. 'The blues got you. They want to talk to you. You got to tell 'em somethin' . . . .' For him the blues was a living presence. For the virtually unrecorded Buster Pickens, 'the only way anyone can ever play blues — he's got to have them . . . you have a tough way in life — that makes you blue. That's when you start to sing the blues — when you've got the blues.' Blues is not only a music, it is also a state of mind. A blues singer plays the blues to get rid of the blues. Blues as an expression of the black experience; this the blues singer was sure was his alone. 'Never was a white man could sing the blues.'

It was even less likely that any European white man would

be able to, and it could be argued that no one ever did. But if there were no European blues singers to compare with the black American innovators of the music, blues was the catalyst that made the creation of a genuine teenage pop music, pop culture, possible. Unlike jazz, which had a considerable influence on European popular music from the twenties to the fifties, and to which a small number of Continental musicians made a real contribution, blues was almost unknown until after World War II. Although one or two blues singers played in the Special Services they were only heard by army audiences. Louis Armstrong and Duke Ellington had brought their orchestras to the London Palladium in the thirties, and jazz had been heard in every European country, including Russia, by that time. Many jazz musicians settled in France and other countries between the wars to bring the live experience of the American music to young European players. But not blues singers.

In an influential booklet published by the Worker's Music Association during World War II, *The Background of the Blues*, Iain Laing wrote that 'the blues is not the whole of jazz, but the whole of blues is jazz, having no existence apart from this idiom.' His statement encapsulated the view of all jazz writers, critics, club owners and concert promoters at that time — insofar as they recognized the existence of blues at all. American jazz authors, whose books were eagerly sought if difficult to obtain, reinforced the jazz association and assigned to the blues a role as precursor of jazz, often positing a pre-Civil War date.

Writing on jazz had been initiated in Europe but few authors made much reference to blues. 'The blues, a product of the spiritual, antedates jazz as a whole', stated the Belgian, Robert Goffin, in 1943; Goffin had been, in 1929, the first author to write on jazz and his word was respected. But the law was uttered by the American, Rudi Blesh, whose *Shining Trumpets* was published in Britain in 1949. He established both a progression and criteria for the blues in his succession of *archaic* (e.g. Blind Lemon Jefferson), *classic* (e.g. Bessie Smith), *contemporary* (e.g. Tommy McClennan), *decadent* (e.g. Jazz Gillum) and *eclectic* (e.g. Billie Holiday). Admirers of Lady Day winced, but his classification and his judgements were hardly questioned: the blues singers whose records were appearing on Chicago labels were 'decadent' and Ma Rainey and

Bessie Smith were 'classic'. When blues was discussed at all it was in jazz magazines, and always in these terms.

In the forties blues was the subject of an esoteric cult, a backwater of interest in 'pure' jazz, which was itself a minority enthusiasm whose adherents opposed 'swing' in vigorous terms. So blues was valued for its ethnicity, its authenticity and its historic importance rather than for its merits as a music.

And then, in the summer of 1949, Leadbelly arrived in Europe at the invitation of the Hot Club de France. Twice convicted of murder, a man of violence (but surely a victim of racial prejudice?) from the penitentiaries of Texas and Louisiana, he was the self-styled 'King of the Twelve-String Guitar Players of the World'. He brought a repertoire of work songs, ballads, Afro-American folk songs and blues, the living embodiment of the pre-jazz folk traditions. But the small audience that heard him realized he was in pain; the giant Leadbelly, Huddie Ledbetter, was struck down with lateral sclerosis. He died in the United States six months later, and the jazz world mourned the loss of the last link with the blues.

Josh White had worked with Leadbelly, so he came to Europe and toured in Britain. The boy who had led a score of blind blues singers through the South and recorded as Pinewood Tom was a virtuoso guitarist and sang with a glottal catch. He opened his velvet shirt to the waist, settled on a high stool and sang *The House of the Rising Sun*, or *One Meat Ball*. Almost as disappointing was Lonnie Johnson, who had once accompanied Texas Alexander, as he smiled his way wistfully through *I Lost my Heart in San Francisco*. And then Big Bill Broonzy arrived. The few blues singers who in the early fifties were brought to Europe, came at the invitation of jazz promoters and played for jazz audiences. They worked as intermission artists and anyway, were cheaper than jazz musicians. A dispute between the British and the American Musicians' Unions did not allow jazzmen to appear in the United Kingdom, but blues singers could come as 'variety artistes' (sic). So Big Bill sang at the Kingsway Hall, Holborn, after a succesful tour in France.

He was introduced by Alan Lomax, who had been with his father John Lomax when he discovered Leadbelly. Big Bill soon found himself cast in the same role, and delved back into his childhood memories to produce ballads and folk songs. ('Folksongs? all songs is folks' songs — I never heard a hoss sing, ' he commented many times.) His hollering made Josh White seem slick and effete; amiably he sat in with Chris Barber's jazz band, or held audiences in the palm of his hand for hours. In 1955 his autobiography, *Big Bill Blues*, written with the Belgian, Yannick Bruynoghe, was published in Britain. 'I know there ain't but a small amount of the real blues singers still living . . . and if I was to stop playing the real old slow blues I don't know what would become of it,' he said.

His audiences were determined to keep playing not only the real old slow blues, but the real old ballads and folk songs, too. They made black country music themselves. There was William Mitchell in Big Bill's book, photographed with his bass made from a washtub, and there was Washboard Sam playing rhythm on an old scrubbing board. Out came the jugs, the washboards, the tubs, the kazoos, harmonicas and comb-and-paper. The three-chord trick on guitar was all that was needed to accompany *Worried Man Blues* or *See See Rider*. But no one expected the runaway success of Lonnie Donegan's *Rock Island Line*. The voice was Cockney/Deep South, the song was Leadbelly's, the singer's name was half Lonnie Johnson's. But the banjo player from Chris Barber's Jazz Band made a 'skiffle' record which stood at number five in the charts in the United States within weeks, and eventually received the accolade of the mimicry of Stan Freeberg.

Skiffle, home-made, blues-based music on improvised instruments, was not quite the first blues form to be popularized in Europe. Early in the war a 'craze' for boogie-woogie enlivened the rhythm clubs. Boogie-woogie was a powerful piano style in which eight-to-the-bar rhythms were played in the left hand and ostinato passages in the right. It was coloured with railroad rhythms and was hidden in Chicago and Detroit for a decade before the discovery of Meade Lux Lewis made *Honky Tonk Train Blues* popular, and Tommy Dorsey made band versions of *Pinetop's Boogie-Woogie*. But boogie rode high on the Swing wave and this 'commercialized' it for the blues coterie. Skiffle was different. It was earthy, authentic. And though it brought the usual outcry against any popular youth music, it was widely recognized as healthy. The Chislehurst Caves rocked to scores of skiffle groups, churches and youth organizations played skiffle, and the Salvation Army strummed for coins in the streets.

If Leadbelly was one hero of skiffle, Woody Guthrie was the other. It was a blend of black and white folk music from America. Alan Lomax led a group in Britain; so too did Peggy Seeger, daughter of the folklorist Charles Seeger. Their Washington house-servant, Elizabeth Cotten, a Negro, was the source of one of the anthems of skiffle, *Freight Train*, and she even got some royalties for it, eventually. Peggy married Ewan MacColl, one of the leaders of the British folk-song revival which was a child of skiffle. Through it young Britishers discovered their own tradition and ultimately influenced English Folk Dance and Song Society policy. In a sense skiffle's folk emphasis was a counter to rock 'n' roll, which was no less a hybrid. Elvis Presley's *Hound Dog* hit the charts at the same time as Donegan's *Rock Island Line*, and the black-jacketed, string-tied rockers in their 'leathers' and their British counterparts, seemed to be exploiting both blues and white folk with a crude primitivism. *Hound Dog* was blues singer Big Mama Thornton's song, but she got no royalties for it. Nor did Big Boy Crudup, the Mississippi blues singer, whose *That's All Right Mama* was Presley's first hit. To the blues enthusiast both skiffle and rock sold the blues down the river.

At the Good Earth Club in Gerrard Street, London, and then at the Roundhouse in Wardour Street, Alexis Korner and Cyril Davis ran a Barrelhouse and Blues Club, dedicated to unadulterated blues. Davis fitted the blues singer image, burly, taciturn, a panel-beater by trade. He was devoted to Leadbelly's recordings and did passable imitations until heavy drinking and performing against doctor's direction brought an early death. His working-class origins were unusual; Korner's professional-class background the norm. Later, Alexis Korner, who never compromised his position, was host to a number of young and successful aspiring blues singers.

Big Bill Broonzy died in 1958, but by this time there were enough blues records around to show that the tradition was not dead yet. Brownie McGhee and Sonny Terry, playing guitar and harmonica respectively, came over that year to a warm welcome; they played country-based blues in the Carolina tradition. Muddy Waters came too. He was originally from Mississippi but had been living for the past decade in Chicago. When he played at the Leeds Folk Festival he played electric guitar, to howls of dismay from the audience. Next time he took the precaution to bring his accoustic guitar with him, only to upset his audience again. By this time they had caught up with the amplification of instruments which had been a characteristic of the Chicago blues bands since the forties. Within the space of a few years nearly every country in Europe had heard a few dozen blues singers and they knew what to expect.

Credit for the visitors in the late fifties goes largely to Chris Barber, jazz band leader but enthusiast for blues, who brought many to England to play intermissions in his concerts. But in Germany Horst Lippmann and Fritz Rau promoted an 'American Negro Folk Blues Festival' in 1962 which brought a 'package' of blues singers and musicians representing rural and urban traditions to the stages of Germany, France, Switzerland, Denmark, Holland and Britain. Blues singers were soon touring in Spain and Scandinavia, Italy and Ireland, and some came to settle. Broonzy's sometime pianist Memphis Slim married a French wife, bought a new villa outside Paris and acted as mentor to new arrivals from the United States. Champion Jack Dupree first settled in Switzerland, then married an English girl and made his home in Halifax. Many blues singers found Europe to their liking; there was less prejudice, they were lionized and in their own field the competition wasn't keen. But some were at a loss: Eddie Boyd chose Sweden after France, while the restless pianist Curtis Jones failed to make an impression in Spain and died penniless in Morocco.

Generally the visiting blues men played to large audiences and enjoyed exultant receptions. They were recorded by such firms as Storyville in Denmark and Blue Horizon in Britain with due regard for their talents and without pressures to make commercial hit records. Some visiting bluesmen, like Little Walter or Sonny Boy Williamson, both harmonica players, required supporting groups and were genuinely surprised and delighted when the young French, German or English groups knew their records by heart and could provide the backing they wanted. Undoubtedly the experience of hearing blues singers in person had a profound effect in developing European taste, ear and skill for the blues, but the way was also prepared by the availability of information on the subject. In 1959–60 Samuel B. Charters' *The Country Blues* and my own *Blues Fell This Morning; the Meaning of the Blues* were the first books to be published in Europe that considered blues outside of a jazz context. Others were to follow, augmented by a large number of specialist blues magazines. The first of these was Belgian: Serge Tonneau's *R and B Panorama*, probably the first blues magazine anywhere. In Britain *Blues Unlimited* edited by Simon Napier and Mike Leadbitter began monthly publication in 1963, and still flourishes. *Jefferson* in Sweden, *Blues Notes* in Austria and *Blues World* in England were among the other regular publications to appear in the sixties. 'Discography' – the listing of all recordings within a given field, was pioneered in France in the thirties by the jazz critic Charles Delauney. Always an exacting undertaking, it was set new standards of accuracy and presentation with the publication of Robert M. W. Dixon and John Godrich's *Blues and Gospel Records 1892–1942*.

Through recordings European enthusiasts could conduct original research in blues, which was enriched by interviews with visiting singers. Some preferred to go to the sources, as did the French blues writers Jacques Demetre and Marcel Chauvard who went to Chicago and Detroit in 1959 and the Belgian Georges Adins who visited St Louis the same year. In 1960 I was able to spend several months doing research in both the northern cities and in the Deep South, recording material for BBC archives in which blues was previously unrepresented, and making the interviews that were compiled in *Conversation with the Blues*. Subsequently, many European collectors from the Netherlands, Germany, Scandinavia and elsewhere made field trips which added to knowledge of the blues and its milieu, and which were published in specialist media.

So the early sixties saw many visiting bluesmen in Europe, an expanding blues literature, still predominately European, many blues recordings being made available, and a growing number of young musicians who were learning to play blues music. The position was comparable to the rediscovery of New Orleans jazz a score of years before, when ageing and forgotten musicians were winkled out of longshore dives and Louisiana salt mines to play to rapt, incredulous white audiences. And conscious that blues research had arrived late on the scene, the blues-hounds tended to seek out the veterans like Sleepy John Estes, Big Joe Williams, or the slightly younger down-home bluesmen like Lightnin' Hopkins — all of whom toured in Europe. Estes sang of being nearly drowned near Brownsville, Williams of President Roosevelt, Hopkins of Tom Moore's farm at Navasota, Texas. It was fascinatingly remote, but also far from relevant to the lives of young whites in Birmingham or Brussels who were trying to sing blues. For every guitar strummer who declared in unfamiliar gutterals that he ain't goin' down that big road by hisself there was another who could sense the incongruity of flaggin' an ole Greyhound to carry him some place else.

In the United States Bob Dylan provided an answer: he drew from the blues and from Woody Guthrie too. Guthrie's 'talking blues' idiom suited Dylan. His *Outlaw Blues* or *She Belongs to Me* were straight twelve-bar blues, but *Motor-Psycho Nightmare* or *Subterranean Homesick Blues* extended the idiom and were filled with vivid, contemporary imagery. But Dylan was 'folknik' and while he showed the way to a more poetic, youth-based song type derived from blues, his earlier compositions were strongly coloured in delivery and character by Guthrie and Jack Elliot. Another way out of the contemporary dilemma had been around for a decade in rock 'n' roll, the music that skiffle hoped to challenge. And out in front of the R 'n' R singers, on the fringes of R & B, were Chuck Berry and Bo Diddley. R & B — rhythm and blues — was the name given to blues by the record companies in the post-war years when the old 'race music' went out with darkies, negroes, and eventually, Negroes. Chuck Berry and Bo Diddley were part rhythm and blues singers but their music was directed unashamedly to a teenage market.

Bukka White might sing of streamline trains and the penitenshu' but they sang of hot-rods and high school. Berry's *It Wasn't Me* even referred to Greek-letter societies, while Bo Diddley's *Gunslinger* made a wry, ironic joke out of the cowboy myth. Ellas McDaniel called himself Bo Diddley (he said) from the rhythm 'bo diddley um dum'; he wore black shades, a bright tartan jacket and played an outrageous vermilion metal guitar with a square body. Chuck Berry was less flamboyantly dressed but his posturings as he played, not to mention short spells of jail for violations of the Mann Act, ensured his notoriety. No one chose to call Chuck and Bo poets, but there were many in Europe who were listening hard to their words as well as the basic rock 'n' roll beat. Unlike most of the rockers they were still recording profusely.

Rhythm and blues covered the sophisticated singing and sleek guitar playing of a T-Bone Walker, it embraced the fierce, raw shouting of Howling Wolf and the down-home singing of Lonesome Sundown; even in the sixties blues singers still used the colourful pseudonyms of the kind that Bat the Hummingbird or Bumble Bee Slim had in the thirties. R & B also included an aspect that had been overlooked by the European blues enthusiasts — the singing of the quartets like the Orioles, the Clovers or the Platters, whose smooth, close harmonizing vocals had derived from the Gospel choirs as much as from the Ink Spots. They were appearing again in Detroit in the sequinned, two-toned suited vocal groups of Berry Gordy's Tamla-Motown label like Martha and the Vandellas or the Four Tops. And there was the Soul amalgam of Gospel inflections with blues lyrics that ignited Aretha Franklin or B.B. (Blues Boy) King, or Ray Charles.

They were all currents in the explosion of pop: the pop music, pop culture revolution that was sparked off in Britain in the sixties. They called it Beat, then.

Beat music, a synthesis of R 'n' R, R & B, Soul and straight blues, with Dylanesque lyrics and some considerable native talent, broke on the world market with the records of the Beatles. They were the Quarrymen once; a skiffle cum rock 'n' roll group who made some poor records in Germany but came back to hit the charts with *Please Please Me* and *From Me to You*. Their indebtedness to the rock singer Little Richard was evident in *Long Tall Sally* or *I'm Down*; to Chuck Berry in *Roll Over Beethoven*. They smoothed out the blues inflections in the twelve-bar *Can't Buy Me Love* but the blues underlay its structure.

In spite of the sensation that the Beatles created at the time, it was the Rolling Stones that became the target of parental animosity as, in helpless frustration, they saw the long-haired, atavistic, sensuous, blatantly lewd Mick Jagger and the group seduce their innocent offspring. Some of the band had worked with Alexis Korner; they knew their blues and paid their dues. Even their name was taken from a Muddy Waters recording, and they adopted the brazen, heavily amplified, harshly uttered urban blues of Muddy Waters, Howling Wolf and Elmore James. Teenage revolt was personified in their performances of blues like *I Just Want to Make Love To You* or *I Can't Be Satisfied* by black bluesmen who were in their fifties. Their own compositions in the rhythm and blues vein like *Satisfaction* or *Get Off Of My Cloud*, especially in performance, built up to a frantic conclusion with Jagger strutting, camping it up, provoking the crowds with sensuous lips and surly asides. It wasn't blues but it was very close to it and the spell worked on the audiences was akin to that of an urban blues band.

There were others in the beat/rhythm and blues movement: notably the Animals, who drew for some of their repertoire on the Mississippi/Detroit singer, John Lee Hooker; and the Yardbirds who took some of their inspiration from Elmore James, before following the Beatles east in pursuit of the sitar. Central to the Yardbirds was Eric Clapton, a brilliant guitarist who was probably the most able blues instrumentalist to come from Britain. He modelled himself on Robert Johnson via Elmore James: James had shaped his whole approach to blues on Johnson's style, amplified it and put it in the Chicago context; now Clapton made it part of the pop music idiom. Clapton left the Yardbirds to form Cream with Ginger Baker and Jack Bruce; a guitar, drums and bass trio of formidable talents who probably played better blues, technically, than did most of the working blues bands in Chicago at the time.

The Move, the Who, John Mayalls' Bluesbreakers, the Graham Bond Organisation, the Pretty Things . . . dozens of beat, R & B psychedelic, acid rock, blues bands appeared in the sixties, taking not only Britain but Europe by storm — and America as well. The irony of the whole pop music revolution was the way that British bands brought the blues back on home to the United States. When Lightnin' Hopkins and Lonesome Sundown eventually got a mention in a Houston newspaper it wasn't because they were local bluesmen, but because the Animals mentioned them in an interview while on tour. White American rhythm and blues bands proliferated, though records by British

groups still topped the charts. To some extent this benefited
the black bluesmen — they found themselves working the college
circuit, and many left the black clubs for the better, but short-
lived, pickings of the blues concerts and pop/rock festivals.

There was a noticeable falling-off of direct blues contact in
Europe; the Lippmann and Rau concerts played to diminishing
audiences on the Continent and began giving the United Kingdom
a miss. The National Blues Federation, resounding in name but
small in scale, was formed to bring over blues singers, but except
for the small coterie, black bluesmen were already losing their
appeal by the late sixties. For one thing, Britain had its own
black exponent of the pop/rock culture in Jimmi Hendrix, a
wild-haired, lean, image conscious guitarist. Actually he was
Seattle born, but his career caught fire when he was brought
to England by Charles Chandler of the Animals. His orgiastic
screaming, his phallic guitar, his psychedelic patterned shirts,
his beads of amber and perspiration had the crowds and the
groupies clamouring for him. Hendrix played flashy guitar but
he had genuine talent with a hard core of blues; though he
denied being a singer he had a blues singer's voice. He was also
well promoted: Charles Chandler later confessed that they only
chose 'the more gruesome shots which made him look like a
big nasty' for the publicity photographs.

A 'wall of sound' blasted from the mass of amplifiers of
the Jimmi Hendrix Experience. Every aspect of his performance,
the appearance of his band, the unleashed violence as he
smashed his guitars (it had worked well for Pete Townshend
and the Who in the Mod period a few years before) — epitomized
the schism between the generations. Hendrix died of the effects
of drugs in 1970 at the age of 24; just about the age of Robert
Johnson when *he* died in 1938. To the teenage pop culture it
seemed like a martyr's death, like Brian Jones's of the Rolling
Stones, or Al Wilson's of the American white blues group,
Canned Heat. But Hendrix hadn't sold out, he hadn't gone soft;
both accusations were made about the Stones. It seems too
neat to say that with the death of Jimmi Hendrix that blues as
an inspirational force in European popular culture died too —
one remembers Leadbelly and Big Bill Broonzy.

But it does seem like it.

This is not to say that the influence of blues had disappeared;

on the contrary, it has been absorbed into pop music until the form, the techniques and the expression of blues have become part of the norm. But blues has given — or rather, has been sucked dry — of all it can offer to pop music. Now pop music is living on itself and has succumbed to the debilitating effects of nostalgia, imitating the early phases, calling it all 'rock'.

For fifteen years though, through the successive phases of skiffle, rock and roll, rhythm and blues, pop, progressive pop, psychedelic pop, acid rock, plain rock, through all this, blues played a dominant part in shaping a music which became the symbol of a culture. Blues was seen as the music of a minority, a sector of society whose segregation was paralleled by the separation of youth from older generations. It was a delusion of course; there was no equivalent in the middle-class, art school trained, well-heeled pop groups of the Marquee, Wardour Street, for the humiliation of racial segregation, for the poverty of the ghettoes of the Black Belts, for the significance of Muddy Waters spelling out, 'I'm a *Man*! spelt . . . M . . . A . . . N . . .' to the black, packed, howling crowd at Smitty's Corner.

But they believed there was. For the teenage audiences the R & B groups, the pop/rock groups were screaming, through wa-wa pedals and fuzz boxes, and wailing slides, amplifiers turned up to maximum, the independence of pop-youth culture from the standard of their parents: blues-based music was shouting about the Bomb, about Vietnam, about grass, acid, scoring, ripping off, shacking up. . . . Cult became culture, blues on transistor radios, on cheap lp's, on posters and publicity became its universal symbol.

It couldn't remain so because blues is a slowly evolving music while the pressures of the teenage market and the commerical interests that catered for it and exploited it required rapid change. Most pop musicians worked their way through more blues styles in a year than the majority of bluesmen do in a lifetime. When it was over it was the rock stars who had the Rolls Royces, the film contracts, the big houses with the swimming pools, and their profiles in *Vogue*; not the blues singers. It was no coincidence that the black audiences quit the blues like it had never been, when the Beatles and the Stones topped the charts.

13

American Popular Culture in the Thirties: Ideology, Myth, Genre

Philip Melling

What Melville said of Captain Vere in *Billy Budd* is pertinent to the role of the American novelist in the 1930s:

There had got to be established in him some positive conviction which ... would abide in him essentially unmodified so long as his intelligent part remained unimpaired. ... His settled convictions were as a dyke against those invading waters of novel opinion, social, political, or otherwise, which carried away as in a torrent no few minds in those days.[1]

The construction of a 'dyke' in the thirties is a problem in aesthetics. This is a particular concern for the writer who assesses the impact of popular culture or the fictional strategies of consumer art; and for the radical novelist who provides an aesthetic at some distance beyond ideology without offence to 'novel opinion' in criticism. Josephine Herbst locates the problem for the Marxist novelist in a letter to David Madden:

I have felt that my own work has been considerably damaged by the category, (proletarian literature) and that the term since the Second World War has been used more as blackmail than as a definitive term with any valid meaning. I think the whole thing needs a more fundamental approach. Where are the roots to the writing in the thirties? Was it all political? .... Language — sex, the exalted role of the body — the confluence of so many diverse elements — how can it be nailed down to Marx or to an angled proletariat?[2]

Herbst complains that the critic and not the artist has determined our frame of reference for the thirties, such as the 'entrepreneurs

[1] Herman Melville, *Billy Budd and Other Tales* (New York 1961) pp. 27–8.
[2] D. Madden, ed., *Proletarian Writers of the Thirties* (Carbondale, Illinois 1968) p. xv.

of writing, the head-boys who have also been mostly responsible for the rehashes'.[3] Herbst may be referring us to the critic Joseph Freeman whose 'vocative' radicalism is well demonstrated in a foreward to *Proletarian Literature in the United States*, published in 1935. Posing the question: 'what constitutes experience?' Freeman assumes that if art 'is to ignore politics and the class struggle' then the only experience left for art to record will be 'the experience of personal sensation, emotion and conduct, the experience of the parasite classes. Such art is produced today by bourgeois writers.' From this premise Freeman declares that only the 'proletarian' writer concerned ideologically with the class struggle can offer a relevant statement.[4] Art must be, therefore, a weapon in the class war, a doctrinal imperative for all proletarian critics between 1930 and 1935, particularly V. F. Calverton in *The Modern Quarterly*, Mike Gold in the *New Republic* and Granville Hicks in *New Masses* editorials.

It is arguable whether the cultural Stalinist had, as Charles Angoff believes, the influence to ' "make or kill" a book or a play that did not follow the proletarian line'.[5] Certainly some novelists writing in the ambience of Marxism were constrained by the need to conform and the disease of careerism. Had the first and last winner of the *New Masses* prize for fiction, Clara Weatherwax, been free to work out her needs and work through her own errors, it is possible that something less tendentious or contrived might have come from the novel, *Marching! Marching!* Too often the demands of a party dogma that kept constantly shifting in the most erratic ways forced Miss Weatherwax and those like her into a wrenching of the observed truth and a vast simplification of human experience. Medodramatic scenes, wish-fulfilment endings and the rejection of internal logic were the tithes the writer paid the party. They led not merely to a literary failing but, far worse, to the moral deceit of passing off the literature of a party disguised as the literature of a class. With little sense of wit and infatuated with violence as the mid-

[3] *Ibid.*, p. xxi.
[4] J. Freeman, ed., *Proletarian Literature of the United States: An Anthology* (London 1935) pp. 12, 16.
[5] Charles Angoff, *The Tone of the Twenties and Other Essays* (New Jersey 1960) p. 229.

wife of history, the strike novel tailored fact to suit fiction and persistently revised the successes for organized labour in the strikes of the period into the fictional defeat of a down-trodden class. Cultural entrepreneurs on the radical periodical resorted, in turn, to what Edmund Wilson describes as an 'ethical' inventiveness. By this he means that they provided 'imaginary versions' of their 'ideal great writers', like John Dos Passos, who at the time was writing a trilogy about the effects of authoritarianism and had, in *The New Republic* in 1930, announced himself, politically a 'middle-class liberal'.[6] The sinister underside of this comic inventiveness is exposed by the dithyrambic Marxism and lunatic moralizing in Mike Gold's attack on Thornton Wilder, 'Prophet of the Genteel Christ',[7] and the culpable dismissal of Henry Roth as 'introspective and febrile' in one *New Masses* review.[8]

Artists on the Left in the thirties never, as Max Eastman had once contended, wrote in uniform. It may be argued that the Communist example gave a societal 'focus to the unformulated radicalism of the 1930s',[9] as is evidenced by those who pledged their support for the Communist presidential and vice-presidential candidates, Foster and Ford, in *Culture In Crisis*. But Marxism was at once more convincing and influential in the novel in a supportive role, an adjunct to those neo-Hegelian prophecies of Oswald Spengler which infiltrate the writings of Dos Passos and Eliot (the English translation of *The Decline of the West* only appeared in 1926); or to the apocalyptic historicism of Henry Adams whose *History* had considerable appeal for F. Scott Fitzgerald. The thirties was an age of apocalyptic faith, according to Malcolm Cowley, the literary editor of the *New Republic* during the period. But to those intellectuals who looked forward to 'the destruction of the old Babylonian order and the establishment of a universal commonwealth',[10] the thirties was the casualty of a failed apocalypse. If Roosevelt

[6] Quoted in Edmund Wilson, 'Marxism and Literature', *The Triple Thinkers* (London 1962) p. 233.

[7] Mike Gold, 'Wilder: Prophet of the Genteel Christ', *New Republic* LXIV (October 1930) pp. 266–7.

[8] *New Masses*, 'Brief Review' XIV (12 February 1935) p. 127.

[9] Daniel Aaron, *Writers on the Left* (New York 1961) p. 403.

[10] Malcolm Cowley, 'The 1930's Were an Age of Faith', in the book review section of *The New York Times*, 13 December 1964.

remained in the wilderness of the art world — with the exception of documentary cinema and Post Office murals — a man whose lack of interest in the aims and energy of the Popular Front rendered him a subject for contempt, the meliorism of the New Deal prevailed, at least until a war economy resolved the depression. Marxism emerged as one of many lost causes in the period, its image soured by the Moscow show trials and the Hitler-Stalin pact. Spain too became an indecisive defeat in a 'marginal' engagement, an event of symbolic promise but not realized fact; what Fiedler records in a sentimental quest for purity in the thirties as part of the 'other memory'.[11]

The sense of an ending, not merely of a historic period, but of a cycle or ethos, is a literary image of the 1930s different in substance from that issued by liberal court historians like Arthur Schlesinger, Jr and official sponsors of the New Deal. Its appeal may be located in that persistent undercurrent of wish-fulfilment and fabulism which led an independent existence beyond ideology. W. H. Auden describes it as a 'disease of consciousness which is incapable of converting wishes into desires. A lie is false; what it asserts is not the case. A wish is fantastic; it knows what is the case but refuses to accept it. All wishes whatever their content, have the same and unvarying meaning — "I refuse to be what I am".'[12] This rejection of self, situation, or position, erodes desire and consumes belief, for whatever the individual wishes, Auden concludes, 'he cannot help knowing that he could have wished something else.' The termination of such pressure is in death since, 'In its final stages the disease reduces itself to a craving for a violent pain',[13] a craving which occurs in Nathanael West's concluding portrait of the age: the ceremonial dance-riot in *The Day of the Locust*.

The ascendancy of wish-fulfilment thinking in the late twenties — the speculative desires for wealth fed by bond salesmen, Old Counsellors, newspaper hucksters — exploded in the

---

[11] Leslie Fiedler, 'The Two Memories: Reflections on Writers and Writings in the Thirties', in Freeman *Proletarian Writers of the Thirties, op. cit.*

[12] W. H. Auden, 'Interlude: West's Disease', *The Dyer's Hand and Other Essays* (London 1962) p. 241.

[13] *Ibid.*

thirties on all levels; for now there lay a far greater distance than ever before between the ideals of society and the democratic possibilities of fulfilling them. Even literature seemed designed, in the popular sector, to provide a major avenue of escape. Malcolm Cowley disagrees. For him, the literature of the thirties was socially committed since there has 'never been a period when literary events followed so closely on the flying coattails of social events'. In particular, he notes: 'Almost all the books published after 1932 belong to the literature of the depression, in the sense that they either revealed its effect on their authors, or studied its causes, or tried to evade it by fleeing to the ends of the earth and the depths of time — only to return with a lesson for tomorrow.'[14] Some writers that witnessed the shaking of the capitalist system were driven by the very momentum of experience to serious examination of their national roots. Historical novelists like Kenneth Roberts in *Arundel* and John Corbin in *The Unknown Washington* used their fiction as instruments of rediscovering national self-belief which, as a result of economic collapse, had become dangerously weak. The Southern Agrarians in *I'll Take My Stand* advocated a return to the past — to 'hierarchical religion, scholasticism and the Cult of Byzantine'[15] — to solve the problems of an industrial present; while the humanists Irving Babbit and Paul Elmer More reacted ascetically against the freedom of the twenties with an eclectic synthesis of Plato and Calvin. But Cowley's assessment of the symbiosis between literature and society from the arbitrary date of 1932, implies a shared awareness of political and economic struggle between the writer and his public which is not borne out by a critical evaluation of consumer demand and 'best seller' lists. Cowley himself points out in the same article that the proletarian novel enjoyed a critical reputation far outweighing its popularity given that average sales hardly exceeded 2,500 copies per book.[16] As James Rorty confirmed, in the preface of *Where Life is Better*, some Americans remained resistant not just to radicalism but

[14] Malcolm Cowley, *Think Back On Us . . . A Contemporary Chronicle of the 1930's* (Carbondale, Illinois 1967) p. 347.

[15] Eric Mottram, 'Living Mythically: The Thirties', *Journal of American Studies* vol. VI, no. 3 (December 1972) pp. 270—71.

[16] Cowley, *Think Back On Us, op. cit.*, pp. 349—50.

to any serious consideration of the problems facing them: 'I encountered nothing in 15,000 miles of travel that disgusted and appalled me so much as this American addiction to make-believe. Apparently, not even empty bellies can cure it.'[17]

Popular literature in the thirties was written on the basis of a shrewd recognition that those who had lost their money and job would crave escapist fiction. On news stands, with circulations ranging up to four million copies a month, pocket-digest magazines or newspapers like Bernarr MacFadden's *Evening Graphic* contained not only an 'Advice to the Lovelorn' but a 'Lonely Hearts' column, in which lonesome girls were enabled to meet equally lonesome boys.[18] Best seller novelists such as Hervey Allen (*Anthony Adverse*), James Hilton (*Lost Horizon*) and Margaret Mitchell (*Gone With The Wind*), exploited with nostrums and anodynes the public passion for surface maturation, conventional romance and local colour, with little if any intention of returning from history to the present. Equally compulsive in its appeal was that euphoric directive by Walter B. Pitkin to followers of the Townsend Plan, *Life Begins at Forty*. The thirties were abundant in social narcotics — *Wake up and Live*; *How to Live Within Your Income*; *How to Win Friends and Influence People*; *How to Make the Most of Your Life*; *Live Alone and Like It*; *How to Live Without a Woman*.

The anguish and weakened confidence of America in the thirties is indexed by the growth of salves, palliatives, fads. Heated interests in dance marathons, tree and flagpole sitting, backgammon and miniature golf flared up.[19] Gambling increased noticeably — the largest salary in the United States in 1934 going to Moe Annenberg, owner of *Racing Form* — as people tried to win back by good luck what, as it seemed, they had lost by bad.[20] At the movies, fantasy was compounded on Banko, Keeno, or Screeno nights when the manager would come on stage and spin a carnival wheel while the audience, like the rest of society, waited anxiously for the winning number.

[17] James Rorty, *Where Life is Better: An Unsentimental American Journey* (New York 1936) p. 13.

[18] Simon M. Bessie, *Jazz Journalism* (New York 1938) p. 134.

[19] James D. Horan, *The Desperate Years* (New York 1962) p. 134; F. L. Allen, *Since Yesterday* (New York 1940) p. 35; Gilbert Seldes, *The Years of the Locust* (Boston 1933) pp. 74—80.

[20] Henry Morton Robinson, *Fantastic Interim* (New York 1943) p. 271.

Thus by April 1931 New York Rabbis were predicting the arrival of a New Moses who would soon be along to end the depression, a prophecy realized only in Will Rogers' adventures in *Steamboat Round the Bend*. In the absence of Moses, the jigsaw craze began. At the close of 1933 more than two million puzzles had been sold. All over the country people were trying to put the pieces together, to get the picture organized. Many of the pieces were missing, thrown away, or never produced and such puzzles, even if completed, would have shown only pictures of chaos.[21]

The call to discipline was both sinister and comic. Each week in over 800 secret fraternal orders half the population transformed itself into an exotic army of Knights, Pharaohs, Redmen, Vikings, Furies, Hermits, Owls, Odd Fellows, Galahads, Maltese and Tibetans; a living historical pageant fighting with all its boredom and inertia to activate a style of fabulism.[22] Movie audiences accepted a blander ritual of security and Hollywood, having discovered a profitable way of deflecting radicalism, gave the fans cake. Film-makers like Walt Disney provided an image of history that the audience could consciously accept as fact and into which it might unconsciously escape from daily routine. The essential con- servatism of Disney, as Richard Schnickel makes clear, lay in his tendency to relieve the complexities of urban industrialism through jokes, musical cues and by emphasizing the cultural traditions of the past. Disney purged nature and society of mystery and substituted a fictitious cuteness for its inherent discord; he affirmed the pioneer values of self-reliance, wit and eternal persistence and indulged in nostalgic longing for small-town amenities.[23] This very process of daydream and myth offered a replacement for positive action. In *Middletown In Transition*, the Lynds contend that the movies became a major source for emulative ideas. In them, escape became the very image of reality, 'authentic portrayals of life' that ultimately consisted of 'a medley of vague and variable im-

---

[21] Horan, *op. cit.*, p. 166.
[22] Charles Merz, *The Great American Band-Wagon* (New York 1939) pp. 23—4.
[23] Richard Schnickel, *The Disney Version* (New York 1968) pp. 51—3, 154—5, 157, 194—5, 210—13, 361.

pressions'.[24] Screened in a darkened baroque theatre, movies
not only romanticized life; they transformed its conditions and
offered simplicity and order. When all else was so bleak twenty
million people, one out of every six Americans, found time to
go to the movies every day of the week.[25]

To Glenway Wescott the problem is one of perception and
the recurrence of an 'old secretiveness'. Man had developed a
'tendency to cringe, and to dream in ideal terms, and to look
down upon little radical facts.'[26] In the fiction of Nathanael
West the lovelorn dream ideally to escape the pain and rupture
of living. But their aspirations, cheapened and commercialized
by movies, radio and newspapers, only intensity their sense of
betrayal. West's people are grotesque in a society that stimulates
and thwarts their desires, his novels are ironic and angry and
trace a pattern from expectation to despair to violence. Riding
through the slums of New York, Miss Lonelyhearts recognizes
his own contribution to the joke:

He saw a man who appeared to be on the verge of death stagger into a movie theater
that was showing a picture called Blonde Beauty. He saw a ragged woman with an
enormous goiter pick a love story magazine out of a garbage can and seem very
excited by her find.[27]

Nathanael West is a writer who examines the tension between
consumer art and consumer frustrations. He assesses the needs
of mass society but does not satisfy them and experiments with
cherished forms of kitsch without becoming a best seller. West
had once considered giving Miss Lonelyhearts the subtitle of 'a
novel in the form of a comic strip',[28] thereby stating an enduring concern with popular culture as a fictional strategy. Certainly
the novel is highly structured and written in imitation of the
cartoonist's methods of showing characters in a series of picture
boxes — the newspaper office, the park, Delahanty's speakeasy,
Miss Lonelyhearts apartment, Betty's apartment, the El Gaucho
club, a Connecticut farm — each of which is complete in itself

[24] Herbert Bluimer, Movies and Conduct (New York 1933) pp. 198—9.

[25] Merz, op. cit., pp. 174—5.

[26] Glenway Wescott, Fear and Trembling (New York 1932) pp. 237, 238, 255.

[27] Nathanael West, The Complete Works of Nathanael West, Introduction by
Alan Ross (New York 1957) p. 115.

[28] Nathanael West, 'Some Notes on Miss L.', Contempo, 15 May 1933, p. 1.

but forms part of a larger story. The novel may lack the straight-forward development of a comic strip. 'Each chapter,' West wrote, 'instead of going forward in time, also goes backwards, forwards, up and down in space like a picture.'[29] But the effect holds the readers interest by making him see rather than merely sense an enclosed landscape. It provides a useful point of con-centration for the anguished fancy and disorder in the novel, a unity of effect through a brief visual image which recalls the poetic method of Edgar Allan Poe. 'Lyric novels,' West argued perceptively, 'can be written according to Poe's definition of a lyric poem. The short novel is a distinct form especially fitted for use in this country.'[30]

The focus of *Miss Lonelyhearts* is not synoptic but that of an 'ecological' hybrid, a genre which for Blanche Gelfant, locates an idiosyncratic response to a confined milieu.[31] West provides us with that response in Mary Shrike's desire to go 'Spanish' at the El Gaucho club: 'Guitars, bright shawls, exotic foods, out-landish costumes,' the newspaper man realizes, 'all those things were part of the business of dreams.'[32] Mary is an absolutist of the imagination; she exemplifies what T. S. Eliot has called, *bovarysme*, the adoption of an aesthetic rather than a moral attitude to life. She recalls those characters in the spatial unit of Albert Halper's *Union Square* who counteract their frustra-tion with an impersonation of style. Mr and Mrs Drollinger go 'Russian', surround themselves with junk, refer to each other as Vanya and Natasha and speak to each other in bad Chekhov. 'The Man Who Walks Backwards' watches the world in mirrors attached to his eye glasses and, 'like so many Americans' during the depression, tries 'to construct a life that made sense from things found in gift shops.'[33] This sense of desperate gaiety is but one step away from the mental instability of the heroes of Benchley, Thurber and Perelman: 'I'm going to the Zoo,' Walter Mitty reports, 'and feed popcorn to the rhinoceros. That makes things seem right, for a while anyway.'[34]

[29] *Ibid.*
[30] *Ibid.*
[31] Blanche Gelfant, *The American City Novel* (Norman, Oklahoma 1954).
[32] West, *The Complete Works, op. cit.*, p. 93.
[33] Kurt Vonnegut, *Slaughterhouse V* (London 1970) p. 3.
[34] James Thurber, *Vintage Thurber* vol. I (London 1963) p. 36.

Whatever we make of Thurber's scenario there is certainly
evidence of a recoil from the problems of life in a complex
civilization that leads to a strange internal fantasy devoid of
any value except that of exoticism. The effect is that characters
who have little sense of history must resort to fantasy in order
to escape the present. They tend to be individuals in
a state of self-creation pursuing a style which their creators
deprive them of. The radical, mute hero of James Gould
Cozzens' neglected novella, *Castaway*, re-enacts the utopian
myth of Robinson Crusoe in the desolate landscape of a
department store fortified against intruders. Lecky encounters
neither the coherency of play nor the challenge of isolation.
He confronts instead, the comic nightmare of a Doppleganger
victim surrealistically adrift amid the gadgetry of a consumer
society. Lecky's fantasy of privacy suggests a need to interrupt,
what Lewis Mumford referred to at the time as 'the inevitable
routine of living';[35] to indulge oneself and exorcize at the
same time those hooded hordes whom Ortega y Gasset, in *The
Revolt of the Masses*, believed were supplanting the values of
a culture-bearing elite.

The confining mentality and accidie of the city can not be
evaded, alternatively, by movement west, as the California
novel in the thirties overtly demonstrates. Steinbeck makes it
clear that his 'Okies' in *The Grapes of Wrath* are initially
betrayed not only because society rejects them but also since
they reject society as it is and construct an ideal image of life
in California, 'where it's easy living'.[36] They are guilty, in
Steinbeck's dialectic, of making 'teleological' rather than 'non-
teleological' decisions; of obscuring fact with preconceived
notions and of thinking in terms of 'what should be, or could
be, or might be', instead of 'what actually' is'".[37] In an
exilic tradition of westward drive and escape into the sunset
they respond not merely to economic and ecological pressures
but to an archetypal race memory. The tragedy of Jody's
grandfather in Steinbeck's 'The Leader of The People' is that

[35] Lewis Mumford, 'From a City Notebook', *The New Republic*, 18 September
1929, p. 125.
[36] John Steinbeck, *The Grapes of Wrath* (New York 1967) p. 63.
[37] John Steinbeck and Edward F. Ricketts, *Sea of Cortez* (New York 1941),
p. 13.

westering 'didn't last long enough'. Like his ageing compatriots
the old pioneer discovers that, 'There's no place to go. There's
the ocean to stop you. There's a line of old men along the shore
hating the ocean because it stopped them.'[38] The democracy
of the frontier has been replaced by an oligarchy of Big Business,
the fluidity of the West succeeded by the standardization of
Main Street. The peripatetic hobo lives out a solitary hegira to
nowhere; like Faulkner's Joe Christmas he is 'doomed with
motion'.[39]

Edmund Wilson's description of the California novelists in
the depression as 'The Boys in the Back Room'[40] gives a tacit
sense of an enclosed but seedy world and a felt presence of
Hollywood which employed many of these writers. In *They
Shoot Horses, Don't They?* California is merely an 'enormous'[41]
room — the belly of a whale at the end of an amusement
pier — which gives ecological focus to the 'picaresque'[42] desire
for drama and self-advertisement through the ceremony and
spectacle of marathon dancing. In literal terms *They Shoot
Horses, Don't They?* finalizes the westward dream of the
depression émigré as a Sisyphean 'merry-go-round'. But more
important is the way McCoy uses popular dance as a feature
of mass art, invests it with mythic significance and utilizes the
divisive energies contained by that dance as a fictional device
to pace and structure the novel. McCoy's use of dance-form
translates motion both as an element in the exhibition of
gesture — the expressive myth of upward social mobility — and
as the balletic articulation of a nomadic impulse. The dance
thus becomes an important space-cult ceremony, what Rudolph
Somner describes as 'an intense space-experience'.[43]

In *They Shoot Horses* the dancers participate in the
horrifying spectacle of a derby race — 'a little novelty guaranteed

[38] John Steinbeck, 'The Leader of the People', *The Long Valley* (London 1970),
p. 214.

[39] William Faulkner, *Light In August* (New York 1959) p. 167.

[40] Edmund Wilson, 'The Boys in the Back Room', *Classics and Commercials: A
Literary Chronicle of the Forties* (London 1951).

[41] Horace McCoy, *They Shoot Horses, Don't They?* (London 1965) p. 23.

[42] Lucy L. Hazard, 'The American Picaresque', *The Trans-Mississippi West*
(Boulder, Colorado 1930) p. 217. Hazard locates the emergence of the 'new-
born American picaresque' in a rejection of 'routine respectability' and a
'mechanized society' in favour of 'the open road'.

[43] Quoted in Susanne K. Langer *Feeling and Form* (London 1953) p. 170.

to pack 'em in' — indulge in arranged marriages to boost the 'showmanship angle'[44] and exhaust themselves with displays of stamina to acquire the material benefits of sponsorship. But whipped into an ecstatic state by the master of ceremonies, Rocky Gravo (who performs with his microphone the same orchestrating function as West's radio commentator outside Kahn's Persian Palace in *The Day of the Locust*) the marathon dancers acquire a destructive sexual appetite which complements that of their audience. These dislocated energies are approximated in turn by the fractured narrative. The textual in-turnings complement the repetitive introduction of film stars, the cadenced rise and fall of the ocean as it quivers against the pilings, and Robert's mystical pirouetting as he pursues a moving ring of sunlight. The early scenes are simple yet cinematic, describing in vivid detail the visual appearance of a slain woman at death. They fade out to reveal a close-up of Robert Syverten and the appearance of a judge who pronounces sentence. The bulk of the novel is a flashback account of the felt reasons for the narrator's crime and the story of his relationship with Gloria Beatty. It suggests a tension between the 'criminal' facts of the narrator's case and a separate set of extenuating circumstances. These facts, as in *Miss Lonelyhearts*, are conveyed through a series of box-like incidents, a city park, a seduction scene, a derby race, a public wedding. They are interspersed with fragments of background life: information from a newspaper cutting, snatches of biography, italicized awakenings of perception from Syverten and the measured reading of the death sentence which concludes on the last page with the phrase: 'MAY GOD HAVE MERCY ON YOUR SOUL. . . . '[45]

By recalling these events Syverten imposes an order on his thoughts and extracts a new understanding from his experience. The process is aided by a tight-lipped 'cablese,'[46] a language of objectivity and pace which grew out of the tickertape style of World War I, and which McCoy perfected under the tutelage of Captain Joe Shaw on the *Black Mask* magazine. The baldness

[44] McCoy, *op. cit.*, pp. 31, 73.

[45] *Ibid.*, p. 125.

[46] 'Cablese' was the 'great language' which so attracted the young Hemingway that he told Lincoln Steffens: I had to quit being a correspondent. I was getting too fascinated by the lingo of the cable. Quoted in Lincoln Stephens, *Autobiography of Lincoln Steffens* (New York 1931) p. 834.

and economy of the style heightens the solitariness and bestiality of Syverten's experience, yet is effective in balancing the typographical and structural tricks. Crisp, muscular and colloquial, the style serves as a prophylaxis for McCoy against an increasingly complex, rapidly changing world where, in Valery's words, 'there are too many facts' and 'where all . . . results speak at once'.[47] Faced with the problem of locating the disparity between idealism and the destructive character of experience, McCoy keeps his emotional distance and his eyes hard on what Hemingway called 'the sequence of motion and fact'.[48] The approach has been called merely 'tough'. But as Richard Bridgman demonstrates, it is a form of colloquial language which descends from Twain, Hemingway, the *Black Mask* school and an arduous apprenticeship in journalism. It employs a simplified diction, limited vocabulary and subtly varied sentence constructions. It stresses dialogue, concrete noun and verb and conveys a sense of objectivity through an avoidance of adjectives and verbs.

The hard boiled genre is a muscular and functional attempt to give organic form to a world view. The twenty-minute egg of that school and McCoy's contemporary, is James Cain. His novel, *The Postman Always Rings Twice*, is a characteristic artifact of the thirties; it reflects a vision of popular culture which Cain's observations of society encouraged. The aesthetic statement in the novel is inseparable from the observed fact and the tremendous pace of the narrative assimilates a world in which violence is 'idiomatic' or 'daily'.[49] The overall impact is that of brevity, urgency and directness; the material is stripped almost 'bald' in its avoidance of emotional cliché and bathos. As Mr Katz wittily remarks: 'It's not how long it lasts. It's what you do while you're in there',[50] a statement which could stand as Cain's way of recognizing Nathanael West's injunction that a writer should: 'Forget the epic, the master work. . . . Leave slow growth to the book reviewers, you only have time to explode. Remember William Carlos Williams' description of the

---

[47] Everett W. Knight, *Literature Considered as Philosphy: The French Example* (London 1957) p. 40.

[48] Ernest Hemingway, *Death in The Afternoon* (London, 1966) p. 6.

[49] Nathanael West, 'Some Notes on Violence,' *Contact* I, no. 3 (1932) pp. 132–3.

[50] James M. Cain, *The Postman Always Rings Twice* (London 1970) p. 82.

pioneer women who shot their children against the wilderness
like cannon balls. Do the same with your novels. A novelist can
afford to be everything but dull.'[51] Pace and improvisation
are vital elements in Cain's novel. Amid his frantic animalistic
whirl with Cora, which he perfunctorily refers to as 'holy',
Frank Chambers is consumed by a pathological hipsterism and
driven along at a pace that prohibits self-evaluation:

Then I saw her . . . except for the shape, she really wasn't any raving beauty, but
she had a sulky look to her, and her lips stuck out in a way that made me want to
mash them in for her.[52]

It is not only the harshness of style that enhances the novel's
authenticity, but also the sordid nature of its environment which
reflects the hard surfaces, expresses the mood and provides an
impersonal statement on American society in the depression.
While too many proletarian novelists wrote about the masses
to the intellectuals, Cain wrote not only about, but mainly to
the masses, dramatizing their temptations and inner drives.
With a purity of vision unimpaired by ideological tithes he
pointed up the closeness of violence to the surfaces of life.
Although W. M. Frohock has accused him of a knowing
exploitation of violence and sex the charge is made without
regard to context. With the violence of the thirties covered
extensively by the news media and fictionalized in mass entertainment, the public became crime addicts. Popular culture
expressed not only the spontaneity of violence, but also
America's eagerness to experience it vicariously as 'entertainment'. But in view of the high incidence of violence in all his
work, Cain lends little power to the long-standing tendency in
mass art to glamorize crime. He is a novelist who transcends
the 'trash category' of horror pornography.[53] As Raymond
Chandler succinctly comments: 'Possibly it was the smell of
fear which these stories managed to generate. Their characters
lived in a world gone wrong, a world in which, long before the
atom bomb, civilization had created the machinery for its own

---

[51] West, 'Some Notes on Miss L.', *op. cit.*, pp. 1—2.
[52] Cain, *op. cit.*, p. 8.
[53] W. M. Frohock, *The Novel of Violence in America 1920—1950* (Dallas, Texas
1950) p. 87.

destruction, and was learning to use it with all the moronic delight of a gangster trying out his first machine gun.'[54]

In his foreward to *The Raymond Chandler Omnibus* Lawrence Clark Powell lists *The Postman* as one of the most memorable novels written about 'the Great Wrong Place'. As a Los Angeles novel Cain's book locates a shifting emphasis from nature to society, from the given world of the open road that Frank must endure to the artificial world of restaurant and mortgaged home that Cora must have to protect herself against the vagaries of the first. Cain introduces another dimension to 'the back room', the detective genre and that fraternity of *Black Mask* writers who adopt a city as their own and record its manners. Thus W. H. Auden sees Raymond Chandler, the Los Angeles novelist, as 'interested in writing, not detective stories, but serious studies of a milieu, the Great Wrong Place, and his powerful but extremely depressing books should be read and judged, not as escape literature, but as works of art.'[55] Chandler himself, in *The Simple Art of Murder*, offers a practitioner's interpretation of the crime novel and acclaims Dashiell Hammett for taking murder out of the English drawing room and dropping it into the seedier alleys of San Francisco. Chandler believes that Hammett wrote authentically 'for people with a sharp, aggressive attitude to life' and 'gave murder back to the kind of people that commit it for reasons, not just to provide a corpse.'[56]

Both Chandler and Hammett provide us with an informative analysis of the city; their private eye's are guides who conduct us on a tour of the underworld, into its alleys and down those mean streets which are dark with something other than night. Hypocrisy in religion, deceit and self-interest in business, corruption in politics, seep into the alleys and create 'messes' that Sam Spade and Philip Marlowe seek to clean up. Viewing life with the sharpness of a picaro at worm's-eye level the detective is both participant in and observer of the city. Strategically placed to objectively describe and implicitly judge it, he dispenses with language that does not enable him to govern the immediate. His is a language from the solar plexus, reflecting a

---

[54] Raymond Chandler, *The Simple Art of Murder* (New York 1964) p. 3.

[55] Auden, 'The Guilty Vicarage', *The Dyers Hand, op. cit.*, p. 151.

[56] Chandler, *op. cit.*, p. vii.

vision of life which is deadpan and cynical, an attitude ironic, dispassionate and neutral, a tone culturally unpretentious and hard boiled. As Leslie Fiedler says, 'The private eye is not the dandy turned sleuth', '. . . he is the cowboy adapted to life on the city streets, the embodiment of innocence moving untouched through universal guilt . . . the honest proletarian, illuminating by contrast the decadent society of the rich.'[57]

In the West Coast novel of crime and detection the gangster and detective live in an inverted world where the possibilities for expression are restricted to the petrified forests of Southern California. Gary Cooper, 1929's Virginian, becomes a beer racketeer in 1931's *City Streets*. The mobster's flaw is contained in the simulated pose of an agrarian in a complex, metropolitan world. He is ignorant, responsive, and instinctive but insists on sharing the untutored individualism of the cowboy in a society where conformity to rules and traditions is the price for security. As a symbol of his environment the gangster exerts a forceful effect on a voyeurish audience which does not know first hand the world of crime. As Robert Warshow puts it: 'The real city, one might say, produces only criminals; the imaginary city produces the gangster: he is what we want to be and what we are afraid we may become.'[58] The gangster expresses an unconscious protest against the sham optimism of a society in collapse. A psychopathic caricature of the Alger stereotype, he rises to success through diligence and self-reliance, hurting people and accepting, in turn, that he must be hurt by others. He attains temporary eminence and power, but his ultimate reward is a punishment for his negation of traditional virtues and is a consequence of his presumption in setting himself apart from the masses. The individual can no longer rise on his own and he who chooses to try — Scarface, Little Rico — is doomed. In traditional picaresque style, the gangster becomes the depression's favourite cultural scapegoat. For, as Warshow explains: 'The whole meaning' of the gangster's 'career is a drive for success' and 'he always dies because he is an individual; the final bullet thrusts him back, makes him after all, a failure.' This is perversely a source of reassurance to the reader/audience

[57] Leslie Fiedler, *Love and Death in the American Novel* (London 1967) p. 489.
[58] Robert Warshow, 'The Gangster as Tragic Hero', *The Immediate Experience* (New York 1962) p. 131.

whose final response to the gangster is 'a response to sadism'.
The reader gains 'the double satisfaction of participating
vicariously in the gangster's sadism and then seeing it turned
against the gangster himself.'[59] Urban passivity is justified;
the twin myths, of cowboy and vigorous urban Darwinist,
prove incompatible.

Raymond Chandler preferred, on his own admission, 'a conservative atmosphere, a sense of the past';[60] which is to say an
urban pastoralism safely accommodating violence. Marlowe is
the traditional American folk-hero who finds 'his destiny in the
West'[61] and attempts to change things through a vanishing code
of voluntary individualism, justice and celibacy. He moves with
integrity and toughness through a lonely world, rarely deviating
from the code of a frontier knight in a society that makes
stringent demands on his manners. Like Owen Wister's Virginian
he identifies himself with a tradition of violence as evidence of
his courage but never accomplishes the brutal effects of Daly's
Race Williams or Hammett's Sam Spade. Marlowe takes
terrific beatings; he is slugged, shot at, doped, strangled and
tempted; yet he survives because it is in his nature as a catalyst
to survive. Marlowe rescues damsels and old men, fights with
pornographic booksellers, psychic consultants and chiefs of
police. There is the occasional cop like Bernie Ohls who is
tough, efficient and honest, but more frequently the police
are dishonest and brutal, a foil for the private eye who risks
life, reputation and license to ensure protection for those for
whom he works. Chandler's credo is set down in *The Simple
Art of Murder*: 'Down these mean streets a man must go who
is not himself mean, who is neither tarnished nor afraid.'[62]
Love, marriage and sex, are, until *The Poodle Springs Story*,
consistently denied the Chandler detective partially, at least,
because a man is less capable of freely offering his life in
defence of others while he has a family at home. In 'Trouble
is My Business' Dalmas is tempted by a redhead with 'bedroom'
eyes' who was once in the social register. He goes out with her

[59] *Ibid.*, p. 131—2.

[60] Philip Durham, *Down These Mean Streets a Man Must Go: Raymond Chandler's
Knight* (Durham, N. Carolina 1963) p. 37.

[61] *Ibid.*, p. 82.

[62] Chandler, *op. cit.*, p. 193.

and sees her four times but then recognizes that he has not 'the money, the clothes, the time or the manners'.[63]

The appeal of the detective, to some extent, resides in an extension of the reader's ego since his most prominent features are shrewdness, wit and a measure of strength. The criminal, conversely, is a personalization of the reader's grievance against society, a scapegoat who justifies his suspicion that all men including those who appear most innocent are really his potential enemies. Hence an audience experiences considerable satisfaction when the criminal is identified, for this denoument confirms to him that he is right to suspect everybody. According to William Aydelotte: 'The detective story does not reflect order; but expresses on the fantasy level a yearning for order; it suggests, then, a disordered world, and its roots are to be sought in social disintegration rather than social cohesion.'[64] This view is borne out by the attitude held by Eric Ambler's novelist-detector, Latimer, in *The Mask of Dimitrios*. Latimer sees the body of Dimitrios, 'not as a corpse in a mortuary but as a man, not as an isolate, a phenomenon, but as a unit in a disintegrating social system.'[65] Order is discovered and imposed by the detective: he is indispensable for he alone can solve the riddle.

Yet it is simply not true to claim as does Aydelotte that the detective dispenses a wish-fulfilment fantasy of 'Power',[66] infallibility and resilience. That dubious honour might be reserved for Erle Stanley Gardner's Perry Mason, or Mickey Spillane's McCarthyite Mike Hammer, an animal man with a need '. . . to take the law into his own hands, to bring to trial, to judge, to condemn [but in his case even personally to execute] those who he singly decides to have been of the Bad'.[67] But Marlowe is neither contemptuous of death nor immune to fear. He is a noble, somewhat witty man, sad and insecure, who is a failure

---

[63] Raymond Chandler, *Trouble Is My Business, And Other Stories* (London 1972) pp. 8, 68.

[64] William Aydelotte, 'The Detective as a Historical Source', *Yale Review* (1949–1950) p. 94.

[65] Eric Ambler, *The Mask of Dimitrios* (London 1971) p. 63.

[66] Aydelotte, *op. cit.*, pp. 77, 86.

[67] Christopher La Farge, 'Mickey Spillane and His Bloody Hammer', in Bernard Rosenberg and David M. White, eds., *Mass Culture: The Popular Arts in America* (Glencoe 1957) p. 177.

in that he cannot make money, and whose closest literary
neighbour is the private investigator of Hammett's *The Dain
Curse*. He has neither the certitude nor the assurance of what
John Paterson terms, the pre-depression 'trascendent sleuth',
and occupies that 'dim uneasy region that lies between the
. . . legitimately constituted social order and the rapacious
criminal underworld.'[68] Unlike Hammer he trusts neither the
one nor the other and is himself not trusted by either. In *The
Big Sleep* Marlowe's eloquent sympathy for General Sternwood
— a 'few locks of dry white hair clung to his scalp, like wild
flowers fighting for life on a bare rock'[69] — is undercut by a
job which ensures that he protect the rich from suffering the
consequences of their misdeeds. The social injustice of the
situation does not elude Chandler. As a minor character in
the novel says to Marlowe:

I'd like to see the flashy well-dressed muggs . . . spoiling their manicures in the rock
quarry at Folsom, alongside of the poor little slum-bred hard guys that got knocked
over on their first caper and never had a break since. That's what I'd like.[70]

Marlowe frequently admits to being scared and lonely. Lying
on a dingy waterfront hotel bed in *Farewell My Lovely*, he
tersely assesses the witless joke of his position:

I needed a drink, I needed a lot of life insurance, I needed a vacation, I needed a
home in the country. What I had was a coat, a hat and a gun.[71]

This observation, neither prepared for nor overstated, reveals
Marlowe not in a state of maudlin self-pity but comically aware
of being without love, and hence vulnerable, which is the price
he must pay for his 'Power'. With 'another day drawing to its
end, the air dull and tired', Marlowe returns to his office in *The
High Window*:

I filled and lit my pipe and sat there smoking. Nobody came in, nobody called,
nothing happened, nobody cared whether I died or went to El Paso.[72]

[68] John Paterson, 'A Cosmic View of the Private Eye', *Saturday Review* XXXVI
(22 August 1953) pp. 7—8.
[69] Raymond Chandler, *The Big Sleep* (London 1973) p. 14.
[70] *Ibid.*, p. 197.
[71] Raymond Chandler, *Farewell My Lovely*, *The Raymond Chandler Omnibus*
(London 1966) p. 285.
[72] Raymond Chandler, *The High Window* (London 1973) p. 162.

Marlowe's toughness consists not in a dumb-ox conquest of feeling but in the conquest of a tendency to spill his emotions in public — what Joseph defines in Saul Bellow's *Dangling Man* as the inhibiting model of 'hardboiled-dom' — which is a question of manners but not sensibility. If Marlowe must be seen as practising a creed distilled from Hemingway the interesting comparison is not with Harry Morgan but with Jake Barnes who cries in private about his shattered manhood and frustrated desire for Brett Ashley. Barnes's discovery that it is 'awfully easy to be hardboiled about everything in the daytime, but at night it is another thing'[73] reverberates throughout a crucial scene in *The Big Sleep* when Marlowe discovers Carmen Sternwood in his bed naked. Marlowe broods about Carmen's threat to his integrity and the sanctity of a home violated. 'Knights had no meaning in this game. It wasn't a game for knights.'[74] But the scene is developed with such controlled ambiguity that it remains unclear whether Marlowe's contempt for Carmen merges with a desire for her flesh, privately released in rage after her departure:

Steps tinkled on the quiet pavement. A car started up not far away. It rushed off into the night with a rough clashing of gears. I went back to the bed and looked at it. The imprint of her head was still in the pillow, of her small corrupt body still on the sheets.

I put my empty glass down and tore the bed to pieces savagely.[75]

It is worth comparing the language and tone of this description with Hemingway's concluding paragraph to chapter IV of *The Sun Also Rises*.

Camus' hypothesis in *The Rebel* that the tough novel is stylized, anti-intellectual and reductive of the interior life, is not adequate. Dilys Powell refers us to the modernist influence of Chandler — his indifference to precise, logical narrative, his descriptive pace and richness of ironic style, his left-out plot links and obscure motives — on a film like Roman Polanski's *Chinatown.*[76] Moreover, the development of character and

---

[73] Ernest Hemingway, *The Sun Also Rises* (London 1958) p. 28.

[74] Chandler, *The Big Sleep, The Raymond Chandler Omnibus, op. cit.*, p. 153.

[75] *Ibid.*, p. 153.

[76] Dilys Powell, 'The Eye of the Master', *The Sunday Times*, 11 August 1974, p. 23.

effacing of personality in Polanski's film cannot be treated as a mere shift in interpretation from the Bogart private eye — saturnine, guttural, lisping — without reference to the underside of character presented to us by Chandler and even Hammett. For if Marlowe is a figure of sometimes intense and terrible loneliness, Hammett's private eyes are possessed by the guilt and anxiety of being spiritually brutalized by the violence which is their idiom. Both the Continental Op and Max Thursday admit to that 'nameless melancholy of the man of action who sees the shadow of thought on the wall.'[77] In *Red Harvest* the Op's lost alternative, of perhaps having resolved the criminal situation in 'Poisonville' — and performed his job — with less bloodshed, grows in poignancy and he begins to doubt his own motives. The Op discovers that he is paying the price for his 'Power' — his morbid fear that he is spiritually infected and going 'blood simple like the natives. Play with murder enough and it gets you one of two ways. It makes you sick or you get to like it,'[78] he says as he tabulates the 16 murders to that moment.

The quintessential myth of omniscience and power in the folklore of the thirties is represented not by Marlowe or Spade, which is the contention of Edmund Wilson,[79] but by the corpuscular space detective, Superman. With his embarkation cry, 'Up! Up! and away-y-y-y!', he traverses millions of miles instantaneously and lands on an ailing planet at the farthest reaches of the cosmic frontier to do battle with creatures similarly endowed with supernatural power. Since he is virtually immortal and can move away in defiance of gravity from the mean city streets and the life of Clark Kent, he enjoys a more glossy appeal than the urban guides of Glendale and Southern California with their strange fears and limitations. Thinking never occurs to Superman; it is just not necessary for the success of his missions and could probably interfere with their executions. Leo Gurko capsulates this adequately: 'Superman is sublimely indifferent, a condition in some ways more devastating than outright repudiation. He is, like Tarzan and most other

---

[77] Ernest Borneman, 'Black Mask', *Go* (February-March 1952) p. 64.

[78] Dashiell Hammett, *Red Harvest* (London 1963) p. 137.

[79] Edmund Wilson, 'Why Do People Read Detective Stories', *Classics and Commercials, op. cit.*, p. 236.

factitiously primitive figures, a symbol of pure motor action, whose profound attraction lies in that very fact! To create personages who are free of the responsibilities of mind and have conquered the terrors of Nature is to provide a measure of release for oneself.'[80]

Superman appeared in 1938 a native of the planet Krypton which blew up one day leaving him floating through the ether, a lone survivor. The timing of his arrival was welcome in a society soon to be jittered by a radio version of H. G. Wells's *War of the Worlds* and threats of holocaust from European power devils. Pressured by an insistent audience during World War II to go to Berlin and drop bombs on Hitler[81] Superman destroyed the West Wall and was promptly branded as a Jew by the Third Reich in *Das Schwarz Korps*. But Superman is nothing if not Aryan. With his magnificently proportioned body and lurking sexuality he is an exotic descendant of Paul Bunyan, Pecos Bill, Jack London's 'Buck' and Tarzan. As the camp equivalent of Charles Lindbergh, Superman occupies the heroic position of cosmic pioneer who liberates the mythology of picaresque folklore by conquering the laws of gravity. He reopens the world of wish-fulfilment and urban escapism in the 1930s but argues against self-limitation and understanding. He, and his pop-culture progenies, Batman, Wonder Woman, Captain Marvel and Kid Eternity, are metaphors of a dream of limitless and juvenile power which gives access to the politicization of myth and the proposition 'that "evil" is a formulated conquerable enemy unable to resist American magic.'[82]

'We remain fixated,' says Joseph Campbell, 'to the unexorcized images of our infancy, hence disinclined to the necessary passages of our adulthood.'[83] The cartoon and comic strip are terminal points in American popular culture which reach out beyond the 'hardboiled-dom' of the thirties and locate, some thirty years later, American foreign policy and the contemporary novel whose stimulus often is that policy. The concept of

---

[80] Leo Gurko, 'Folklore of the American Hero', *Heroes, Highbrows and The Popular Mind* (Indianapolis, Indiana 1953) p. 175.

[81] *Ibid.*, p. 174.

[82] Mottram, *op. cit.*, p. 228.

[83] Joseph Campbell, *The Hero with a Thousand Faces* (New York 1956) p. 11.

frontierism and 'Diplomacy in Eden'[84] incinerates Vietnamese and confuses the difference between contemplating God and playing God. Its by-product is the nightmare fiction of a cartoon world: the personless comedy of Joseph Heller and the soft-centred Populism of Ken Kesey. Brian Patten is pessimistic but for the wrong reasons, when he writes:

The serials are all wound up now,
Put away in small black boxes
For a decade or so. Superman's asleep in
    the sixpenny childhood seats. . . .
And Flash Gordon likewise wanders lonely
Weeping over the girl he loved 7 universes ago.

We killed them all simply because we grew up. . . . [85]

---

[84] Charles L. Sanford, *The Quest for Paradise* (Urbana, Illinois 1961) ch. 12.

[85] Brian Patten, 'Where are you now Superman', in Edward Lucie-Smith, ed., *The Liverpool Scene* (New York 1968) p. 44.

14

Gentlemen of Principle, Priests of Presumption

Benjamin DeMott

This chapter is offered as a survey of problems in political writing that have surfaced in ways direct or oblique during the Watergate crisis. The spectrum covered is wide and the literature of politics will doubtless seem to come slighted as compared with the subliterature.

One further prefatory word — of acknowledgement. The prompting to literary reflection on Watergate came in part as a result of the appearance during the Ervin Committee sessions of a figure absent for decades from the American political scene — the politician as embryonic novelist. Again and again Mr Baker of Tennessee foreswore standard-form factfinding in favour of the pursuit of inner configurations of response. 'I am probing into your state of mind,' he declared to one or another witness. 'How do you feel now?' Intent on probing the textures of response, ingratiatingly patient but persistent, shaking off distractions of dates and names and deeds, concerned for the quality of a qualm, Mr Baker invited witnesses to speculate on their own emotions as recollected, to make him privy to events as known from inside. Now and then he was rewarded with some halting word about how it all felt — 'I kind of drifted along,' said Mr Herbert Porter — whereupon the senator leaned forward eagerly, catching what Lawrence would have called the momentaneous on the wing: 'Now,' Baker was heard to say, 'now you have reached now precisely that point I would like to examine and I intend to examine. . . .' The Senator's interest

*This chapter was written in 1973. Given the nature of Benjamin DeMott's concerns no attempt has been made to update the references. Ed.

in motive and condition of temperament did not please every
observer (Mr I. F. Stone complained that some of Baker's
questions were 'fuzzy and pretentious'.) But on the whole the
Tennessean's notices were good. And if his performance can't
be thought to improve the prospect for rapprochement
between novelistic art and politics, it did as I admit launch the
train we ride.

The problems I wish to review are of several sorts, obscurely
but genuinely interrelated, and can be grouped conveniently in
the discredited high, middle and low brow categories of yester-
year. At subliterary levels the problems flow from the structure
and modes of organization of commercial effort to provide the
public with sound political intelligence about the times. At a
level above that of day-to-day newspaper reportage they flow
from the middlebrow writer's irremediable dependency on the
tattered rhetorical ready-to-wear of myth and epic. And in the
high literary culture the problems include an overly crude
theory of knowledge and an irrational pique at the sound of
the public voice.

Let us begin with the simplest and most obvious problem:
the poverty of journalistic means. Upwards of a hundred lawyers
are now engaged in research and allied adventures, under the
direction of Special Investigator Cox. They were led to this
task not by a hundred or so members of the White House Cor-
respondents' Association working in concert but rather, as
everyone knows, by two young men — Messrs Bernstein and
Woodward of the *Washington Post*. The story of these reporters'
labours has recently been told with agility and style by Mr
Timothy Crouse, late of *Harvard Crimson*, now a contributing
editor of *Rolling Stone*, in a handy press critique called *The
Boys on the Bus* (published by Random House in 1973). Mr
Crouse points out what the reporters themselves have emphasized in conversation — that the conventional beat system on
their paper, as on all others, would have prohibited any news-
paperman on national assignment from probing as they probed.
Bernstein and Woodward were city side men, small potatoes as it
were, inexpensive and free from the obligation to 'cover' pseudo-
events contrived by ingenious 'spokesmen for the President'.
They were also — a less trivial matter than might be apparent —

men passing through divorces, hence free of an evening, as they
themselves remark, deprived of home lives, eager for distraction,
able to work round the clock on interviews in private houses,
away from inhibiting official settings. There was no backup team,
no corps of investigative journalists bent on disclosing the Whole
Story. Two men on an assignment that from the first clearly
demanded dozens: proof not of the vitality of American
journalistic institutions but of the serious underfinancing of
independent investigative enterprise.

Lack of means is but one side of the journalistic coin; the
other reads, lack of impact. The participants in a recent BBC
roundtable on the press and Watergate — they included Mr
Ben Bradlee, editor of the *Post* — ran on boastfully about 'the
power and integrity of American newspapers' and 'their sleep-
less vigilance' and the like. Yet as Mr Ian Hamilton remarked, if
this power was real, should not the Watergate story have had at
least some effect on the Nixon landslide? (The story was fully
ventilated in the papers by 10 October, weeks before the
national election.) It is surely also relevant that the *Post*
reporters, in their interview with Crouse, spoke bitterly about
their own inability, despite repeated efforts, to interest other
reporters and Washington bureau chiefs in the story they were
uncovering. (Bradlee himself has acknowledged that for months
the story could not get beyond the *Post*'s 'own circulation
area'.) What is more, much more, Watergate is in fact a rerun:
the first time through, owing to the failure of the press, the
story simply did not take. The record of press impact in disclosing an earlier and related scandal — that involving
International Telephone and Telegraph, the San Diego Democratic Convention, Dita Beard, *et alia* — testifies that damaging
facts spread large in the American newspapers are, under
ordinary circumstances, no threat whatever to the directors of
conglomerates and the Cabinet officials disposed to serve them.
The particulars of the ITT intrigue, involving contributions to
underwrite a West Coast Democratic National Convention
(desired by the President) by ITT, in exchange for a negotiated
settlement of a Justice Department action requiring the conglomerate to detach itself from a major insurance company —
these were spelled out in a series of newspaper columns, and in
testimony before a Senate committee. (The cast included

Senators Gurney and Ervin, and it was during these hearings that Ervin developed his helpful detestation of the doctrine of executive privilege.) The investigating journalist was Mr Jack Anderson. The evidence he produced was never undermined or countered: to reread his ITT articles — they are now available in a little book called *The Anderson Papers* — is to grasp anew the absurdity of boasts about the power of the American press. An absolutely damning report on corruption in the highest places, fully documented, is printed in over a hundred newspapers; the key Justice Department anti-trust official is posted comfortably off to a Chicago judgeship; the Attorney General has no comment; headlines for a few days but no public outcry; the matter slides quietly out of sight. The moral is that, except in absolutely extraordinary circumstances, the power of the press is nihil, and subliterary foundations for a penetrating literature of politics cannot truly be said to exist.

When we advance a step to middling rungs we are, as I said, face to face with zombie epic. Far the most successful pre-Watergate work in zombie epic was Mr David Halberstam's *The Brightest and the Best*. An effective indictment of that book was in print long before the Ervin Committee sat to its labours — the words of Miss Mary McCarthy. Miss McCarthy insisted that Halberstam's picture of 'an anguished President locked in combat with his conscience' required 'some comparison with reality'. Her comment deserves fuller representation:

A man divided in his mind between dispatching combat troops, increasing Special Forces, and trying out one of three bombing scenarios is scarcely a figure of Greek tragedy. . . . Yet Halberstam's design necessitates a big central figure ('There were many Johnsons; the complicated, difficult, sensitive man'; 'terrible decisions',) and the incessant manufacture of suspense. Rubicons being crossed, traps closing, doors shutting forever, I do not know how many 'turning points' are reached in the narrative or how many crossroads. His determination to view Vietnam as an American tragedy means that the outcome is ineluctable, foreordained (cf. the 'woulds' and 'were to bes'), and that all those Rubicons should be invisible to the participants; nobody ever says, 'Well, the die is cast.' Since, like the spectators of a Greek tragedy, the reader knows anyway what the end is going to be, suspense must be created artistically, and inner conflict heightened where little may have existed in real life.

But this skepticism deterred few midcult Watergate watchers. Time and again the thumb went on the scale and the eye read heroic weights. For such behaviour met in the gentlemen of principle sitting on the Watergate committee isn't surprising. Encountering purposes and values contrary to his own, a gentleman of principle holding office is bound to remark of the person opposite him, 'What a liar!' When, on the other hand, he meets clarities concerning the Just and the Good precisely paralleling his own, he cries out with the proverb that 'an honest man is the noblest work of God'.

Bad as it was with the elected men of principle, so it became with commentators granted space enough to lay out their fantasies in the morning paper. Two younger American novelists were invited by the key organ of contemporary opinion, the opinion-editorial page of the *New York Times*, to deliver their views concerning the chairman of the special Senate subcommittee. Each writer had produced a successful political romance, the one achieving Book of the Month Club selection, the other, serialization in a ladies magazine. Mr Willie Morris set up an opposition between Senator Ervin and Messrs Haldeman and Erlichman on the basis of a regional difference, contrasting the grace and dignity of the Old South, with the rawness and amorality of the West Coast, finding for 'Senator Sam' partly on the basis of qualities Morris claimed to remember from boyish days when he dated the Senator's 'charming granddaughters'. Mr Lelchuk, a shade more beamish, was roused by Mr Ervin's Shakespeheriana to an 'affection approaching family feeling. 'My dear Senator,' he wrote:

It's been a long, long time in our national life — for myself, for many of us, almost twenty years, when we first learned about democracy through an elfin, whitehaired gentleman lawyer who took on and defeated another egomaniacal tyrant on national television — a long time since we've had someone to look up to, respect, laugh with, and finally even, love. Someone whom we'd want to sit down to dinner with, as well as one to lead us. . . . It's been you, dear wise Senator, making Watergate over into the Tyrant's Waterloo, against the wishes of the Department of Justice, the Administration, even Harvard prosecutors, you, Senator, who have toughed the hero-chord in an age when heroism has been deservedly demythologized and heroes exposed as papier mâché figures. Now in the process you've revitalized democracy, replacing empty rhetoric and lies with true democratic substance. . . . You help us redefine the meaning of the heroic; the joining of the ordinary (downhome stories) with the extraordinary (your knowledge of the Constitution and the laws); the opportunity to meet a great challenge and take on a monstrous opponent; the acknowledgment of vulnerability while getting the job done. . . In the midst of dealing with lies, coverups, crimes, mechanical hacks and conscienceless bureaucrats, cheats, extortionists, perjurers, burglars, bagmen and blackmailers, while dealing with the low sordid crimes of the Tyrant (the higher ones, of Indochina, as you well know, needs another courtroom), you have remained just, cultured, intelligent, graceful, learned.

No impulse here to breathe along the nerves of a leader, to know his innerness, to suffer the full power of his vanities and frustrations and blindness as one's *own* afflictions. Those who remember Mr Ervin in the 1960s as firmly dedicated to the proposition that the poor and powerless should continue to be punished for being poor and powerless, because the Constitution so recommended, could not fully share this perception.

The absence of keenness was no less marked in midcult journalistic accounts of the witnesses than in encomia bestowed on the interrogators. A portion of the blame for this may perhaps be laid to the need to objectify and characterize what is properly described as trade association mentality. We may return to Mr Baker's questioning of Mr Herbert Porter, who disbursed huge sums unquestioningly for the Committee to Reelect the President and, like virtually all the others, never blew a whistle — we might return specifically to the question, 'What was your state of mind, how did you feel?' Mr Porter's face betrayed a touch of surprise at these questions, as well it might, for these are not queries of the kind familiar to trade association persons, and Porter and the rest — Dean, Magruder, Mitchell, Erlichman, Haldeman, others — seem to have been genuine trade association men. Of what mentality do we speak when we use this phrase? Suppose yourself an employee of the Independent Grocers Association lobby in Washington: how exactly do you deal with events or experience or questions from without? As follows: by referring them to the welfare of the Independent Grocers. An oil shortage, a riot in Detroit, the conviction of a Congressman for taking bribes from con- tractors, a decision about federal control of advertising rates on cable TV channels, a new food stamp program, a drought in East Africa — about each of these issues, about all matters, a trade association aide is never confused. The essential question before him cannot be moral, philosophical, professional. There is but the one question: unvarying, superbly comforting: 'How will this affect us?' Whatever and whenever an event occurs, the grid for its reception is prepared, the filter is fixed: 'Where is our interest?' And as for one's insides: well, the sense of personal justification and responsibility is firm. To ask the question, 'How will this effect us?', is to be doing one's job, faithful to one's charge, loyal, principled, dutiful. The moment of Mr Baker's question was a moment of juxtaposition, incongruity. All at once, here was an inquisitor asking about tinges, qualms of conscience — one could not respond with, say, 'Buzz off.' One knew that somehow some other vocabulary and consideration was in play, some context . . . wrong-doing? . . . But one couldn't in these shoes quite cut off all show of surprise, puzzlement, incredulity. To be asked how one felt at a time when one was only doing a good trade association man's job. . . . It is a little like waiting in your car as a traffic violator for a cop who, when he finishes writing a summons, hands it to you accompanied by a bit of a Verdi aria. Mr Porter is jostled. He falls back on the old worn Nixon organizational words — team player, member of the group. The media seizes on the words, we are once again off on the weary culture critique of the 1950s, conformity, etc. But the life of this instant of questioning, as of many others, lay elsewhere in the patch of moral surprise, and this life could have been touched by an alert journalist.

One can, to be sure, press too hard. I do not claim to have 'the explanation,' nor do I say that I know that crowd to their bottom — the prevalence of a trade association mentality explains all. America, lacking institutions, lacking a clergy, army, aristocracy, lacking professions knit tightly enough to enforce standards, has in their place trade associations, and the problem is that they are inevitably heedless of any and all larger goods. I believe such talk, laid on too heavily, isn't sound reporting, it is editorializing, culturology. What one is after is the instant of penetration, the answer to the question, 'Why did he look surprised?' — the interpreter catching and explaining a bit of feeling on the wing. And of this there is very little.

It may readily be granted that Watergate turned a searchlight on sub- and middle-literary assumptions, with a bearing on the

alteration of politics; but only a solemn head would propose
that the searchlight reached as far as the high literary culture.
Still the hearings *were* oddly helpful — obliquely helpful — in
calling to mind features of the currently dominant aesthetic
that are at least tangentially connected with problems of
imagination in political inquiry. Gleefully non-referential, this
aesthetic takes as the highest good the exploration through
parody of the postures of literary truthseeking. At its best it
produces a Mary McCarthy responsive to the genius of
Nabokov and supremely hostile to the mythy kitsch of Halberstam. At its less good — well, the implicit epistemology may be
characterized — unkindly — as schoolboy positivist. It announces
in tones of revelation that all talk, all writing, 'all expressed
forms of life, reality and history [are] fiction . . .,' that 'life,
reality and history exist only as discourse . . .' and that no
form of discourse 'can *be* life, reality or history.' From here it
advances to a chuckle at the lunacy of believers in historical or
political understanding. 'What is the Civil War and how do we
know it?' asks Professor Poirier in 1968. 'Where is Lyndon
Johnson and how does anyone know him? Is he a history book,
an epic poem or a cartoon by David Levine? Who invents
Lyndon Johnson, when and for what immediate purpose? . . .
And what about Richard Nixon, the living schmoo? Where
does the fiction end and the historical figure begin? . . . How
do we know . . . the Vietnam war . . . any more than we know
Lyndon Johnson or Richard Nixon?'

It would be pointless to abuse partisans of these views in
the name of one or another naive realism or other epistem-
ological simplism. What matters is not in this instance acts of
assessment but an act of recognition — awareness that the
influence of the antireferentialists has tended to elevate truths
of the labyrinth, of frustration and enclosure, to sacramental
status, while dismissing as delusory truths of the clearing, of
satisfaction and release. The latter truths are, to be sure — R.
E. Collingwood once explained this — individual and local,
hinged to transitory states of feeling — but no more so than
the truths of the labyrinth. And valuing the one immensely
above the other has the effect, among others, of inhibiting
imaginative inquiry into political experience. Where is
Robert Haldeman and how does one know him? One knew an

instant of him — something not to be confused with words — as Mr Weicker read back his marginalia. Good! Great! One saw a person knowing in a discrete instant that he was being perceived as caught out, feeling within himself that he had been deceived, hating his deceiver, half-shamed yet not by what it was held he should be ashamed — a complex of experience, in short, different for Haldeman than for Weicker, or for the viewer. Pondering all this in the present context one is less comfortable with the contemporary passion for the inaudible, the inexpressible, the unknowable; less tolerant of the ceaseless crying down of theories of literary reference that actually haven't had standing for two centuries or longer. Well and good to mock, in fine 'litry' style, the Watergate cliché: 'at this moment in time'. Dangerous, though, ever to forget that authenticity about 'this moment in time' is among the strongest literary suits. Lawrence himself — I note this in passing, and in embarrassment, yet am persuaded of its relevance — repeated those words often in his discourse, as for example on the explosive truth of the relation between Van Gogh and sun-flowers, a truth 'at that quick moment in time', 'at that living moment'. He was no voice of simple minded mimesis like those the politicians of self-parody conjure as their enemy — yet there is surely nothing in his aesthetic to deny the possibility of a vibrant imaginative work in political settings.

A counterpart of belief in salvation by parody is the con-viction that public voices, which by definition speak seriously and attempt to imagine or incarnate national energies in a 'mere' literary tone, are tastelessly presumptuous. 'I am the only President you have,' said Mr Johnson, later Mr Nixon: and with a gesture of relief the emergent high literary culture agrees. Perhaps partly in response, aspirants to a national voice regularly perceive themselves as hilarious clowns — challengers afflicted with loony presidential aspiration ('My ambition is to be President despite the fact that I'm a Catholic,' says Allen Ginsberg in 'America') — or as spokesmen on the margin, voices of special interest or local hate. Even when deformed, the ambition of such aspirants can be exhilarating (or at least funny). The democratic nerve trills when Norman Mailer gazes at Henry Cabot Lodge striding across the Saigon airport, and invents a Mr Ambassador who feels himself to be 'necessarily superb'. The intensity and rhetorical blaze of LeRoi Jones's 'Black Art' raises that poem to levels higher than those of ordinary Black Power tracts.

Yet the presumption I refer to isn't finally a mere spirit of impudence, like that which speaks loudest on Mailer's political page, and it is invariably more inclusive than any attitude framed in the poems of LeRoi Jones. The sound is that of summons, a demanding address to the energies of a potentially national best self. The capacity to produce this sound depends on belief in an alternative continent of power, a reservoir of sanity or of proper protest basely ignored by the authorities.

I do not imply — in order to achieve a rising tone — that the episode we are passing through is creating such a power, an audience 'beyond'. I would note that there have been hints in recent months of the formation of a popular risk-all, daretaking, deeply contrary moral judgement — that which alone can enable modest men and women to contemplate with terror total change, disruption, impeachment. But it is one thing to note this phenomenon and another to dream of imminent cultural reconciliation — between the newly alienanted judgemental middle classes and the permanently alienated literateurs. The country's two best-regarded literary creators have been committed for years to a 'Hegelian suspicion,' as one critic puts it, 'that the world itself is governed by self-generating political plots and conspiracies more intricate than any [that writers] could devise', and utterly beyond the comprehension of the public at large. Watergate intensifies this belief, not weakens it.

Still the mind turns and turns. Our literary culture possesses, to this day, as England does not, a poetry of political incantation. Among our gifted younger writers are some who can imagine astounding solidarity with the outs, the bottom dogs, who can live into a snippet of near speech — a poor black father to son, at the zoo, see, they feed the lion now — live into it, dilate it, pack it with furious force, becoming in the process priests of presumption, touching resonances of Whitman and Blake.

Out of burlap sacks, out of bearing butter,
Out of black bean and wet slate bread,
Out of the acids of rage, the candor of tar,

Out of creosote, gasoline, drive shafts, wooden dollies,
They Lion grow.

Out of the gray hills
Of industrial barns, out of rain, out of bus ride,
West Virginia to Kiss My Ass, out of buried aunties,
Mothers hardening like pounded stumps, out of stumps,
Out of the bones' need to sharpen and the muscles' to stretch,
They Lion grow.

Earth is eating trees, fence posts,
Gutted cars, earth is calling in her little ones,
'Come home, Come home!' From pig balls,
From the ferocity of pig driven to holiness,
From the furred ear and the full jowl come
The repose of the hung belly, from the purpose
They Lion grow.

From the sweet glues of the trotters
Come the sweet kinks of the fist, from the full flower
Of the hams the thorax of caves,
From 'Bow Down' come 'Rise Up,'
Come they Lion from the reeds of shovels,
The grained arm that pulls the hands,
They Lion grow.

From my five arms and all my hands
From all my white sins forgiven, they feed,
From my car passing under the stars,
They Lion, from my children inherit,
From the oak turned to a wall, they Lion,
From they sack and they belly opened
And all that was hidden burning on the oil-stamed earth
They feed they Lion and he comes.

I am imagining here a link between the spirit of this poem, the power of its assumed alliance and compassion, and the curious and moving national willingness — how it has awed Europe! — to consider taking our leaders out to their and our own edge. I am imagining this and holding it forth, upward from the tangle of problems and obstacles, claiming it as our growing point. For the nurture of a literature of democratic politics, suitable for this nation as conceived, who knows better soil?

Index

DATE DUE

GAYLORD			PRINTED IN U.S.A.